Executive Compensation in Imperfect Financial Markets

ELGAR FINANCIAL LAW

Series Editor: Takis Tridimas, *Queen Mary, University of London, UK*

This important series comprises high quality monographs on a wide range of topics in the field of financial law, hosting work by established authors of international reputation, alongside younger and more emerging authors. The series is synonymous with original thinking and new, challenging research. The subjects under consideration range from financial services law, through securities regulation, to banking law and from financial fraud, through legal aspects of European Monetary Union and the single currency, to the legal workings of international financial institutions.

Titles in the series include:

Law and Corporate Finance
Frank B. Cross and Robert A. Prentice

Secured Transactions Reform and Access to Credit
Edited by Frederique Dahan and John Simpson

Financial Regulation in Crisis?
The Role of the Law and the Failure of Northern Rock
Edited by Joanna Gray and Orkun Akseli

Law Reform and Financial Markets
Edited by Kern Alexander and Niamh Moloney

Regulating Credit Rating Agencies
Aline Darbellay

Executive Compensation in Imperfect Financial Markets
Jay Cullen

Executive Compensation in Imperfect Financial Markets

Jay Cullen

University of Sheffield, UK

ELGAR FINANCIAL LAW

Edward Elgar

Cheltenham, UK • Northampton, MA, USA

Published by

Edward Elgar Publishing Limited
The Lypiatts
15 Lansdown Road
Cheltenham
Glos GL50 2JA
UK

Edward Elgar Publishing, Inc.
William Pratt House
9 Dewey Court
Northampton
Massachusetts 01060
USA

A catalogue record for this book
is available from the British Library

Library of Congress Control Number: 2014943899

This book is available electronically in the ElgarOnline.com Law Subject Collection, E-ISBN 978 1 78254 929 1

MIX
Paper from responsible sources
FSC® C013056

ISBN 978 1 78254 928 4

Typeset by Columns Design XML Ltd, Reading
Printed and bound in Great Britain by T.J. International Ltd, Padstow

For Marcus, the world is yours

Contents

Preface

When I first thought of writing this book, a few years ago, it was at a time when I was also attempting to get a foot on the property ladder in the UK. The idea to write the book and my experience in buying my first property were explicitly linked. As the well-known aphorism declares: 'an Englishman's home is his castle' and having secured my first job in academia, I was looking forward to joining the throng of first-time buyers clamouring for mortgage finance, issued in ever greater volumes by the UK's cluster of large commercial banks. The housing market was experiencing the greatest boom in its history, and many people – myself included – were in danger of being left behind. Due to ever increasing house prices, and surveying the mortgage field from a position of inexcusable ignorance, I thought initially that my fairly meagre (or generous, depending on your point of view) lecturer's salary would get me nowhere near affording even an entry-level property in an area in which I wished to live based on a traditional ratio of income to purchase price. In more prudent days, of course, banks were willing to lend around three times salary to would-be purchasers of properties, whilst often also demanding a hefty deposit. On these terms, I would never have reached even the first rung of the property ladder.

Never fear! The Great Moderation was here! Funded by a seemingly endless supply of cheap money and consistently stable interest rates, first-time buyers like me were able to raise mortgages of many, many multiples of income – often with no deposit required – and thus experience the wealth effect that only proprietorship of a home can generate. Bankers were being rewarded handsomely for extending these loans, and bank shareholders were reaping large dividends and handsome share sale profits, as bank stocks soared in value throughout the 2000s. These trends were aided particularly by the raft of banking conglomerations and financial deregulations which characterised the pre-2008 period. Moreover, on a macroeconomic scale, it appeared that the spectre of instability which had haunted the world of finance since the mid-1960s had forever been consigned to history.

Yet, something didn't quite add up; the joy with which I signed my first mortgage agreement was tempered by a drop of fear. Of course, the desire to own a home was powerful, but I was also sure, even as a non-economist, that property prices could not continue to appreciate inexorably. These doubts were fuelled further by articles by so-called doomsayers in the popular press predicting that real estate prices would eventually begin to fall, and by my chance encounter with the work of a little-heralded economist (at least, at that time), Hyman Minsky. Minsky's work, in particular, struck a chord with the prevailing economic conditions of the mid-2000s: this was, of course, a time of supposed great financial stability, an era consistently heralded as the point when the cycles of boom-and-bust had ended. Nonetheless, despite some doubts, in 2007 I signed the mortgage papers on my first house, putting down a small deposit as a buffer against any future fall in value. Naturally, of course, I was hoping within a few years to have a nice slice of home equity.

The rest, as they say, is history.

The house I bought is now, of course, in negative equity (with no guarantee that it will ever be worth more than the outstanding mortgage). Accordingly, the experiences of 2007–2010 were chastening. For me and many others, they raised basic questions about the assumptions of mainstream economic theories and financial market modelling, which had essentially predicted that financial crashes of this variety were next-to-impossible. It has since become clear that these so-called 'orthodox' theories are, in fact, highly limited in explaining how financial markets operate. On a practical level, these limitations were reflected in the collapse in value of many asset markets over the half-decade following 2007 – from stocks to real estate, from commodities to sovereign bonds. Moreover, the huge rewards on offer at financial institutions – based, as they are, to a great degree on rewarding executives and senior managers through (often) short-term incentive systems – seemed to be prime culprits in creating the conditions in which these asset values could become inflated. On this basis, it is my view that there are further and serious questions to be asked of financial regulation systems and bank corporate governance regimes – which of course inform compensation packages – which proceed from a theoretical position that demonstrably fails to reflect economic reality.

Above all, this book attempts to add to the debate concerning the contribution of executive compensation at financial institutions to the greatest financial crisis of recent times. As will hopefully become clear during the book, I consider the pattern of ever more financial concentration and conglomeration, ever higher financial leverage levels, ever greater short-termism from shareholders, and ever increasing banker compensation levels to be four sides of the same financial instability pyramid. The continued existence of this prism has been aided and abetted by the construction of an exceedingly powerful narrative concerning the supposed efficiency of markets and the virtues of individual liberty, leading to a concerted retreat of the state, to be replaced by private contracting. The mantra that centralised regulation is unnecessary due to the corrective powers of market discipline, self-interest and the profit-motive-created conditions under which the capacity of financial institutions to generate instability increased exponentially. Many bankers profited enormously from this intellectual failure. It is my contention in this book that this was not an entirely unconscious enterprise.

Despite the experiences of the past few years, at the time of writing, in the UK a new property bubble appears to be emerging, concentrated in London but affecting the entire country. Prices are approaching 2007 levels, even though wage growth has been stagnant since the great crash. Moreover, almost unbelievably, this latest property bubble is being overtly supported by government, through generous taxpayer-underwritten mortgage schemes, proffered in the main by the same broken banks which still enjoy explicit state guarantees. I admit to having severe misgivings concerning this trend, and fear for a future economic path founded on ever greater levels of mortgage debt. Notwithstanding these fears, how long it is likely to be before this boom turns to bust is probably best answered by an economist, not a lawyer, and I have therefore not addressed in this book the latest developments in the mortgage markets.

Although the genesis of this book may be traced to the pre-crisis world, it was written almost exclusively over the 18 months up to April 2014. During that time, I have had some truly enlightening experiences, none more so than attending the 22nd Annual Hyman Minsky Conference in New York City in April 2013. I encountered scholarship and organisation magnitudes above that which I was previously used to, and am forever indebted to the conference participants and the Levy Economics Institute, each of whom opened my eyes to visions of the world of finance founded on principles of justice and common sense. I am of the firm belief that economics and law still have much to learn from one another, and this feeling was confirmed to me during that trip.

In researching and writing this book, I have been extremely fortunate to have benefitted from discussions and assistance from some of the best and brightest people I have ever encountered. First of all, I would like to thank Andrew Johnston of the University of Sheffield who, despite his hectic work life and his own punishing publication schedule, found time to review my work, comment on its flaws, and explain some of the more difficult concepts of law and economics to me. We benefit from a shared passion for the work of Minsky and his academic successors, and this book is much the better for Andrew's input. I am also grateful to Trevor Pugh who, in his former life as a high-level banker, garnered more than enough knowledge and expertise to provide me with some excellent advice and thoughtful criticism when needed. If I manage in my lifetime to learn a tenth of what Trevor knows about the financial system, I shall be very happy.

Thanks, of course, also go to Emilios Avgouleas, my former PhD supervisor, (occasional) co-author, and long-time mentor. Now at Edinburgh, Emilios was extremely helpful to me during my time at Manchester, and has assisted me greatly in both my career as a lecturer, and my development as an academic. His guidance has been invaluable, and this book would not have been possible without his support (although he may not agree with everything I say in it!). Emilios – *sas efharisto poli*. I have also enjoyed some informative and inspiring discussions with other colleagues, both past and present, who have offered (often) kind words and support to me over the duration of the project. Special thanks in this regard go to Lorie Charlesworth, George Mair, Tony Harvey and Jamie Murray, each of whom has brought their own (unique) views of both me and the subject matter to keep my feet firmly on the ground, especially at those times when I threatened to dissolve in a haze of confusion, both legal and economic.

I would also like to thank the staff at Edward Elgar, who have been more than patient with me over the last 18 months, and have not refused a single appeal for help or the inevitable request for a short extension(!).

Finally, there are three sets of people to whom I must pay the utmost thanks. First, to my Mum and Dad, Pauline and Jim, who have constantly but gently urged me on with this task. The words of encouragement I received spurred me on a number of occasions when I wanted to throw the whole lot in the proverbial (desktop recycling) bin. Although Dad is a retired lawyer, this area of law and regulation must be as far removed from his area of practice as possible, yet his enthusiasm for my progress has been infectious, and Mum has been full of reserved yet consistent support.

Second, to my wife, Sarah, who has been as patient with this project as she has been with everything else in our lives. Sarah has been a constant source of love, attention and sacrifice during the time we have known one another, and I shall be eternally grateful for the way in which she has allowed me the time and space to complete this book. She has looked after me and encouraged me in my work, often single-handedly raising a family, running a home, and continuing with her own academic career.

Wonder Woman has nothing on Sarah. I hope one day I will be able to repay that support in kind.

Third, to my children, Neve and Marcus. You are each a daily inspiration to me, and a very welcome distraction from the rigours of work. I am thankful for every day we have together.

Abbreviations

ABCP	asset-backed commercial paper
ABS	asset-backed security
AMH	Adaptive Markets Hypothesis
BCBS	Basel Committee on Banking Supervision
BDT	Behavioural Decision Theory
BHC	bank holding company
BIS	Bank of International Settlements
CAPM	Capital Asset Pricing Model
CB	countercyclical buffer
CCB	capital conservation buffer
CDO	collateralised debt obligation
CDS	credit default swap
CSR	corporate social responsibility
EBA	European Banking Authority
EMH	Efficient Market Hypothesis
EU	European Union
FASB	Financial Accounting Standards Board
FCA	Financial Conduct Authority
FDIC	Federal Deposit Insurance Corporation
FIH	Financial Instability Hypothesis
FSB	Financial Stability Board
GFC	Global Financial Crisis
IIF	Institute of International Finance
LCFI	Large Complex Financial Institution
M&M	Modigliani-Miller Theorem
MBS	mortgage-backed securities
REIT	real estate investment trust
RoA	return on assets
RoE	return on equity

RPE	relative performance evaluation
RWA	Risk-Weighted Assets
RWH	Random Walk Hypothesis
RWO	risk-weight optimisation
SEC	Securities and Exchange Commission
SOX	Sarbanes-Oxley Act
TBTF	too-big-to-fail
VaR	Value at Risk

1. Introduction

INTRODUCTORY REMARKS

We are now six years from the peak of the worst financial crisis for several generations. Scores of books, articles and reports, and millions of pages of copy have been produced by the printed press detailing the mishaps, blunders and greed which characterised the lead-up to the Global Financial Crisis (GFC) which caused it. Much of the literature has centred on the role of executive compensation in causing – at least partially – the collapse of hundreds of financial institutions, and the near death of the global financial system.

The cascade of recent crises would suggest that something is clearly wrong with Western corporate governance and, by extension, with the way in which corporate executives are rewarded. Concentrating on the size of bankers' pay, and the supposed perverse incentives that massive bank executive compensation packages generated, has become de rigeur in many popular and policy-making circles.[1] Criticism of the supposed outsized pay of bankers and other senior employees of financial institutions merely intensified once the effects of the GFC on national economies became clear. Governments assumed the burden of rescuing the financial system and its constituents – at extreme costs to taxpayers – whilst pay practices in the City of London, Wall Street and other major financial centres seemingly remained largely unaffected. When the compounded effects of large fiscal government deficits and reduced tax receipts due to increased unemployment and lower economic output began to bite, disbelief at the scale of the mismanagement involved soon morphed into intense public and political outrage at the 'business as usual' approach to bankers' compensation that appeared to characterise the post-GFC environment.

---

[1] For a flavour of this, see Jill Treanor, 'Banks Risk Further Fury As Bonus Season Begins In the City' *The Guardian* (London, 13 January 2013) http://www.guardian.co.uk/business/2013/jan/13/banks-fury-bonus-season-city.

Anger and resentment at executive pay levels in the financial sector has therefore characterised much of the reform to the regulation of compensation structures since 2008, yet – as shall be explained later in this book – a natural consequence of reliance on market pricing to determine pay awards gives rise to large amplifications in executive remuneration, independent of incentives. The repeated misconception that market pricing, which is highly imperfect and subject to considerable distortions, may be used to underpin systems of compensation which reduce the incentives of managers and senior executives to adopt excessive risk has meant that despite some considerable changes to the rules governing executive compensation at banks, flaws in remuneration systems remain and corporate collapses are perpetuated. Moreover, these flaws were easily exploited by knowledgeable executives, who repeatedly demonstrated their adeptness at extracting value from corporations based on negligible value creation, the adoption of excessively risky business strategies, or outright fraud.

Naturally, the easiest sticks with which to beat the financial sector have been that of 'greed' and 'recklessness', as politicians and senior industry regulators have moved to condemn compensation practices to which they had readily consented just a few years earlier. Based on this platform, much progress in the realm of executive compensation at financial institutions has been made. In 2012, in proposing caps to senior bankers' bonuses, a senior EU banking official claimed that '[t]his crisis, which is not over yet, shows the risk and problems posed by some excessive bonuses in the financial sector'.[2] These comments presaged an EU-wide cap on bankers' bonuses, which was introduced at the beginning of 2014.[3] On the opposite side of the Atlantic, laws restricting pay at financial institutions have been in place since the passage of the Dodd-Frank Act 2010.[4] Moreover, international standard-setters for financial institutions have issued prescriptive rules and guidance on the

---

[2] MarketWatch, 'EU Officials Debate Crackdown on Banker Bonuses' (Market Watch, 13 June 2012) http://www.marketwatch.com/story/eu-officials-debate-crackdown-on-banker-bonuses-2012-06-13-7485329.

[3] Amendments were made under Directive 2013/36/EU of the European Parliament and of the Council of 26 June 2013 on access to the activity of credit institutions and the prudential supervision of credit institutions and investment firms, amending Directive 2002/87/EC and repealing Directives 2006/48/EC and 2006/49/EC [2013] OJ L176/338. For discussion, see Andrew Johnston, 'Preventing the Next Financial Crisis? Regulating Bankers' Pay in Europe' (2014) 41 J. LAW & SOCIETY 1.

[4] Dodd-Frank Wall Street Reform and Consumer Protection Act, Pub. L. No. 111/203 (July 21, 2010) Pub. L. No. 124 Stat. 1376.

composition of bankers' remuneration, which place restrictions on the composition and frequency of performance-related compensation awards.[5] Each of these sets of regulations has been informed by the perception that large bonuses and performance-linked pay created the conditions necessary for the GFC, and that crises are less likely to erupt if incentives for risk created by compensation systems are restricted.

On the one hand, executive remuneration in the banking and financial sectors was, and remains, massive.[6] Certainly from a purely distributional position, the rewards of top executives seem extraordinary in comparison to the rewards on offer to the average banking employee.[7] Moreover, this trend is replicated across industries in developed countries, and has long been a topic of political and ethical discourse.[8] On the other hand, there is considerable empirical evidence to suggest that incentive-based pay plays a fundamental role in encouraging executives to perform to the highest levels and to create value for their companies,[9] and thereby for national economies. It is an (often uncomfortable) truth that senior executives at financial institutions are often rewarded commensurately with the value they create for the companies, and thereby their investors.

Moreover, it is clear that the compensation of senior executives at financial institutions, in most circumstances, is determined by two factors which arguably bestow clear legitimacy upon the prevailing levels of remuneration at banks in the pre-GFC era. Firstly, the relative size of pay

---

[5] For example, see Financial Stability Board, *FSF Principles for Sound Compensation Practices: Implementation Standards* (2009).

[6] For example, the aggregate compensation of the CEOs of two of the highest-profile casualties of the GFC, Bear Sterns and Lehman Brothers in the five years prior to the GFC was over $1 billion. See Lucian A. Bebchuk, Alma Cohen & Holger Spamann, 'The Wages of Failure: Executive Compensation at Bear Stearns and Lehman 2000–2008' (2010) 27 YALE J. REG. 257.

[7] In the US, the ratio between the median compensation of CEOs and the median salary of the 'average' employee is 273:1. See Lawrence Mishel & Natalie Sabadish, 'CEO Pay In 2012 Was Extraordinarily High Relative To Typical Workers And Other High Earners' (2013) Economic Policy Institute Issue Brief No. 367.

[8] For example, in the UK, see UK High Pay Commission, *Cheques With Balances: Why Tackling High Pay Is in the National Interest: Final Report* (2012).

[9] For the classic papers on this issue, see Michael C. Jensen & Kevin J. Murphy, 'Performance Pay and Top-Management Incentives' (1990) 98 J. POLIT. ECONOMY 225; Michael C. Jensen & Kevin J. Murphy, 'CEO Incentives: It's Not How Much You Pay But How' (1990) 3 HARV. BUS. REV. 138; Eugene F. Fama, 'Agency Problems and the Theory of the Firm' (1980) 88 J. POLIT. ECONOMY 288.

packages is largely determined by non-salary elements such as bonuses and stock options. Of course, these provide high-grade incentives for executives to promote the success of their companies, and create value for investors. Simultaneously, the fact that options and bonuses tie so much individual success to corporate value intensifies the risk to executives' personal wealth and, as importantly, their reputational capital. It is therefore debatable whether restricting the capacity of executives to profit in tandem with investors would have welfare-enhancing effects, because motivating executives to take risk would prove difficult. Secondly, and perhaps most significantly, in developed jurisdictions with free movement of capital and labour, it is the market which sets the competitive rate of pay, at all levels. Unless there are regulations restricting the compensation of senior executives (as are present in some jurisdictions in the case of financial institutions in receipt of governmental support), or the state has a hand in the relevant industry, executive pay levels are legally decided by free and unencumbered bargaining between the board of directors and investors.

Notwithstanding for now the merits or otherwise of the claims concerning the contribution of executive compensation to the GFC, it is clear that the latest crisis exhibited many of the taxonomic features of recent preceding scandals and financial collapses. These episodes included the technology company crash (the so-called dot.com bubble of around the year 2000), the option-rigging scandals which beset many Western companies in the late twentieth century, and the gargantuan frauds which laid waste to huge corporations (most notably Enron) in the early part of the twenty-first century.[10] The asset bubbles which collapsed financial institutions in 2008 centred on the housing sector, but it is clear from empirical research that global asset and commodities markets were almost universally inflated in the lead-up to the GFC, which provided further potential for instability to result from price collapses, each of which in some way may be linked to individual incentives.[11] More

---

[10] 'In each of [the global] crises, the activities which gave rise to them has enriched many individuals involved, while the aftermath imposed substantial and widely dispersed costs on people outside the industry.' See John Kay, 'Should we have 'narrow banking'?' in Adair Turner, Andrew Haldane, Paul Woolley, Sushil Wadhwani, Charles Goodhart, Andrew Smithers, Andrew Large, John Kay, Martin Wolf, Peter Boone, Simon Johnson & Richard Layard (eds), *The Future of Finance: The LSE Report* (LSE, 2010) 230.

[11] L. Randall Wray, 'The Commodities Market Bubble: Money Manager Capitalism and the Financialization of Commodities' (2008) Levy Economics Institute of Bard College Public Policy Brief No. 96.

recently, the Libor-rigging scandal threatened to plunge several large financial institutions back into crisis.[12] At the time of writing, massive central bank injections of cash into financial markets (so-called 'quantitative easing') have led to surges in equity markets, whilst the housing market in the UK appears destined for yet more inflation-busting price rises.

Each time these episodes have threatened Western capital and stock markets, regulators have responded with demands for the introduction of ever higher corporate governance norms, higher financial reporting standards and increased market disclosure. Yet, despite the presence of some of the most prescriptive corporate governance standards in the world, jurisdictions including the US, UK and several large European countries saw their financial sectors decimated by the reckless behaviour of senior bank executives, even as those executives were lionised by politicians.[13] Moreover, bankers have themselves recognised the toxic impact prevailing compensation and incentive systems had in causing the crisis.[14]

Accordingly, it is the contention of this book that we are faced with a problem that cannot be solved simply by tinkering around the edges of

---

[12] For discussion, see Andrew G. Haldane, 'Constraining Discretion in Bank Regulation', Paper given at the Federal Reserve Bank of Atlanta Conference on 'Maintaining Financial Stability: Holding a Tiger by the Tail(s)', Federal Reserve Bank of Atlanta, 9 April 2013, http://www.bankofengland.co.uk/publications/Documents/speeches/2013/speech657.pdf.

[13] Gordon Brown, then UK Chancellor of the Exchequer, infamously saluted the UK banking industry in 2007, commenting that 'The financial services sector in Britain and the City of London at the centre of it, is a great example of a highly skilled, high value added, talent driven industry that shows how we can excel in a world of global competition. Britain needs more of the vigour, ingenuity and aspiration that you already demonstrate that is the hallmark of your success … [in this] era that history will record as the beginning of a new golden age for the City of London.' See Gordon Brown, Speech by the Chancellor of the Exchequer, the Rt Hon Gordon Brown MP, to Mansion House, 20 June 2007, http://webarchive.nationalarchives.gov.uk.

[14] In one of the most wide-ranging surveys into the causes of the GFC, the International Institute of Finance surveyed 37 global banks regarding their attitudes to compensation and risk taking. Their conclusion was unambiguous: '98% of survey respondents believe that compensation structures were a factor underlying the crisis. To improve the functioning of financial markets, practitioners highlight that compensation needs to be addressed in concert with other issues, especially risk management.' See International Institute of Finance, *Compensation in Financial Services: Industry Progress and the Agenda For Change* (2009) 3.

corporate governance codes, or demanding increased market oversight of corporate disclosure. We cannot rely on greater regulation of executive behaviour by the market: each episode of crisis, more forcefully than the last, has revealed the inability – or indeed, the unwillingness – of market participants to enforce behavioural standards. Instead, the task of real reform requires wholesale changes to the way in which we view the market itself.

On this basis, it is the modest aim of this book to highlight why this change in perception is so important. We, as regulators and proponents of efficient and just exchange, ought to preserve those aspects of the market which give rise to welfare-enhancing trading and developmental outcomes. The market is adept, in most circumstances, at producing allocative efficiency and achieving fair value. In these tasks, it remains supreme. Yet it is also flawed, and its flaws often lead to crises which may have been prevented. One flaw which must be addressed is the virtual wholesale reliance currently placed on the pricing mechanism relating to financial markets to deliver value-based compensation contracts. These prices are in some instances subject to distortions, and permitting financial institutions to rely on them to incentivise their management has cost the economy dear. Reducing this reliance will not only lower the risks to investment, but will improve general economic and social prosperity, a cardinal aim of corporate governance.[15]

Whilst lessons to be derived from the GFC are legion, some of the most salient can be mined from the corporate governance failures which afflicted financial institutions, and led to the embedding of poor incentives across compensation contracts in the sector. Of course, remuneration systems in financial institutions created perverse incentives, particularly short-termism, which encouraged recklessness. However, further limits to executive compensation efficiency exist due to market price distortions, which may persist for protracted periods. Therefore,

---

[15] 'Good corporate governance underpins market confidence, integrity and efficiency, and hence promotes economic growth and financial stability.' See Grant Kirkpatrick, *Improving Corporate Governance Standards: The Work of the OECD and the Principles* (OECD, 2004) 2; 'Corporate governance is concerned with holding the balance between economic and social goals and between individual and communal goals. The governance framework is there to encourage the efficient use of resources and equally to require accountability for the stewardship of those resources. The aim is to align as nearly as possible the interests of individuals, corporations and society.' See Adrian Cadbury, *World Bank: Corporate Governance: A Framework for Implementation* (2000) Foreword.

whilst many of the criticisms of existing compensation arrangements are merited, they ignore crucial questions concerning the integrity of the market pricing mechanism, which remains a central aspect of the methods used to calculate remuneration awards.[16] It will be demonstrated by this book that the market pricing mechanism is, on occasion, highly flawed, and this undermines the use of many forms of incentive-based pay because market prices are often used as benchmarks with which to assess performance (usually through metrics such as stock prices or asset prices):

> A salient example [of supposed good corporate governance] can be found in the recent enthusiasm for 'incentivizing' corporate officers and directors by compensating them primarily, or even solely, through options and stock-based compensation schemes. If market prices do not closely reflect actual expected risks and returns, this single-minded focus on share price is a recipe for mismanagement.[17]

This book will provide strong evidence that the predominant view of financial market operation is limited in explaining both investor behaviour and the formation of market prices. On this basis it contends that compensation packages pegged to the short-term whims of financial markets are an inefficient form of corporate remuneration; they do not provide corporate executives with the necessary incentives to motivate them to maximise corporate value or provide long-term growth and sustainability. Instead, they incentivise executives to adopt short-term, high-risk business strategies, particularly through the use of leverage and credit, or through data manipulation. On this theme, the UK Parliamentary Commission on Banking Standards, formed following several banking scandals in the UK, commented:

> Remuneration has incentivised misconduct and excessive risk-taking, reinforcing a culture where poor standards were often considered normal. Many bank staff have been paid too much for doing the wrong things, with bonuses

[16] European Central Bank president Jean-Claude Trichet recently pointed out: 'A large number of aspects of the observed behaviour of financial markets is hard to reconcile with the efficient market hypothesis.' See 'Reflections on the Nature of Monetary Policy Non-standard Measures and Finance Theory', Jean-Claude Trichet, President of the ECB, Opening address at the ECB Central Banking Conference, Frankfurt, 18 November 2010, http://www.ecb.europa.eu/press/key/date/2010/html/sp101118.en.html.

[17] Lynn A. Stout, 'The Mechanisms of Market Inefficiency: An Introduction to The New Finance' (2003) 28 J. CORP. L. 635, 641 (hereinafter Stout, 'Mechanisms'.

> awarded and paid before the long-term consequences become apparent. The potential rewards for fleeting short-term success have sometimes been huge, but the penalties for failure, often manifest only later, have been much smaller or negligible. Despite recent reforms, many of these problems persist.[18]

What each driver of market pricing failure in relation to the relevant instances has in common is the wholesale destruction of corporate value in the wake of huge preceding gains for senior executives. These instances have serious ramifications for the almost singular focus on corporate data such as stock prices in determining executive remuneration, as they demonstrate that market inefficiencies are not only common, but often give rise to crises, which may become so grave as to threaten the entire financial system. If links may be established between market pricing failure, compensation incentives and crisis, a strong case may be advanced for greater regulation of executive remuneration.

THE STRUCTURE OF THIS BOOK

This book is divided into six substantive chapters aside from this brief introduction, and a brief conclusion. The next chapter deals with the issue of executive compensation in modern markets on a theoretical basis, by surveying the theories which dominate the system of executive compensation in modern corporations. Executive compensation packages at public companies comprise common elements such as a base salary and performance-target-related pay. This, theoretically, ought to mitigate potential conflict between the principal and agent, by making a proportion of the executive's pay contingent on firm performance. This aligns the interests of shareholders (superior firm performance and increased profits) with those of management (commensurate performance-adjusted rewards). This performance-related pay often includes an element with a specific link to the stock price of the corporation that the executive is employed by. Thus the more shareholder value that executives create, the more pay they receive. Executive remuneration rewards are therefore based, to a great extent, on the market price of companies (or their market capitalisation).[19] However, the widespread adoption of equity-based compensation has led to a damaging obsession with short-term

---

[18] Report of the Parliamentary Commission on Banking Standards, *Changing Banking For Good* (Vol. I), HL 27-I; HC 175-I, 9 (2013).

[19] Calculated by multiplying the number of outstanding shares in a company by the current per-share market price.

market price movements, contributing to corporate scandals based on systematic abuse of financial reporting, and financial structures.

Chapter 3 both discusses modern finance theory and analyses the various challenges to the hegemony of modern finance theory in explaining financial market behaviour. In doing so, it highlights the challenges that face the use of predictive tools concerning individual behaviour in formulating executive compensation levels in contemporary public securities markets. In fact, the utility of compensation contracts is entirely based on a system of near-flawless market pricing. This chapter therefore addresses the notion that market pricing is flawless; that is, the price of a security is always equal to its value (the so-called Efficient Markets Hypothesis, or 'EMH'). If the value of securities is flawless so, by proxy, must be a firm's market capitalisation. The EMH bases its predictive qualities upon the rational investor model.[20] A further and essential tenet of the EMH is that there is no such thing as an 'over-valuation' of assets: market prices are always correct because agents are rational and will arbitrage away any price anomalies extremely quickly. Financial crisis is therefore unpredictable – and therefore unavoidable – and crashes simply mark departures from equilibrium. In this vein, the chapter proceeds to discuss both behavioural finance and other theories of financial market operation which highlight instances in which the market pricing mechanism has failed to deliver efficient pricing, and accordingly undermined equity-based compensation systems. In particular, the chapter considers the most obvious challenge to the notion that market prices are efficient: asset bubbles. Standard financial theory does not recognise the possibility of asset bubbles, yet every major financial crisis has been preceded by one.[21] Each of the theories conceived to explain these phenomena, in contrast to the EMH, provides explanations for the departure of price from value for sustained periods, although each is limited in providing

---

[20] In relation to the supposed futility of governmental fiscal policy, for example, neoclassical economic theory holds that '… markets will adjust instantaneously [to new information]. For because expectations are rational, optimizing agents will take predictable countercyclical government fiscal and monetary policy into account in their behaviour. Policy can only have effects if it "surprises" agents, and rational expectations ensure that policy that systematically surprises agents is not possible.' See Simon Mohun, 'New Classical Economics' in William Outhwaite (ed), *The Blackwell Dictionary of Modern Social Thought* (John Wiley & Sons, 2002) 433.

[21] Charles P. Kindleberger & Robert Z. Aliber, *Manias, Panics And Crashes: A History of Financial Crises* (6th edn, Palgrave Macmillan, 2011).

solutions for the normative design of more appropriate financial regulatory structures.

On this basis, Chapter 4 analyses Minsky's so-called 'Financial Instability Hypothesis' ('FIH'), which I consider to be the most comprehensive and accurate explanation for the fact that financial markets experience periods of boom and bust, and thereby undermines the view that financial markets are stable and equilibrium-seeking. The FIH holds that euphoric expectations of future expansion will affect an economy's debt structure, leading to financial instability and eventual widespread corporate distress. The chapter will address the way in which the capital structure of corporations – particularly banks – may be arranged so as to increase their profitability, based purely on asset expansion and leverage. This permits executives to capture gains derived from changes in leverage levels, and through recourse to financial measurements of performance which may be inflated through use of more leveraged capital structures. Tinkering with capital structure in this way will often appear to improve short-term profitability, but will do so at the expense of long-term stability.

Chapter 5 proceeds with an examination of the contribution of executive remuneration to the GFC, which arguably exploded modern finance theory and supports the consideration of a new economic paradigm. The GFC demonstrated that, consistent with the predictions of the FIH, common causes drive most significant financial crises, and exposed the role of debt-fuelled expansion in creating financial conditions of fragility. Equity-based compensation provided executives at financial institutions with serious incentives for this expansion. Many investors were caught up in the market euphoria of the years preceding the crash despite warning signs that a financial crash was imminent being sounded before 2007, when the crisis began. The market pricing mechanism did not reflect the likelihood that this was the case. Market discipline was insufficient to guard against consequences which flowed from poor incentives and rent seeking. Economic units, particularly financial institutions, migrated towards unstable financial structures, as entities in the shadow banking system and traditional banks sought to increase returns via unprecedented credit expansion. To support this position, the chapter utilises data from the financial sector which demonstrates that leverage in the financial system increased significantly in the build-up to the crisis and the sub-prime mortgage backed asset market was expanding at a rate which did not reflect underlying fundamentals. At the same time, executive pay levels, based on weak incentives for risk management and related to a large extent on the inflation of asset values, burgeoned. This chapter also notes a further paradox in relation to this theme; the very compensation policies that executives push for (equity-based remuneration) may in themselves drive financial institutions to become more unstable, and thereby may distort the market pricing mechanism.

The final two substantive chapters, in light of previous discussions of the integrity of market pricing, consider both the reforms made to compensation systems in the financial sector, and make some proposals for reform to executive compensation contracts, to reduce reliance – directly or indirectly – on market prices. Chapter 6 discusses the reforms made in the major/Western financial centres since the GFC. Chapter 7 considers further reforms to existing compensation mechanisms, in some cases simply augmenting those already present in the banking sector. Markets are prone to extreme oscillations in price and it may require observation for a protracted period for fundamental value to emerge in order to 'screen out' the possible effects of market irrationality and failed investor learning. Added complexity in business and financial markets has provided executives with the opportunities to exploit methods through which to capture additional rents. The proposed reforms will arguably increase the level of protection for the financial system by reducing the opportunities for this conduct.

2. An analysis of the role of executive compensation

INTRODUCTORY REMARKS

As referred to briefly in the introductory chapter, it is common for market prices to be used as a reference point for calculating executive compensation. Regulatory and legal provisions in Anglo-American markets are based on the view that the market is efficient, and that market prices capture true value, even in the short term. This view of the efficiency of the market has been a central axiom of corporate regulation for more than 50 years, and is explicitly recognised in much legislation.[1] Whilst recent events in financial markets have demonstrated some of the fallibilities of these views, the notion that prices convey fundamental value remains a powerful assumption.

Moreover, there are strong political and economic traditions at play. In the US, in particular, the regulation of private contractual bargaining is frowned upon: there is a generally held view that the market should be left to regulate the conduct of participants and, thereby, corporations, and their employees.[2] The private sector is trusted to deliver superior competitive efficiencies, which ought to translate into greater total accumulated wealth, and increased economic prosperity. On this basis, progressively more politically conservative governments on each side of the Atlantic have rolled back government regulation and replaced it with privatisation of regulation and market-driven codes to regulate behavioural standards and free economic actors from so-called 'excessive' regulation. The stated rationale for this is simple: private market actors are in possession of the greatest incentives to deliver services and ensure

---

[1] For discussion, see Henry T.C. Hu, 'Efficient Markets and the Law: A Predictable Past and an Uncertain Future' (2012) 4 ANN. REV. FIN. ECON. 179.

[2] Ludwig von Mises, 'Economic Calculation in the Socialist Commonwealth' in Friedrich A. Hayek (ed), *Collectivist Economic Planning: Critical Studies on the Possibilities of Socialism* (first published 1935, The Ludwig Von Mises Institute, 2009).

corporations pursue the most desirable objectives for investors, thus protecting investment and preserving capital value.[3]

On a more practical level, of course it is clear that no private or public institution could possibly supplant the role of the market as an epistemic monitor of corporate affairs. The complexity and sophistication of modern securities and financial markets, together with the extreme costs of monitoring that any central monitoring system would bring, mean that corporations are regulated largely by market participants, with few legal constraints upon corporate behaviour beyond those pertaining to accounting and disclosure.[4] A consequence of this is that market-driven codes of corporate governance continue to characterise the regulation of Anglo-American public corporations.[5] Indeed, lawmakers have consistently emphasised the importance of retaining the market-based view of corporate governance regulation, even as crises have threatened entire economies. The failure to dispense with the view that the market can never be second-guessed is, in my view, a key failure of post-2008 reform.

EXECUTIVE COMPENSATION: AN OVERVIEW

From these brief observations, it is clear that in Anglo-American markets, corporate governance systems proceed upon the assumption that markets – and by proxy, market prices – are to be trusted to convey fundamental value. According to this position, the use of market prices as metrics with which to judge executive performance is entirely logical. Notwithstanding the merits or otherwise of this view, it is crucial at this stage to identify the precise role of market pricing in determining executive compensation rewards at Anglo-American public corporations. It will become clear that the exercise of setting executive pay relies to a great degree on market prices, because a large proportion of compensation is

---

[3] In legal terms, this summarises the consequences of the legal theory of contractarianism, expounded most notably by Easterbrook and Fischel in Frank H. Easterbrook & Daniel R. Fischel, *The Economic Structure of Corporate Law* (Harvard University Press, 1991) (hereinafter Easterbrook & Fischel, *Economic Structure of Corporate Law*).

[4] Emilios Avgouleas, *Global Governance of Financial Markets: The Law, the Economics, the Politics* (CUP, 2012) 120.

[5] Sol Picciotto, 'Regulatory Networks and Multi-Level Global Governance' in Olaf Dilling, Martin Herberg & Gerd Winter (eds), *Responsible Business: Self-Governance and the Law in Transnational Economic Transactions* (Hart, 2008).

determined by securities prices (i.e. the market capitalisations of corporations). The actual and perceived merits of the market pricing system itself will be considered in a later chapter.

The following analysis will address key elements of the role of remuneration contracts. It will identify the function of executive compensation (beyond the obvious function that very few employees provide their services for no monetary reward) and discuss the structure of executive compensation and the various elements which comprise performance-related executive pay. It will proceed to analyse the extant literature on the key weaknesses of existing compensation arrangements at public companies. The chapter concludes by introducing the problems with executive compensation generated by imperfect market pricing, which damage the utility of current methods of remuneration. This analysis will contextualise the issue of executive remuneration, explain how the market mechanism is embedded in corporate governance systems, and provide critical commentary on flaws in the prevailing paradigm.

(i) The Function of Executive Compensation

Compensation fulfils several functions. Of course, the most significant is as a measure of the marginal product of employee labour, which further allows those same employees to purchase goods and services from others.[6] Employees are generally rewarded with salaries commensurate with their roles and functions, and levels of remuneration are often equated with the market rate for corporate talent. In Anglo-American markets, virtually all compensation arrangements are determined by market forces, including those where employees retain significant shareholdings in their employer corporations. In this situation – in the case of top executives, in particular – compensation awards may appear excessive.[7]

---

[6] Gian Luca Clememti, Thomas F. Cooley, Matthew Richardson & Ingo Walter, 'Rethinking Compensation in Financial Firms' in Viral V. Acharya & Matthew Richardson (eds), *Restoring Financial Stability: How To Repair A Failed System* (Wiley, 2009) 197.

[7] For a flavour of this view, see the UK High Pay Commission, *Cheques With Balances: Why Tackling High Pay Is in the National Interest: Final Report* (2012), which comments at 7: '1980 top bosses were well rewarded, but they had not pulled so far away from the rest of society. Since then some of them have enjoyed an increase of over 4000% to what are now multi-million pound packages. Those in respectable middle class jobs such as secondary school

Beyond this basic function, in relation to the corporate governance of large public corporations with dispersed ownership structures, the main role of executive compensation is to ameliorate risk to shareholder equity. It does this by providing incentives for executives to act in ways which favour shareholders, in preference to expropriating benefits for themselves. The concept of using executive compensation to achieve broader aims beyond simple remuneration for labour and services underpins 'shareholder value theory', which dictates that corporations ought to be run in the financial interests of their owners: the chief objective for the corporation is 'the conduct of business activities with a view toward enhancing corporate profit and shareholder gain'.[8] Shareholder value theory derives its power from the premise that shareholders, as the owners and ultimate risk bearers of corporations, have the greatest incentives to maximise the value of the corporation.[9] Thus, their interests ought to be prioritised by executives of the corporation, as enhancing shareholder wealth will benefit both investors and wider society, through wealth creation, allocation of resources, and by encouraging entrepreneurial drive. Shareholder value theory demands that management ought to run the corporation in the interests of shareholders *only* – and remain accountable to the owners of the firms they manage and to no further constituencies: 'a manager told to serve two masters (a little for the equity holders, a little for the community) has been freed of both and is answerable to neither'.[10] By proxy, the pursuit of shareholder value is viewed as a method of creating more efficient firms, summarised famously by Milton Friedman in 1962:

---

teachers and policemen have seen their income rise by a much more modest amount with average wages increasing from £6,474 to just £25,900 over the same period.'

[8] American Law Institute, *Principles of Corporate Governance: Analysis and Recommendations* (1994) S.2.01(A).

[9] Prior to the passage of the Companies Act 2006 in the UK, a minister commented that 'The Company Law Review considered and consulted on two main options. The first was "enlightened shareholder value", under which a director must first act in the way that he or she considers, in good faith, would be most likely to promote the success of the company for its members … The Government agrees this is the right approach. It resolves any confusion in the mind of directors as to what the interests of the company are, and prevents any inclination to identify those interests with their own. It also prevents confusion between the interests of those who depend on the company and those of the members.' See comments of Lord Goldsmith, Lords Grand Committee, *Company Law Reform Bill* (HL 2005–06, 190-I) 255.

[10] Easterbrook & Fischel, *Economic Structure of Corporate Law*, 38.

> There is one and only one social responsibility of business – to use its resources and engage in activities designed to increase its profits … Few trends could so thoroughly undermine the very foundations of our free society as the acceptance by corporate officials of a social responsibility other than to make as much money for their stockholders as possible.[11]

'Shareholder value theory' at first glance appears remarkably plausible as a method of aligning managerial and investor interests and reducing risk to shareholder wealth. On the other hand, however, recent history would suggest that there are flaws in this view, particularly that executives may be incentivised successfully to pursue business strategies which favour the long-term interests of shareholders. There are several reasons for this. Shareholder value theory requires that executive behaviour be monitored to ensure that executives are pursuing strategies beneficial to corporate owners. However, many corporate failures may be attributed to the flawed belief in the power of market participants to closely and accurately monitor the behaviour of corporate executives, and the supposed 'mystical' power of market discipline.[12] Market participants fail to fulfil this role for many reasons, some of which will be explored in later chapters. It is also clear that creating 'value' for shareholders may mean different things to investors with heterogeneous investment horizons. Many executives have shown themselves to be adept at creating short-run increases in share prices which have proved ephemeral, and short-termism has often been the catalyst for corporate collapse.[13]

Moreover, shareholder value theory, as a way of explaining how to incentivise executives, does not entirely mitigate the 'agency costs' associated with the separation of ownership and control which characterises the modern Anglo-American corporation.[14] In classic corporate governance theory, it is posited that managers (agents) are in a position to

---

[11] Milton Friedman, *Capitalism and Freedom* (University of Chicago Press, 40th Anniversary Edition, 2002) 133.

[12] David T. Llewellyn, 'Inside the Black box of Market Discipline' (2005) 25 ECON. AFFAIRS 41.

[13] See Anup Agrawal & Sahiba Chadha, 'Corporate Governance and Accounting Scandals' (2005) 48 J. LAW & ECON. 371.

[14] NYSE, *Report of The New York Stock Exchange Commission on Corporate Governance* (2010) 12. Individuals held 93% of US equities in 1950; by 2006 this had dropped to approximately 33%; and by 2009, it was just 25%. See American Bar Association, *Report of The Task Force of the ABA Section of Business Law Corporate Governance Committee* (2009) 15. The UK experience of share ownership change has been even more pronounced. In 1957 individuals owned nearly 70% of quoted equities; by 1989 this had fallen to around 20%. Today the figure is 14.8%, with institutional investors holding over 50%, and

exploit shareholders (principals) by exercising their control over firm resources to benefit themselves.[15] Berle and Means highlighted this facet of the corporation in 1932: directors in joint-stock companies, they argued, could not be expected to be as careful with other people's money as they were with their own.[16] Further work by Jensen and Meckling found that managers will seek to engage the firm in activities that are not in the firm's best interests, in financial terms, in order to maximise their own wealth.[17] These private benefits are not enjoyed by stockholders in the firm and, in this way, can be viewed as 'excess'.[18] The agency conflict arises because of the differing priorities placed on the objectives of the firm by the owners and management. Principals are compelled to expend financial resources to monitor their agents, which reduces their return on investment. This not only deprives shareholders of potential dividends but reduces allocative efficiency in the economy, as valuable resources are diverted from increasing the competitiveness of firms to the supervision of management. Moreover, the process results in an overall deadweight loss to society, as managers appropriate rents which properly belong to investors and which could be harnessed more efficiently. Appropriate corporate governance structures are thus required to reduce the requirement for monitoring and to prevent managers from abusing their status.[19]

It is posited that the market mechanism is best placed to regulate the conflict between managers and principals, by exposing management to

overseas holders (including institutions) accounting for 31.9%. See Jonathan P. Charkham, *Keeping Better Company* (OUP, 2005) 307.

15 See George P. Baker, Michael C. Jensen & Kevin J. Murphy, 'Compensation and Incentives: Practice vs. Theory' (1988) 43 J. FIN. 593; David S. Scharfstein, 'The Disciplinary Role of Takeovers' (1988) 55 REV. ECON. STUD. 185; Michael C. Jensen, 'The Agency Costs of Free Cash Flow: Corporate Finance and Takeovers' (1986) 76 AM. ECON. REV. 323; Eugene F. Fama & Michael C. Jensen, 'Separation of Ownership and Control' (1983) 26 J. LAW ECON. 301; Michael C. Jensen & William H. Meckling, 'Theory of the Firm: Managerial Behaviour, Agency Costs, and Ownership Structure' (1976) 3 J. FIN. ECON. 305 (hereinafter Jensen & Meckling, 'Agency Costs'); Stephen A. Ross, 'The Economic Theory of Agency: The Principal's Problem' (1973) 63 AM. ECON. REV. 134.

16 Adolf A. Berle & Gardiner C. Means, *The Modern Corporation and Private Property* (Macmillan, 1932).

17 Jensen & Meckling, *Agency Costs.*

18 Sanjai Bhagat & Roberta Romano, 'Reforming Executive Compensation' (2009) 26 YALE J. REG. 359.

19 Marianne Bertrand & Sendhil Mullainathan, 'Agents With and Without Principals' (2000) 90 AM. ECON. REV. 203.

the disciplining effects of the market and ensuring they are fulfilling their duties to their principals.[20] Because *only* shareholders have the profit incentive and investment-risk awareness to implement the most effective corporate governance arrangements to protect their interests, investors ought to be facilitated in the buying and selling of shares.[21] In the absence of an active market for shares, the agents would continue to extract rents from their principals without fear of removal. However, investors are able to exert indirect pressure on managers through stock trades by engaging in takeovers, thus displacing inefficient managers, and through signalling to markets that managers are inefficient by having them removed or by selling shares of underperforming companies.[22] The prevailing market structure thus requires an active 'market for corporate control' where shares may be freely traded.[23] Managers of poorly performing firms will be acutely aware of the possibility that new investors in a firm may decide to remove them for underperformance. This is an efficient method of monitoring management in comparative terms; creditors and other investors are often in a better position to monitor the performance of management than the stockholders in a firm whose shareholding is widely dispersed. Removing restrictions on the market for corporate control[24] therefore ought to improve corporate governance as it will expose managers of poorly performing firms to external discipline.[25] Based on this view, the key developmental insight of work on corporate governance in the 1970s – particularly that of Jensen and Meckling – was to recognise that executive compensation contracts could be used as an element to achieve the alignment of principal–agent interests: agents, it was posited, ought to be judged on the basis of the value they created for their principals, and the most appropriate measure of that value was the stock price of the firms they

---

[20] Eugene F. Fama, 'Agency Problems and Residual Claims' (1980) 26 J. LAW ECON. 327.

[21] Raaj K. Sah & Joseph E. Stiglitz, 'The Architecture of Economic Systems: Hierarchies and Polyarchies' (1986) 76 AM. ECON. REV. 716.

[22] Lynne L. Dallas, 'Two Models of Corporate Governance: Beyond Berle and Means' (1988) 22 UNIV. MICH. J. LAW REFORM 19, 23–24.

[23] See, for example, Larry E. Ribstein, 'Market vs Regulatory Responses to Corporate Fraud: A Critique of the Sarbanes-Oxley Act 2002' (2002) 28 J. CORP. L. 1.

[24] Oliver Hart, 'Corporate Governance: Some Theory and Implications' (1995) 105 ECON. J. 678.

[25] Eugene F. Fama, 'Agency Problems and the Theory of the Firm' (1980) 88 J. LAW ECON. 288.

managed. Higher stock prices increase shareholder wealth.[26] Therefore, the greater the gain of shareholders, the greater the gains that ought to flow to those managing shareholder interests. If they did not, the market for corporate control would operate to ensure those managers would be removed.

Shareholder value, in tandem with a fully operational market for corporate control, therefore came to be regarded as the most effective way of solving the agency problem because it reveals the extent to which shareholders benefit from firm ownership. Beginning in the late 1970s, executive remuneration structures which rewarded shareholder gains were introduced across Anglo-American corporations and stock prices became the standard metric of executive success.[27] As will be noted in the next section, this trend persists until the present day, and the pay of virtually all top executives at Anglo-American corporations is determined to some extent by the share price of their firms. However, as will be explained in the following sections, executive compensation may be viewed as both an agency risk and a solution to the agency problem. It is a solution because it may be designed in an appropriate fashion to align the interests of equity owners in the firm with those of company management.[28] It is a risk because, if designed inappropriately, it may exacerbate the tendency of management to sacrifice long-term corporate performance to secure short-term personal rewards.

(ii) The Structure of Executive Compensation

As identified in the previous section, one of the key functions of governance is to link individual and collective executive remuneration to corporate performance. Performance-related pay remains the dominant approach to setting executive pay levels, principally because a substantial body of research into US companies reveals a statistically significant link between the pay of senior executives and corporate performance.[29]

---

[26] Henry Hansmann & Reinier Kraakman, 'The End of History for Corporate Law' (2001) 89 GEORGETOWN LAW J. 439.

[27] Much of this may be attributed to the work of Michael Jensen, who published several seminal studies into the effectiveness of pay-for-performance mechanisms in promoting shareholder value theory.

[28] Randall Morck, Andrei Shleifer & Robert W. Vishny, 'Management Ownership and Market Valuation: An Empirical Analysis' (1998) 20 J. FIN. ECON. 293.

[29] See John F. Boschen, Augustine Duru, Lawrence A. Gordon & Kimberly J. Smith, 'Accounting and Stock Price Performance in Dynamic CEO Compensation Arrangements' (2003) 78 ACC. REV. 143; Kevin J. Murphy, 'Executive Compensation' in Orley Ashenfelter & David Card (eds), *Handbook of Labor*

Largely thanks to this research, performance-based pay has received Congressional approval in the US,[30] and the use of equity as a reward mechanism rather than cash payments grew quickly throughout the 1980s and 1990s.[31]

Most companies therefore employ executive remuneration settlements which include an explicit link between stock price performance and the compensation that an executive receives. This notion is partially designed to mitigate agency costs, but it is also designed to provide a framework under which appropriate levels of remuneration may be calculated, allowing the market to set a rate of executive pay; owners wish to maximise the return on their equity by structuring CEO pay to reward

---

Economics (Elsevier, 1999); Brian J. Hall & Jeffrey B. Liebman, 'Are CEOs Really Paid Like Bureaucrats?' (1998) 113 Q. J. ECON. 653; John F. Boschen & Kimberly J. Smith, 'You Can Pay Me Now and You Can Pay Me Later: The Dynamic Response of Executive Compensation to Firm Performance' (1995) 68 J. BUS. 577; Michael C. Jensen & Kevin J. Murphy, 'Performance Pay and Top-Management Incentives' (1990) 98 J. POLIT. ECONOMY 225; Michael C. Jensen & Kevin J. Murphy, 'CEO Incentives: It's Not How Much You Pay But How' (1990) 3 HARV. BUS. REV. 138; Eugene F. Fama, 'Agency Problems and the Theory of the Firm' (1980) 88 J. POLIT. ECONOMY 288.

[30] The incentive function of executive compensation was recognised in the elimination of corporate income tax deductions for executive salaries in excess of $1 million, since the limitation applied only to non-incentive-based remuneration. See I.R.C § 162 (m) (2006). This deduction, however, applies to fixed-price options only.

[31] Randall S. Thomas & Kenneth J. Martin, 'The Determinants of Shareholder Voting on Stock Option Plans' (2000) 35 WAKE FOREST LAW REV. 31, 38 ('[S]tock options help align managers' interests with those of shareholders. Stock-based pay, therefore, is claimed to be superior to more fixed components of compensation, such as salary and bonuses, because it rewards managers for thinking like shareholders') (citation omitted). See also John C. Coffee, Jr., 'Understanding Enron: It's About the Gatekeepers, Stupid' (2002) Columbia Law School, The Center for Law and Economic Studies Working Paper No. 207 (hereinafter Coffee, 'Understanding Enron'). In the UK stock options were not used as prevalently in the US; however, stock- and bonus-related compensation is still used extensively. For example, in large UK corporations, the average CEO salary in 1999 was £256,000, whereas the variable compensation was £241,000. By 2003, the average UK CEO salary had increased to £328,000, yet variable compensation had reached £603,000. Perhaps because of the US corporate scandals in 2002, the level of variable compensation fell to £462,000 in 2005, and stock options made up a lower proportion of that variable compensation. For discussion, see Neslihan Ozkan, 'CEO Compensation and Firm Performance: an Empirical Investigation of UK Panel Data' (2011) 17 EUR. FIN. MAN. 260, Table 1.

profits yet also wish to avoid paying the CEO more than is required.[32] 'Performance-based pay' may comprise a wide array of remunerative methods[33] and may be judged based on several metrics, for example: 'Internal measurements could be based on budgeted targets, absolute standards, and/or strategic milestones. External measurements could be based on total shareholder return and/or a designated performance measurement versus an appropriate peer group of companies.'[34] To this end, there are two main forms of compensation used by the modern corporation to achieve this, and each is determined by reference to securities prices (one of the main subjects of this book). Firstly, performance-based bonuses are used. Indicatively, these bonuses would relate to the internal measurement of performance of the company based upon its market capitalization and an external measurement of performance based upon its position relevant to other companies in its peer group.[35]

Secondly, and most commonly, there are stock options. A traditional stock option is a privilege granted to an employee by a company which gives the buyer the right to purchase a stock at a price agreed on at the date the option is granted. In practice, this usually means that an option is granted to an executive at a firm at the market value of the share at the time the option is granted.[36] An option is regarded as a 'long-term' incentive because the period in which it vests rarely comprises a minimum period of less than one year (as later analysis will demonstrate,

---

[32] Janice Kay McClendon, 'Bringing The Bulls To Bear: Regulating Executive Compensation To Realign Management And Shareholders' Interests And Promote Corporate Long-Term Productivity' (2004) 39 WAKE FOREST LAW REV. 971.

[33] The list of performance measurement standards is too exhaustive to give here. For a full discussion of these measurements see Bruce R. Ellig, *The Complete Guide to Executive Compensation* (McGraw-Hill, 2007) 51–69 (hereinafter Ellig, *Complete Guide*).

[34] Ibid. 54.

[35] Ellig notes: 'These measurements are typically relative to own company performance and could use any of the measurements identified internal to the company … An excellent example of this is the stock chart required to be included in the company proxy statement for publicly traded companies. It could be a company-defined group of companies, an industry sub-set within the appropriate stock exchange, or the composite performance of the entire stock exchange. Such measurements are for shareholder value.' See ibid. 67.

[36] The option itself has a value. The value is usually determined by the Black-Scholes option-pricing formula. For further details on the pricing of options, see http://www.black-scholes.co.uk.

however, the use of stock options has often inculcated anything but long-term management strategies). With a traditional option plan, when the options vest and become exercisable, the executive is required to pay the exercise price for each option; that is, the 'strike' price as agreed at the date the option was granted. It is the manager's choice when to cash the stock in. If the stock price increases during the intervening period between the grant and the right to sell the option, the manager might realise substantial financial rewards; the executive concerned will, of course, only exercise the option if the stock price has appreciated between the date of the grant and the exercise date.

On this basis, it is argued that stock options align managerial incentives with those of stockholders; the higher the stock price, the greater the financial rewards for each party,[37] thereby making options a form of profit sharing that links the professional manager's financial success to that of the shareholder. They are regarded as an efficient and appropriate incentive for three reasons: '(1) the executive must put up some of his/her own money, (2) the value, like the shareholder's, is at risk with the price of the company stock, and (3) assuming no discount, there is no charge to corporate earnings.'[38] The rationale for these plans is therefore clear: options are only of value to an executive if the company's stock price at the date of vesting is higher than it was on the date the options were granted.

The market value of these options at the exercise date may be many multiples of the base salary that an executive receives.[39] The late twentieth century witnessed an explosion in their use; at the 2,000 largest firms listed on US exchanges, the value of stock options rose from $50 billion in 1997 to $162 billion in 2000, and between 1992 and 2002, options rose from 5 per cent of the outstanding shares in US public

---

[37] Cynthia E. Devers, Albert A. Cannella Jr., Gregory P. Reilly & Michele E. Yoder, 'Executive Compensation: A Multidisciplinary Review of Recent Developments' (2007) 33 J. MAN. 1016.

[38] Ellig, *Complete Guide* 457. A variation on the traditional option is the use of 'restricted stock'. This involves no payment from the executive to the company at the date of the option grant; instead the executive is granted 'performance shares' which are frozen for a period, preventing the executive from trading them. If agreed performance targets are met by the end of the agreed 'freeze' period, the executive will become entitled to the restricted stock, and receive any profits. See Stacey R. Kole, 'The Complexity of Compensation Contracts' (1997) 43 J. FIN. ECON. 79.

[39] For example, the CEO of Lehman Brothers, Dick Fuld, received a base salary of $750,000 in 2008 yet earned $26,620,000 in the exercise of stock options. See: http://www.forbes.com/lists/2008/12/.

equity markets to 15 per cent.[40] Perhaps more significantly, between 1985 and 2001, equity-based CEO pay increased from 1 per cent to 66 per cent of total compensation.[41] As Professor Coffee noted in relation to the stock options outstanding in 2000: '... if $162 billion is the value of all options in these 2,000 companies, aggressive accounting policies that temporarily raise stock prices by as little as ten per cent create a potential gain for executives of over $16 billion – a substantial incentive'.[42] Following the widespread introduction of these option plans, it is arguable that forces were unleashed which were 'very difficult to control and ... [would] ... almost certainly destroy value'[43] and the incentives to boost stock prices to capture short-term value thereby became pronounced.[44] It is clear that these incentives may have exerted pressure on managers to adopt short-termist behaviour; some of the critical flaws to this brand of shareholder value governance in Anglo-American markets will now be addressed.

ISSUES WITH EXECUTIVE COMPENSATION: ASSUMPTIONS AND FLAWS

As this chapter noted in its introduction, designers of executive pay packages make certain assumptions concerning the integrity of the market pricing system when formulating the composition of compensation. Later chapters will reveal some of these assumptions to be erroneous. In contrast, the remainder of this chapter analyses some of the practical constraints which afflict the use of stock options and other performance-based pay elements. Whilst there is an established and

---

40 See Gretchen Morgenson, 'Corporate Conduct: News Analysis; Bush Failed to Stress Need to Rein in Stock Options', *New York Times* (New York, 11 July 2002); see also Gretchen Morgenson, 'Market Watch: Time For Accountability At the Corporate Candy Store' *New York Times* (New York, 3 March 2002).

41 Brian J. Hall, 'Six Challenges in Designing Equity-Based Pay' (2003) NBER Working Paper No. 9887, 4.

42 Coffee, *Understanding Enron* n 31.

43 Michael C. Jensen, 'Agency Costs of Overvalued Equity' (2005) 34 FIN. MAN. 5, 7 (hereinafter Jensen, 'Overvalued Equity').

44 Patrick Bolton, Jose Scheinkman & Wei Xiong, 'Executive Compensation and Short-Termist Behaviour in Speculative Markets' (2006) 73 REV. ECON. STUD. 577.

well-versed literature in relation to these limitations,[45] it is necessary to survey those criticisms in order to build an analysis of the disadvantages and drawbacks of current compensation arrangements. Moreover, whilst some of the issues to be discussed have been mitigated recently (through recent legislative responses to stock-options scandals and pay-driven corporate collapses), serious problems with stock-based incentive pay still exist – not least the dangers to financial stability which these systems may create when utilised in large financial institutions.

There are three primary practical flaws in the use of stock options which damage the utility of their use. Firstly, valuing options is difficult, and therefore most firms use 'at-the-money' options – that is, with a strike price equal to the company's stock price on the date of the grant. This is despite the fact that 'out-of-the-money' options – that is, options with a strike price at a higher level than the market value – generate much greater pay-for-performance sensitivity than do conventional options.[46] Moreover, studies demonstrate that CEOs value stock options at approximately half their market value. Thus, it is twice as costly to pay a CEO in options as it is in cash. On this basis, too many options are granted to top executives; that is, the incentive benefits of some of the options granted to CEOs are worth less to shareholders than the costs of granting them.[47] CEOs who are paid more and are less 'pressured' by shareholders take less risk, allowing them to pursue strategies which shield the stock price from short- or medium-term negative impact to preserve the value of their remuneration.[48] Thus, the exercise price of the

---

45 This literature is evaluated and well summarised by Bebchuk and Fried in their bestselling book. See Lucian A. Bebchuk & Jesse M. Fried, *Pay Without Performance: The Unfulfilled Promise of Executive Compensation* (2nd edn, Harvard University Press, 2006) (hereinafter Bebchuk & Fried, *Pay Without Performance*).

46 Radhakrishnan Gopalan, Todd T. Milbourn & Fenghua Song, 'Strategic Flexibility and the Optimality of Pay for Luck' (September 2008) http://ssrn.com/abstract=1012975; Shane A. Johnson & Yisong S. Tian, 'The Value and Incentive Effects of Non-Traditional Executive Stock Option Plans' (2000) 57 J. FIN. ECON. 3; Brian J. Hall, 'A Better Way to Pay CEOs?' in Jennifer Carpenter & David Yermack (eds), *Executive Compensation and Shareholder Value* (Kluwer Academic Publishers, 1999); Richard A. Lambert, David F. Larcker & Robert E. Verrechia, 'Portfolio Considerations in Valuing Executive Compensation' (1991) 29 J. ACC. RES. 129.

47 Michel A. Habib & Alexander Ljungqvist, 'Firm Value and Managerial Incentives: A Stochastic Frontier Approach' (2005) 78 J. BUS. 2053.

48 Carl R. Chen, Thomas L. Steiner & Ann Marie Whyte, 'Does Stock-Option-Based Compensation Induce Risk-Taking? An Analysis of the Banking

option is a critical factor in motivating executive decision making.[49] Whether an option encourages an incentive-driven executive to assume an appropriate amount of risk depends on the amount he/she stands to gain financially from the strategy relative to the risk attached to the strategy.[50]

Secondly, options may be repriced.[51] Option repricing in Anglo-American markets has been the source of many recent corporate scandals[52] and the practice is more prevalent at firms with poor corporate governance.[53] Firms may engage in options repricing or 'backdoor repricing' by issuing new options at a lower exercise price. This, of course, distorts the pay-for-performance model. Option repricing is most commonly undertaken when the stock price drops to levels which render the option related to the stock valueless. The justification for stock option repricing is that if a stock becomes 'out of the money', the incentive effects of the stock-based compensation are removed as the sensitivity of pay and performance decreases.[54] Defenders of these practices often point to the fact that repricing may be used to motivate executives whose firms lose value because of factors beyond the control of management: for example, general market swings which drag the price of a particular stock down. However, research supports the view that most option repricing is not driven by market or sector performance but follows the poor performance of the specific individual firms which engage in it.[55] Further, repricing also frequently follows the release of good or bad

---

Industry' (2006) 30 J. BANK. FIN. 915; Bengt Holmstrom, 'Pay Without Performance and the Managerial Power Hypothesis: A Comment' (2005) 30 J. CORP. LAW 703.

[49] Rajesh Aggarwal & Andrew Samwick, 'The Other Side of the Trade-Off: The Impact of Risk on Executive Compensation' (1999) 107 J. POLIT. ECONOMY 65; David Yermack, 'Good Timing: CEO Stock Option Awards and Company News Announcements' (1997) 52 J. FIN. 449.

[50] Tom Nohel & Steven Todd, 'Stock Options and Managerial Incentives to Invest' (2004) 1 J. DERIVATIVES 29.

[51] Brian J. Hall & Thomas A. Knox, 'Managing Option Fragility' (2002) NBER Working Paper No. 9059.

[52] John C. Coffee, 'A Theory Of Corporate Scandals; Why the US and Europe Differ' (2005) 21 OX. REV. ECON. POL. 198 (hereinafter Coffee, 'Corporate Scandals').

[53] Donald M. Chance, Raman Kumar & Rebecca B. Todd, 'The "Repricing" of Executive Stock Options' (2000) 57 J. FIN. ECON. 148.

[54] Mary E. Carter & Luann J. Lynch, 'An Examination of Executive Stock Option Repricing' (2001) 61 J. FIN. ECON. 207 (hereinafter Carter & Lynch, 'Stock Option Repricing').

[55] Menachem Brenner, Rangarajan K. Sundaram & David Yermack, 'Altering the Terms of Executive Stock Options' (2000) 57 J. FIN. ECON. 103.

firm-specific news.[56] Option repricing has therefore received significant regulatory attention. In the US, the Financial Accounting Standards Board (FASB) now requires firms to expense repriced options, making companies more reluctant to engage in repricing.[57] Further, since 2003 shareholder approval to changes in executive compensation schemes has been required under the listing rules of the NYSE and NASDAQ.[58] Shareholders must be made aware of the reasoning behind any exchange offer and may require full disclosure of the impact of any proposed change. However, despite these legislative changes, recent investigations show that backdating of options remains frequent amongst public companies, with around 15–20 per cent of US-listed public companies continuing to engage in the practice. This form of backdating created executive windfalls of approximately 10 per cent.[59]

Thirdly, executives may use their inside information to exploit their investment advantages over outside investors in order to boost their compensation by preventing the dissemination of information to the market.[60] Or, insiders may conceal price-sensitive information which will

---

[56] Sandra Renfro Callaghan, P. Jane Saly & Chandra Subramaniam, 'The Timing of Option Repricing' (2004) 59 J. FIN. 1651 (hereinafter Callaghan et al, *The Timing of Option Repricing*).

[57] The adoption of accounting rule FAS 123R increased the accounting cost of a one-for-one option exchange and eliminated any accounting advantage that stock options had over other forms of equity compensation.

[58] SEC Release No. 34-48108 Self-Regulatory Organizations; New York Stock Exchange, Inc. and National Association of Securities Dealers, Inc.; Order Approving NYSE and Nasdaq Proposed Rule Changes and Nasdaq Amendment No. 1 and Notice of Filing and Order Granting Accelerated Approval to NYSE Amendments No. 1 and 2 and Nasdaq Amendments No. 2 and 3 Thereto Relating to Equity Compensation Plans (30 June 2003), http://www.sec.gov/rules/sro/34-48108.htm.

[59] Jesse M. Fried, 'Options Backdating and Its Implications' (2008) 65 WASHINGTON & LEE LAW REV. 853, 884. Where repricing the relevant options has not been financially attractive, companies have utilised other strategies to reward executives with stock grants; firstly, through granting executives *additional* options with a lower exercise price; or secondly, a contract for a 'value-for-value' exchange which provides the holder of options the opportunity to dispense with 'out-of-the-money' options in exchange for an immediate grant of new shares with an exercise price equal to or less than the fair market value of the stock. See Justin Fox, 'Amazing Stock Option Sleight of Hand' *Fortune* (London, 25 June 2001) 86.

[60] Jesse M. Fried, 'Reducing the Profitability of Corporate Insider Trading through Predating Disclosure' (1998) 71 S. CALIFORNIA LAW REV. 303, 315;

affect their rewards negatively.[61] The power of the CEO is an obvious further factor in the timing of price-affecting information releases.[62] CEOs and other top executives will have substantial discretion over the timing of information disclosure and release which may affect the price of their company stock and thereby the value of their options. Managers, in general, time voluntary announcements which reduce the stock price of their firms to produce the optimal return to them from the exercise of their grants:[63]

> Executives have the incentive and opportunity to manage the timing of their communications of inside information to the market during the period just prior to the date of their stock-option grant so as to reduce the exercise price of their options. Executives benefit from temporary stock price decreases before the grant date and by stock price increases after the grant date. Executive stock option grants create a unique opportunity for insiders to profit by manipulating the timing of information flowing to the market without engaging in insider trading.[64]

The link between the stock price of the relevant firm and executives' personal enrichment is contingent on the quality of information disseminated to the market; thus, executives may use selective information to artificially inflate or deflate prices. That both earnings restatements and equity-based compensation increased significantly throughout the 1990s is indicative of a link between short-termism in markets and information quality and 'corroborates [the] interpretation that managerial behaviour changed, because [of] a significant change in motive'.[65]

J. Seligman, 'The Reformulation of Federal Securities Law Concerning Nonpublic Information' (1985) 73 GEORGETOWN LAW J. 1083, 1095–96.

[61] Callaghan et al, *The Timing of Option Repricing*.

[62] Kevin J. Murphy, 'Explaining Executive Compensation: Managerial Power vs. the Perceived Cost of Stock Options' (2002) 69 UNIV. CHICAGO LAW REV. 851 (hereinafter Murphy, 'Explaining Executive Compensation').

[63] David Aboody & Ron Kasznik, 'CEO stock option awards and the timing of corporate voluntary disclosures' (2000) 29 J. ACC. ECON. 73.

[64] Keith W. Chauvin & Catherine Shenoy, 'Stock Price Decreases Prior to Executive Stock Option Grants' (2001) 7 J. CORP. FIN. 53, 76.

[65] John C. Coffee, 'Gatekeeper Failure and Reform: The Challenge of Fashioning Relevant Reforms' (2004) 84 B.U. L. REV. 301, 315 (hereinafter Coffee, 'Gatekeeper Failure'). A link between the frequency of shareholder class action lawsuits based on accounting manipulation and the rise of stock-related executive pay has been postulated on this basis. See Lin Peng & Ailsa Roell, 'Executive Pay and Shareholder Litigation' (2008) 12 REV. FIN. 141.

There is therefore a strong prima facie case that it was the explosion in the use of stock-based compensation which drove these developments. Several studies find systematic links between the timing of information disclosure and options grants: there is 'strong evidence that executives [time] option exercises relative to private information to enhance the returns from [their] exercise strategies …'.[66] Option grant timing strongly favours the board members at firms; CEOs and independent directors receive an abnormally high number of grants at the lowest price of any particular month. These so-called 'lucky' grants 'are associated with higher CEO compensation from other sources, and are correlated with a lack of majority independent directors on the board, no independent compensation committee with an outside blockholder, or a long-serving CEO'.[67] Evidence also exists that managers adopt disclosure practices which increase 'sentiment-driven overvaluation' to generate short-term spikes in a stock price in order to capture the windfalls from exercising their options.[68] Bebchuk and Fried summarise thus: 'Like managers with control over the timing of their option grants, managers with control over the timing of disclosures and earnings accruals receive options with an exercise price below the company's true value at the grant date.'[69]

MARKET MANIPULATION

The previous section discussed the structural limitations inherent in contracts which use stock-based awards for compensation. It was noted that the design of compensation systems may indirectly reward conduct which does not enhance firm value, and that executives may employ legal

---

[66] David C. Cicero, 'The Manipulation of Executive Stock Option Exercise Strategies: Information Timing and Backdating' (2009) 64 J. FIN. 2627, 2628; see also David Aboody, John S. Hughes, Jing Liu & Wei Su, 'Are Executive Stock Option Exercises Driven by Private Information?' (2008) 13 REV. ACC. STUD. 551; David Yermack, 'Good Timing: CEO Stock Option Awards and Company News announcements' (1997) 52 J. FIN. 449.

[67] Lucian A. Bebchuk, Yaniv Grinstein & Urs Peyer, 'Lucky CEOs and Lucky Directors' (2010) 65 J. FIN. 2363. See also Lucian A. Bebchuk, Jesse M. Fried & David I. Walker, 'Managerial Power and Rent Extraction in the Design of Executive Compensation' (2002) Harvard Law School Discussion Paper No. 366.

[68] Nicholas Seybert & Holly I. Yang, 'The Party's Over: The Role of Earnings Guidance in Resolving Sentiment-driven Overvaluation' (2012) 12 MANAGEMENT SCI. 308.

[69] Bebchuk & Fried, *Pay Without Performance* 164.

(if not entirely legitimate) means to ensure that their compensation awards are maximised. In contrast to the examples cited in those sections, which concerned 'judicious' use of information or the exploitation of legal and regulatory loopholes to maximise executive rewards, market manipulation refers to a direct and illegal effort to undermine the integrity of market information.[70] The term 'market manipulation' is often used generically to cover many forms of market abuse and a precise legal definition is therefore difficult to formulate.[71] It is, however, the economic effects of market manipulation, rather than their legal character, which are most relevant for present purposes.[72]

As the purpose of most abusive practices is to provide misleading information (including the publication of false accounting statements or deliberate obfuscation of materially significant information from the market), it necessarily undermines the informational content of securities prices. Moreover, it is clear that potential manipulators may use a mixture of devices with which to distort information. The fact that there is such a wide array of methods available to potential manipulators to distort prices simply makes the case for market inefficiency more convincing.

In the context of this book, of particular note are the incentives created by modern executive compensation contracts to engage in corporate fraud. These incentives appear to have been operative in many recent cases of market manipulation. The widespread occurrence of these frauds in the 1990s and 2000s certainly appears to have coincided with a shift in managerial compensation structures toward an extension of the use of equity-based remuneration, surveyed in the initial sections of this chapter. It is plausibly argued that stock-based compensation (whether this

---

[70] The classic definition was provided in the US case of *Cargill Inc. v Hardin* (452 F 2d 1154, 1163, 1167–70 (1971)), where market manipulation was defined as any scheme or artifice that deliberately influences the price of a financial asset, resulting in a price other than the one that would have resulted in the absence of such intervention. In legal circles this definition has not been universally accepted as adequate. See Frank H. Easterbrook, 'Monopoly, Manipulation and the Regulation of Futures Markets' (1986) 59(2) J. BUS. 103.

[71] Emilios Avgouleas, *The Mechanics and Regulation of Market Abuse: A Legal and Economic Analysis* (OUP, 2005) 104 (hereinafter Avgouleas, *Mechanics & Regulation*).

[72] In this context, the effects of market manipulation are to 'lead the price of [financial] investments to an artificial level and/or enable the perpetrators of the behaviour to materialize, from interests held in the specific or related investments, financial gains that would not be possible, in the absence of such behaviour.' See ibid. 116.

consisted of stock options or of stock-related performance pay) contributed to a culture of short-termism in the corporate sphere, which incentivised managers to prioritise immediate shareholder returns over long-term sustainable growth. This arguably placed severe pressure on executives to create short-term upward price movements, which, although unsustainable over the medium to long term, were used to justify the award of large compensation packages in the short term. Some of these techniques, whilst dubious, were legal. However, perhaps inevitably, under pressure from shareholders, analysts and markets, many corporate executives also resorted to fraud in order to prop up or inflate securities prices and, in many respects, the genesis of these episodes may be traced to the adherence to the dominant view of enhancing shareholder value, which attained cardinal importance in Anglo-American markets in the late 1990s and early 2000s.[73]

There has been much theorising about the precise nature of the capacity of corporate executives to engage in schemes designed to distort prices.[74] However, perhaps the most accurate characterisation of these abuses, where senior managers used their position to extract wealth from less-informed and less-powerful constituencies, is as a species of 'control fraud'.[75] These are frauds perpetrated by those in control of seemingly legitimate organisations, with the organisations themselves used as agents for the commission of fraud. The incentives to commit fraud for those in control of the relevant organisations are normally financial, and realised through seemingly normal compensation systems. The CEO (or other officers with some degree of firm 'control') is able to exploit the corporation, its creditors and shareholders by virtue of the control he/she has over the corporation's disclosure and internal monitoring systems. These control frauds may even involve external monitors of firm conduct, who may become complicit in the manipulation of accounts; indeed, the most 'profitable' control frauds are normally those with the outward

---

73 For example, the frauds at WorldCom, Parmalat, Global Crossing, Tyco and Enron destroyed billions of dollars in shareholder wealth.

74 For discussion on managerial power theories, see Renee B. Adams, Heitor Almeida & Daniel Ferreira, 'Powerful CEOs and Their Impact on Corporate Performance' (2005) 18 REV. FIN. STUD. 1403; Marianne Bertrand and Antoinette Schoar, 'Managing with Style: The Effect of Managers on Firm Policies' (2003) 118 Q. J. ECON. 1169.

75 William K. Black, *The Best Way to Rob a Bank is to Own One: How Corporate Executives and Politicians Looted the S&L Industry* (2nd edn, University of Texas Press, 2014).

veneer of legitimacy, gained through the blessing of an industry gatekeeper or other financial watchdog.[76] On this basis, most of these frauds are maintained via accounting and financial manipulation:[77] 'Accounting fraud is the looter's "weapon of choice." The CEO uses it to overstate the company's profits and net worth in order to convert company assets to his personal use through seemingly normal and legitimate corporate mechanisms (e.g., salary, bonuses and stock options).'[78] Most corporate crises of this nature therefore involve management manipulation of accounts and financial statements to extract increased wealth from their compensation arrangements, and/or to ensure that their corporations are able to satisfy borrowing requirements imposed by capital markets (thereby maintaining a certain stock price level), rather than direct appropriation of firm assets.[79] The resulting reporting inaccuracies cost substantial sums to shareholders and, of course, contribute to market pricing distortions,

---

[76] John C. Coffee, *Gatekeepers: The Professions and Corporate Governance* (OUP, 2006) (hereinafter Coffee, *Gatekeepers*).

[77] The former chair of the SEC, Arthur Levitt, has commented: '[i]n the zeal to satisfy consensus earnings estimates and project a smooth earnings path, wishful thinking may be winning the day over faithful presentation. As a result, I fear that we are witnessing an erosion in the quality of earnings, and therefore, the quality of financial reporting. Managing may be giving way to manipulation; integrity may be losing out to illusion … A gray area where the accounting is being perverted; where managers are cutting corners; and, where earnings reports reflect the desires of management rather than the underlying financial performance of the company.' Remarks by SEC Chairman Arthur Levitt, 'The Numbers Game' NYU Centre for Law and Business (28 September 1998) http://www.sec.gov/news/speech/speecharchive/1998/spch220.txt. In the US, 10% of listed companies were forced to restate their financial statements at least once between 1997 and 2004. Statistics indicate that the actual number of corporate restatements rose from 91 in 1998, to 330 in 2002. The number of companies listed on the three US exchanges decreased by 20% in this period, from 9,275 in 1997 to 7,446 in 2002, resulting in a larger proportion of public companies being forced to restate their financial accounts. By 2004, the number of restatements had risen to 414. See U.S. Gen. Accounting Office, Pub. No. 03-138, *Financial Statement Restatements: Trends, Market Impacts, Regulatory Responses and Remaining Challenges* (October 2002) 4 (hereinafter U.S. Gen. Accounting Office, *Financial Statement Restatements*). For further discussion, see Coffee, 'Corporate Scandals'.

[78] William K. Black, 'When Fragile becomes Friable: Endemic Control Fraud as a Cause of Economic Stagnation and Collapse' in K. Naga Srivalli (ed), *White Collar Crimes: A Debate* (ICFAI University Press, 2007) 169.

[79] John C. Coffee, 'What Caused Enron?: A Capsule Social and Economic History of the 1990s' (2004) 89 CORNELL LAW REV. 269.

undermining the use of market prices as useful indicators of value.[80] Moreover, the fact that these abuses may occur without detection, in some cases for many years, suggests that there is a strong link between weak standards of governance and the incidence of market abuse. Between mid-2001 and 2002, for example, nine of the largest 100 US-listed corporations were subject to formal investigation by the Securities and Exchange Commission (SEC) for fraudulent financial reporting.[81]

The Enron scandal, in particular, revealed acute issues relating to the accuracy of securities prices, and the role of accounting manipulation in corporate frauds. It also showed how a corporation heavily involved in financial markets (Enron's derivatives business was worth approximately $20 billion) could obfuscate financial performance through complexity and extreme financial engineering. Perversely of course, the incentive systems at Enron led management to engage in long-term value-destroying actions to maintain the company's stock price in the short run. As an example of this, the financial strategy that Enron embarked upon in 2001 – and the market valuation that supported this – required the company to grow its free cash flow by 91 per cent every year for six years.[82] In the event, the *only* way Enron's management could achieve

---

[80] Estimates based on available statistics suggest that the 689 publicly traded companies which announced financial restatements between January 1997 and March 2002 lost over $100 billion in market capitalisation. See Huron Consulting Group, *2004 Annual Review of Financial Reporting Matters: Final Report* (March 2005) http://www.huronconsultinggroup.com. Financial restatements are indicators of – amongst other things – flawed internal financial structures, inappropriate audit controls, and sub-standard reporting mechanisms, and the market views them with distaste. A restatement typically results in an immediate negative return on shareholder value of 9%. See Zoe-Vonna Palmrose, Vernon J. Richardson & Susan Scholz, 'Determinants of Market Reactions to Restatement Announcements' (2004) 37 J. ACC. ECON. 59, 61. Further research indicates that over a three-day window surrounding the corporate restatements, a firm stands to lose 11% of its previous value and, if one examines the median share price of a firm encompassing the 120 days prior to, and following, the accounting readjustment, 'firms lose on average 25 per cent of market value over the period examined and this is concentrated in a narrow window surrounding the announcement of the restatement'. See Scott A. Richardson, Irem A. Tuna & Min Wu, 'Predicting Earnings Management: The Case of Earnings Restatements' (2005) 4, http://ssrn.com/abstract=338681.

[81] Paul W. MacAvoy & Ira M. Millstein, *The Recurrent Crisis in Corporate Governance* (Palgrave Macmillan, 2003) 83.

[82] As noted by Jensen: 'My guess is that at the time of Enron's peak market value of $70 billion, the company was actually worth about $30 billion. It was a

this sort of growth was to engage in earnings management, and many of the financing techniques Enron utilised were used simply to shift debts from its balance sheet.[83] In fact, net profits at the company were fictitious: Enron's profits of 2000 were revealed by its bankruptcy examiner to have been overstated by 95 per cent.[84]

On the basis of Enron and other large corporate scandals during this period, it was rightly concluded that corporate governance fragility was systemic, and Anglo-American regulators reacted with (in some cases, far-reaching) legislative measures. However, despite some similarities between the purpose of these frauds and the motivations for the practices which arguably led to the GFC (such as to increase executive compensation or hide leverage), regulatory changes made following the options scandals in the early twenty-first century were ineffective in preventing later grand-scale corporate collapses in the banking sector.[85] These observations naturally have serious implications for the principal–agent

---

good, viable business; the company was a major innovator. But senior managers' efforts to defend the $40 billion of excess valuation (which was nothing but a mistake that was going to go away anyway) effectively destroyed the $30 billion core value.' See Jensen, 'Overvalued Equity' 4.

[83] For example, it is highly likely that Enron used dubious valuation methods to account for futures and derivatives contracts, which indirectly boosted its reported earnings, without changing its underlying financial strength. Enron's use of mark-to-market accounting allowed it to artificially present future revenues from trades as current revenues: '… Enron reported the entire value of each trade on which it was a counterparty as its revenue, rather than reporting as revenues only its trading or brokerage fees. Traditional trading firms such as Goldman Sachs and Merrill Lynch use a more conservative 'agent model' of revenue reporting, in which only the trading or brokerage fee would be reported as revenue … The … effect of [this] was that Enron's revenues and cost of goods sold, reported in the income statement were increased as much as fifty times compared to what they would have been under more traditional accounting … [If Enron had used the more conservative accounting model its] reported revenues [would have dropped] to $6.3 billion in 2000 instead of the reported $100.8 billion.' See Bala G. Dharan & William R. Bufkins, 'Red Flags in Enron's Reporting of Revenues and Key Financial Measures' in Nancy Rapoport & Bala G. Dharan (eds), *Enron: Corporate Fiascos and Legal Implications* (Foundation Press, 2004) 102–103. See also S. Gillan & J.D. Martin, 'Financial Engineering, Corporate Governance, and the Collapse of Enron' (2003) University of Delaware Working Paper No. 2002-001.

[84] Second Interim Report of Neal Batson, Court-Appointed Examiner, In *re. Enron Corp*., No. 01-16034 (Bankr. S.D.N.Y Jan. 21, 2003).

[85] As will be discussed in a later chapter, this was because the focus of the legislative response to the 2001–02 corporate collapses, particularly the Sarbanes-Oxley Act 2002 (which concentrated mainly on imposing criminal

relationship of the firm. The dispersed ownership structures prevalent in Anglo-American markets, where there are few large shareholders involved in the management of the corporation, appear to facilitate fraud based on accounting manipulation and may explain the species of scandal that generally affects firms with these ownership arrangements. The risk-averse nature of managers, whose individual human capital is tied up with the fortunes of one corporation, makes the incentives for manipulation more acute. Managers are necessarily less interested in long-term returns than shareholders because their continued tenure is not assured, and they may therefore prioritise short-term profits to extract wealth during their 'window of opportunity'.

These incentives are naturally even more serious if executives are compensated through stock-related remuneration, which may create incentives for short-term manipulation of financial statements.[86] Executives are aware that, unless a company collapses, it is unlikely that an accounting restatement will affect them negatively.[87] Research shows a strong link between equity-based compensation and market manipulation.[88] For example, there is a strong correlation between higher levels of equity compensation and earnings management and financial restatements.[89] Where firm CEO pay is comprised of a 'significant fraction' (options worth 20 times his/her base salary) of stock options, the likelihood of a financial restatement rises by 55 per cent.[90] A significant positive relationship exists between a firm's use of stock options and

---

liability for falsely certifying certain financial and accounting statements) was misdirected.

[86] As noted: '... the options craze created an environment that rewarded executives for managing the share price, not for managing the business. Options gave executives strong incentives to use accounting tricks to boost the share price on which their compensation depended.' Arthur Levitt, *Take on The Street* (Pantheon Books, 2002) 111.

[87] See J. Bradford De Long, Andrei Shleifer, Lawrence H. Summers & Robert J. Waldmann, 'Positive Feedback Investment Strategies and Destabilising Rational Speculation' (1990) 45 J. FIN. 379.

[88] Lucian A. Bebchuk & Oren Bar-Gill, 'Misreporting Corporate Performance' (2002) Harvard Law School Discussion Paper 400.

[89] Shane A. Johnson, Harley E. Ryan & Yisong S. Tian, 'Managerial Incentives and Corporate Fraud: The Sources of Incentives Matter' (2009) 13 OX. REV. FIN. 115.

[90] Jap Efendi, Anup Srivastava & Edward P. Swanson, 'Why Do Corporate Managers Misstate Financial Statements? The Role of Option Compensation and Other Factors' (2007) 85 J. FIN. ECON. 667.

securities fraud allegations being levelled against the firm.[91] Further, corporate managers who hold a high proportion of options which they are likely to exercise in the short term are more likely to report earnings that meet – or just exceed – analyst expectations and are more likely to engage in accounting management.[92]

STOCK-BASED PAY, SHORT-TERMISM AND FINANCIAL MARKET PRICES

Although stock options and other performance-based compensation awards are designed to mitigate the problems inherent in the principal–agent relationship, they instead often provide executives with the incentives to manage information and engage in practices which, over the long term, are destructive to shareholder value, despite the fact that shareholder and managerial interests were supposed to become more aligned through the use of stock-based pay. This naturally has serious implications for market efficiency and the integrity of the market pricing mechanism.[93]

The failure of Enron and scandals at other large public corporations during that period highlighted the shortcomings of the model of corporate governance adopted in Anglo-American markets and the problems associated with reliance on market discipline. As Stout notes, there '[are] ironic aspects … to [the] prediction that [the focus on shareholder value] would prove permanent. For one thing … Enron's collapse provided a dramatic object lesson in the perils of management obsession with share

---

91 David J. Denis, Paul Hanouna & Atulya Sarin, 'Is There a Dark Side to Incentive Compensation?' (2006) 12 J. CORP. FIN. 467.

92 Qiang Cheng & Terry B. Warfield, 'Equity Incentives and Earnings Management' (2005) 80 ACC. REV. 441.

93 Another example of the side-effects of poorly structured executive compensation systems occurred in 2004. It was discovered that Royal Dutch Shell, the global oil company, had misstated its proven oil and gas reserves by inflating its volumes by approximately 30%. The SEC and FSA fined Shell $120 million and £17 million respectively for what the FSA termed 'disseminat[ing] false or misleading information as to the true extent of its proved reserves'. See FSA, *Final Notice: The 'Shell' trading and Transport Co., p.l.c.,* 24 August 2004, http://www.fsa.gov.uk/pubs/final/shell_24aug04.pdf. Comment at the time reflected the view that '[s]hareholders [had] suggested that the executive bonus system might have encouraged managers to overbook the reserves'. See Bernard Taylor, 'Shell Shock: Why Do Good Companies Do Bad Things?' (2006) 14 CORP. GOV. 181.

price.'[94] The factors discussed previously lend credence to the notion that financial incentives can lead to serious distortions in the efficiency of market valuation of firms thanks to an excessive over-reliance on short-term performance targets. Shareholder value theorists had contended that external monitoring of corporations was unnecessary in capital markets because managerial incentives, shareholder monitoring of executives, and the market for corporate control would replicate the effects of external regulation. However, excessive focus on the share performance of companies leads to damaging short-termism.[95] Share-price governance promoted an '[e]xcessive focus on quarterly results, scarce attention to value-creation strategies, and failure to probe deeply enough into long-term performance …'.[96] This can result in over-valued stock prices, which reward management in the short term but penalise shareholders in the long term. Where executives are able to inflate short-term earnings through accounting and market manipulation, they will be able to capture short-term appreciations in stock price and exercise their options to sell. This will leave the residual shareholders as bearers of the losses when the stock price invariably deflates. These incentives not only impair executives' view of the long-term health of the company, but may also encourage them to engage in behaviour which undermines the system of pay for performance.[97] The result is often distortion of information provided to investors by companies and, in some cases, the collaboration of analysts with this distortion.[98] It also drives management to pursue strategies which are not in the long-term interests of the company. For example, projects at companies which guarantee short-term income streams might be favoured over other projects which might be more sustainable yet would not impact on company share price over the short term.[99] The problems that these factors cause for business in Anglo-American markets are significant, and

---

[94] Lynn A. Stout, 'New Thinking on Shareholder Primacy' (2011) UCLA School of Law, Law-Econ Research Paper No. 11-04, 5 (hereinafter Stout, 'New Thinking').

[95] Coffee, *Gatekeepers.*

[96] Matteo Tonello, 'Revisiting Stock Market Short-Termism' *The Conference Board Research Report No. R-1386-06-RR* (April 2006) 5 (hereinafter Tonello, 'Revisiting Short-Termism').

[97] Michael C. Jensen, 'Corporate Budgeting is Broken – Let's Fix It' (2001) HARV. BUS. REV. 94.

[98] Gene D'Avolio, Efi Gildor & Andrei Shleifer, 'Technology, Information Production, and Market Efficiency' (2001) Harvard Institute of Economic Research Paper No. 1929.

[99] Tonello, 'Revisiting Short-Termism' 5.

have led some theorists to reject the predominant remuneration paradigm: '[We] must give employees and managers a structure that will help them resist the temptation to maximize short-term financial performance (as typically measured by accounting profits or, even worse, earnings per share). Short-term profit maximization at the expense of long-term value creation is a sure way to destroy value.'[100]

SECTOR-WIDE RATHER THAN FIRM-SPECIFIC PERFORMANCE: IMPERFECT MARKETS

The obstacles discussed previously are largely related to the power that senior management enjoys over the corporation as a direct consequence of the operation of the firm or flaws in the design of compensation contracts. In other words, they comprise factors relating to executive pay arrangements at individual firms. This does not, however, explain the ways in which managerial pay is decoupled from performance due to factors beyond the control of management, the board of directors or the shareholders, thanks to the aggregate operation of global or regional stock markets. Optimal compensation contracts would determine the level of pay based on variables under the control of firm management, rather than on factors beyond their control, thus rewarding executives for corporate performance, both in a relative and absolute sense.[101] The main weakness with the use of stock-based pay and stock options is that executives often capture windfalls through compensation which are not firm-specific; instead they are derived from rising equity markets or sector-specific increases in firm valuations. Indeed, the structure of executive compensation at most corporations results in the potential for executives to be rewarded for average or mediocre performance.[102] This

---

[100] Michael C. Jensen, 'Value Maximization, Stakeholder Theory, and the Corporate Objective Function' (2001) 14 J. APPL. CORP. FIN. 8, 16.

[101] Michael Weisbach, 'Optimal Executive Compensation versus Managerial Power: A Review of Lucian Bebchuk and Jesse Fried's Pay Without Performance: The Unfulfilled Promise of Executive Compensation' (2007) 45 J. ECON. LIT. 419.

[102] Warren Buffett, one of the world's leading investors, has commented that: 'Of course, stock options often go to talented, value-adding managers and sometimes deliver them rewards that are perfectly appropriate. (Indeed, managers who are really exceptional almost always get far less than they should.) But when the result is equitable, it is accidental. Once granted, the option is blind to individual performance. Because it is irrevocable and unconditional (so long as a manager stays in the company), the sluggard receives rewards from his options

is because, in most cases, the exercise price of the option is fixed at the date of the grant and remains fixed for the entire option period; often for as long as 10 years. Executives holding options cash in on the gains if the share price rises above the exercise price. Fixed-price options therefore reward executives for any increase in the stock price of their firms, even if the increase is below or only comparable to their competitor firms or the market as a whole. On this basis, fixed-price options contravene a central axiom of the pay-for-performance paradigm as they fail to insure agents against uncertainty from factors beyond their control, or penalise them for sub-standard relative performance.

External factors which drive executive pay may be strongly associated with the stock price of firms in sectors that experience growth which is due to factors extrinsic to the actions of any manager or firm.[103] CEO pay, for example, is at least as sensitive to exogenous factors ('luck') as to individual performance ('skill').[104] One study indicates that only 30 per cent of the movement of a company's stock price is driven by corporate performance; the remaining 70 per cent is reflective of general market conditions,[105] including macroeconomic factors such as the rate of inflation and interest rate levels;[106] equity-based compensation is rarely corrected for industry or market sector stock index movements.[107] The exercise prices of stock options are rarely – if ever – adjusted for the vesting period. This has the consequence that, particularly in the case of

precisely as does the star …' Warren Buffett, Letter to Shareholders in Berkshire Hathaway, 1985, http://www.berkshirehathaway.com/letters/1985.html.

103 Perhaps the most apposite example of this was the growth in the technology market around the year 2000, often referred to as the 'dot.com boom'.

104 Marianne Bertrand & Sendhil Mullainathan, 'Are CEOs Rewarded for Luck? The Ones Without Principals Are' (2001) 116 Q. J. ECON. 901.

105 SCA Consulting Study cited in Simon Patterson & Peter Smith, 'How to Make Top People's Pay Reflect Performance' *The Sunday Times* (London, 9 August 1998).

106 Interest rate rises, for example, reduce stock market value as investors move funds from stocks into savings accounts. See Alfred Rappaport, 'New Thinking on How to Link Executive Pay With Performance' (1999) 77 HARV. BUS. REV. 91, 92.

107 John E. Core, Wayne R. Guay & David F. Larcker, 'Executive Equity Compensation and Incentives: A Survey' (2003) 9 ECON. POLICY REV. 27; Lucian A. Bebchuk, Jesse M. Fried & David I. Walker, 'Executive Compensation in America: Optimal Contracting or Extraction of Rents?' (2001) NBER Working Paper Series No. 8661; John M. Abowd & David S. Kaplan, 'Executive Compensation: Six Questions That Need Answering' (1999) 13 J. ECON. PERSPECTIVES 145.

long-term options, executives will almost always earn money from stock options, as the value of stock markets generally increases. This further hampers the concept of pay for performance; if the stock price increases due to the effects of inflation or a general bull equity market, the gains driven by executives' individual performance become less apparent: 'Managers who receive options issued at-the-money and exercisable over a ten-year period will make money as long as the stock price goes up nominally over the ten-year period. As a result, the managers can benefit even if shareholders' real returns were tiny or even negative.'[108] Moreover, where these pay awards are not benchmarked to the performance of competitor companies, executives may capture remuneration which is unrelated to their individual performance.[109] As noted by Bebchuk and Fried: 'While connecting pay to executives' relative performance can provide good incentives, tying pay to stock price or earning increases that are unrelated to executives' effort does not.'[110] Of course, markets may experience negative movements entirely unrelated to the performance of a particular executive or CEO which impacts their potential remuneration;[111] however '[a]t worst negative shocks would make the managers' options worthless. On the other hand, positive shocks can boost the value of options by an unlimited amount.'[112] Research further shows that executives benefit more from good sector performance than they lose from poor sector performance.[113] It is also clear that CEOs and senior executives design compensation packages which remain non-sensitive to performance, and allow them to expropriate rents from their firms.[114]

---

[108] Lucian A. Bebchuk & Jesse M. Fried, 'Executive Compensation as an Agency Problem' (2003) 17 J. ECON. PERSPECTIVES 71.

[109] Shane A. Johnson & Yisong S. Tian, 'Indexed Executive Stock Options' (2000) 57 J. FIN. ECON. 35, 36 (hereinafter Johnson & Tian, 'Indexed Options').

[110] Bebchuk & Fried, *Pay Without Performance* 123.

[111] R. Glenn Hubbard, 'Pay Without Performance: A Market Equilibrium Critique' (2005) 30 J. CORP. LAW 717.

[112] Bebchuk & Fried, *Pay Without Performance* 139.

[113] Gerald T. Garvey & Todd Milbourn, 'Asymmetric Benchmarking in Compensation: Executives are Rewarded for Good Luck But Not Penalized for Bad' (2006) 82 J. FIN. ECON. 197.

[114] Carlos E. Jiménez-Angueira & Nathan V. Stuart, 'CEO Bonuses, Relative Performance Evaluation, and Pay-for-Luck' (2010) http://ssrn.com/abstract=1691154.

One solution to this issue is to design stock options which screen out the market trend effects exerted on stock prices[115] through relative performance evaluation (RPE), or indexed options;[116] that is, the price of options should be adjusted for movements in the particular sector concerned, or to a peer group of companies.[117] On this view, payments related to the price of company stock ought to be calibrated to remove the 'noise' effects in the performance measurement of executives without removing incentives.[118] Unlike fixed-price options, indexed options do not reward the poor relative performance of executives in situations where the market is rising generally.[119] This would arguably make compensation more efficient and preserve shareholder wealth:[120] the costs of options which do not exclude the effects on stock price resulting from general market swings to shareholder value are as much as 41 per cent.[121] Further, indexed options do not penalise strong relative performers in markets which are in decline; indexed options filter out the

---

[115] Ana M. Albuquerque, 'Peer Firms in Relative Performance Evaluation' (2009) 48 J. ACC. ECON. 69.

[116] Robert Gibbons & Kevin J. Murphy, 'Relative Performance Evaluation for Chief Executive Officers' (1990) 43 IND. LABOR RELATIONS REV. 30.

[117] See Mark A. Clawson & Thomas C. Klein, 'Indexed Stock Options: A Proposal for Compensation Commensurate with Performance' (1997) 3 STANFORD J. LAW BUS. & FIN. 31, who note at 47: 'While there are a variety of stock option structures designed to accomplish a number of different objectives, the most rational approach attempts to capture the benefits of private company options by creating incentives for the executive to influence the value of the option without transferring unearned value to the executives … the most rational stock option plan is to adjust the exercise price of the stock option up or down, depending on the performance of the index …'.

[118] Bengt Homstrom, 'Moral Hazard in Teams' (1982) 13 BELL J. ECON. 74.

[119] The favourable tax treatment of fixed options in the US makes the use of indexed options rare. See Accounting Principles Board, 'Opinion 25: Accounting for Stock Issued to Employees' (October 1972) superseded by FASB Statement 123r, para. D7. For a discussion, see Brian J. Hall and Kevin J. Murphy 'The Trouble with Stock Options' (2003) 17 J. ECON. PERSPECTIVES 49.

[120] Rajesh Aggarwal & Andrew Samwick, 'Executive Compensation, Strategic Competition, and Relative Performance Evaluation: Theory and Evidence' (1999) 54 J. FIN. 1999.

[121] James J. Angel & Douglas M. McCabe, 'Market-Adjusted Options for Executive Compensation' (2005) 4 GLOBAL BUS. ECON. REV. 1.

common risks associated with stock price movements, in both appreciating and depreciating markets.[122]

However, notwithstanding the apparent benefits of indexed options, very few firms take steps to condition the vesting of options on the achievement of performance targets in relation to competitors. Therefore, even where executives do not achieve targets for relative performance-based awards, their stock options still vest and, in rising markets, they may profit from increases in share prices:[123] 'Options are a free ride for management – no cost, no risk on the down side, only wins – and in those cases where the market goes the wrong way, repricing and a new start.'[124] Of course, even peer-benchmarked pay may be inefficient.[125] Assuming the peer company operates in the same areas of the economy as the company in question (which, if not, would seem paradoxical) benchmarking pay does not screen out the effects of sector-driven stock-price growth, and the commensurate gains achieved from stock options.[126] This suggests that flaws in the prevailing stock option system cannot be cured simply through the 'silver bullet' of indexing.

CONCLUSION

On the basis of foregoing discussions, it is apparent that there are significant issues with the predominant executive compensation paradigm, especially the use of stock-based compensation as traditionally employed by public corporations. Incentive-based pay is theorised as a

---

[122] Companies would have to ensure that management remained incentivised appropriately where the financial rewards on offer were more at risk; executives view options as riskier than cash and thus discount proportionately the value of their options. Executive indexed stock options have an average value of 34% of conventional options when calculated on the basis of the Black-Scholes algorithm. See Johnson & Tian, 'Indexed Options'; see also Murphy, 'Explaining Executive Compensation'.

[123] In 2003 only 8.5% of US firms made the vesting of stock options in the CEO contingent on him/her meeting performance targets. See Joann S. Lublin, 'Why the Get-Rich-Quick Days May Be Over' *Wall Street Journal* (New York, 14 April 2002).

[124] Robert A.G. Monks, 'Executive and Director Compensation 1984 REDUX' (1998) 6 CORP. GOV.: AN INT. REV. 135.

[125] Ellig, *Complete Guide* 70.

[126] 'There is no question in my mind that mediocre CEOs are getting incredibly overpaid. And the way it's being done is through stock options.' Comments of Warren Buffett, cited in Shawn Tully, 'Raising the Bar' *Fortune* (London, 8 June 1998) 272.

solution to the agency problems which afflict firms and may be used to align the interests of managers and owners to ensure efficient compensation contracting and induce value-enhancing behaviour. The value created by executives for shareholders is the usual yardstick with which to measure performance and therefore incentive-based pay is generally comprised of stock-based bonuses, or direct awards of company shares. This chapter has also noted that these grants have often created perverse incentives for executives to manipulate share prices, or pursue short-term price-boosting strategies that are not in the interests of long-term sustainability in order to capture excess compensation (rents). This has often involved direct stock price distortion through the manipulation of corporate disclosure. Furthermore, there are also significant obstacles to the efficiency of privately ordered compensation contracts in the financial services sector, which has structural features that blunt market discipline in a much more profound way than other sectors. Whilst the mechanisms have occasionally differed in creating distress at large public corporations during the numerous collapses witnessed since 2000, it is clear that the motivations across these scandals have been largely congruent: the underestimation of risk by both investors and senior executives, and the use of accounting techniques to disguise borrowing in order to capture inflated short-term returns.

Moreover, whilst the concept of relating pay to performance is doubtless of utility, the mechanisms discussed make a fundamental assumption concerning the operation of securities markets: that prices reflect value. Notwithstanding the drawbacks of current compensation structures outlined above, these criticisms neglect further fundamental assumptions concerning the operation of market pricing mechanisms and thereby the integrity of prices. Each of the solutions suggested to remedy the issue of mitigating the risk generated by the principal–agent problem – even indexed options – is based on the assumptions of standard financial market theory and, by proxy, that market prices are flawless. However, in the following chapter, this book will demonstrate that price is not always synonymous with value and that financial and asset markets are susceptible to forces which drive markets away from intrinsic value for protracted periods, resulting in periodic 'booms' and 'crashes'.

Where prices are distorted, the pay-for-performance paradigm, particularly in the financial sector, breaks down. If prices in securities and/or financial markets do not always equal value, the limits of stock-based governance (in financial institutions in particular) are serious and the focus on share price as a criterion for judging executive performance is highly one-dimensional. The most benign effect of these incentives may be that executives recognise that the market pricing of shares is imperfect and/or contribute to market inefficiencies by manipulating corporate reporting and, by proxy, share prices themselves. However, the issue may also be of vital importance to economic stability; the incentives that exist for the manipulation of data may produce behaviour which, if left unchecked, may be highly damaging to the financial system. For example, not only does the use of stock options increase risk to individual firms, it has been shown to increase systemic risk due to the incentives created to manipulate information.[127] This is particularly true in sectors in which high degrees of financial leverage are used, and it is clear that executive compensation has had a role to play in several major recent financial crises, most notably the GFC (discussed in detail in Chapter 5). Moreover, as will be become clear in later chapters of this book, as risky and/or abusive practices become endemic within a particular sector, driven by compensation incentives, they may themselves contribute to the creation of financial crises.

On this basis, executive compensation systems in financial institutions, including the regulation of executive stock-based compensation, ignore three crucial points:

(i) markets often price risk inefficiently and are vulnerable to behavioural-driven swings in sentiment;
(ii) leverage, in general, increases the stock prices of financial institutions but it may provide incentives for short-termism and expose those institutions, and the financial system, to latent longer-term dangers; and
(iii) focusing only on quantitative metrics of performance embeds poor incentives in compensation contracts, which may have the consequence of inculcating value-destroying behaviours.

These factors highlight extreme flaws in the executive compensation paradigm in the financial sector. It is clearly arguable that the various structural problems which afflict financial markets, in combination with flawed assumptions concerning investor behaviour, may lead to inefficient market prices.

---

[127] Chris S. Armstrong & Rahul Vashishtha, 'Executive Stock Options, Differential Risk-Taking Incentives, and Firm Value' (2012) 104 J. FIN. ECON. 70.

3. Theories of securities market operation: principles and flaws

INTRODUCTORY REMARKS

The previous chapter outlined the mechanisms through which executives in modern public corporations are rewarded. It explained that, due to the nature of the current dominant pay-for-performance paradigm, executives to a great extent owe their pay to the levels of stock market and securities prices. The chapter further discussed some of the intrinsic flaws concerning the use of popular remuneration mechanisms, such as stock options, and bonuses contingent on the performance of company stock.

These compensation mechanisms, of course, rely on basic assumptions concerning the efficiency of securities prices. If securities prices convey fundamental value, equity-related compensation – in whichever form – may claim to be based on objectively assessed data arrived at through the operation of an efficient market, and therefore demand legitimacy. I have previously highlighted the mainstream criticisms of the systems used to calculate pay, especially stock-based compensation. Whilst these criticisms are certainly warranted, they do not place an appropriate level of emphasis on market pricing imperfections. This is a most important factor for analysis in respect of remuneration policies, as a massive portion of executive compensation is based generally on stock prices and asset price levels.[1] If it can be demonstrated that market prices and, *ceteris paribus*, stock prices are inefficient – including over the long term – this will cast doubt on the rationale for using remuneration mechanisms linked to stock price performance or market capitalisation, at least in the form these compensation systems take presently.

This chapter will therefore provide a description of the main orthodox theory used to explain the market pricing mechanism: modern finance

[1] In the financial sector, approximately 75% of senior executive compensation is determined by reference to the stock price of the firm, or bonus payments often contingent on share price performance. This will be discussed in more detail in Chapter 5.

theory. Modern finance theory, at least until recently, has occupied a place at the heart of Anglo-American financial regulation. The theory was given ringing endorsements from some of the world's most powerful central bankers, academics and public policymakers, and its tenets justified the dismantling of large swathes of the regulatory apparatus governing financial markets. Of course, following the events of 2007–09, focus has shifted to other theories to explain the operation of the market pricing mechanism. The chapter will then proceed to provide an analytical account of some of the recent challenges raised to both the assumptions and the conclusions of modern finance theory, especially those highlighted by behavioural finance. Behavioural finance contradicts some of the central assumptions of modern finance theory, and has been used to explain some of the more puzzling phenomena that occur in financial markets, especially asset bubbles. However, behavioural finance arguably suffers from its own set of limitations, particularly the difficulty in constructing a coherent set of regulations based upon its main principles.

Other theories of financial market behaviour have attempted to plug these gaps in our understanding of the forces involved in shaping financial market behaviour and the dynamics which give rise to financial instability and asset bubbles, and this chapter will briefly outline those contributions. However, the chapter will conclude by arguing that each of these accounts of financial market operation also has limitations, and set the stage for an analysis of the most comprehensive alternative theory to explain the operation of financial markets and the financial system, the Financial Instability Hypothesis, which will be discussed in the following chapter.

MODERN FINANCE THEORY

Modern finance theory is the generic term used to describe the collective set of four theories, which include the Efficient Market Hypothesis (EMH),[2] the Capital Asset Pricing Model (CAPM),[3] the

---

[2] Initially developed by Paul Samuelson in his seminal article, 'Proof that Properly Anticipated Prices Fluctuate Randomly' (1965) 6 IND. MAN. REV. 41. See also Benoit Mandelbrot, 'Forecasts of Future Prices, Unbiased Markets, and Martingale Models' (1966) 39 J. BUS. 242.

[3] The original concept was by Harry Markowitz, and was developed by William F. Sharpe, 'Capital Asset Prices: A Theory of Market Equilibrium Under Conditions of Risk' (1964) 19 J. FIN. 425.

Modigliani-Miller Theorem[4] and the Black-Scholes option-pricing model.[5] Whilst the latter three theories are highly significant, and used extensively in finance, their legitimacy rests largely on the operation of the EMH, which, for this reason, will be the focus of this chapter. The central claim of the EMH is 'the simple statement that security prices fully reflect all available information'.[6] The hypothesis was tested empirically with much success during the 1960s and 1970s and became 'the central proposition of finance for nearly thirty years'.[7] In short: 'An "efficient" market is defined as a market where there are large numbers of rational, profit-maximizers actively competing, with each trying to predict future market values of individual securities, and where important current information is almost freely available to all participants.'[8] Market efficiency may take one of three forms: 'strong', 'semi-strong' and 'weak'.[9] Each of these forms assumes that markets are fundamentally efficient, but each to different degrees, based upon the speed with which information is incorporated into prices. The strong-form EMH holds that securities prices reflect all available information, both public and private, and therefore no trader may earn excess returns even where they trade on private information. The semi-strong version holds that securities prices reflect all publicly known information, and adjust instantaneously to the production of new information. Profit from trading on private information is therefore possible, but the window for profit is tightly constrained. Moreover, neither fundamental analysis nor technical analysis may help an investor beat the market. Finally, the weak version of the EMH holds that prices reflect only information historically relevant to the securities concerned. Therefore, traders may make profits on private information gathering, but cannot out-perform

---

[4] Franco Modigliani & Merton H. Miller, 'The Cost of Capital, Corporation Finance and the Theory of Investment' (1958) 48 AM. ECON. REV. 261.

[5] Fischer Black & Myron Scholes, 'The Pricing of Options and Corporate Liabilities' (1973) 81 J. POLIT. ECONOMY 637.

[6] Eugene F. Fama, 'Efficient Capital Markets: II' (1991) 46 J. FIN. 1575.

[7] Andrei Shleifer, *Inefficient Markets: An Introduction to Behavioral Finance* (OUP, 2000) 1 (hereinafter Shleifer, *Inefficient Markets*); Michael C. Jensen, 'Some Anomalous Evidence Regarding Market Efficiency' (1978) 6 J. FIN. ECON. 95 (hereinafter Jensen, 'Anomalous Evidence').

[8] Eugene F. Fama, 'Random Walks in Stock Market Prices' (1965) 21 FIN. AN. J. 55, 56 (hereinafter Fama, 'Random Walks'). Fama is perhaps the chief advocate of the EMH, and was recently awarded the Nobel prize in economics for his work on market efficiency.

[9] Eugene F. Fama, 'Efficient Capital Markets: A Review of Theory and Empirical Work' (1970) 25 J. FIN. 383.

the market for consistently long periods. Operating upon the assumptions that transaction costs are low, and that arbitrage is possible in order to correct potential mispricings, the weak-form EMH holds that sophisticated traders[10] exploit opportunities for profit and return prices to value. Weak-form efficiency is supported generally by empirical studies, although questions remain concerning whether information is impounded into securities prices accurately.[11]

There are two general predictions by the EMH which would support the theory that markets are efficient. Firstly, prices should react quickly to news regarding a security and the effects of this news should be incorporated rapidly and correctly (i.e. should not 'over-react or under-react'). The crucial question for the legitimacy of market efficiency is therefore the speed with which new information is processed into prices. Relative market efficiency is, therefore, calculable by reference to the speed with which the two equilibria ('real world' and theoretical 'fully informed' world) match. This velocity, by implication, can also measure the arbitrage opportunities available to investors.[12] Secondly, prices should not move away from value unless the news itself related to the fundamentals of the security. In other words, news that does not affect the fundamental value of a security should not affect its price. On this basis, the EMH excludes the potential for money to be made from 'stale' information; profit cannot be made from trading on past news, as all historical information on a security will already have been incorporated into its price. In valuing securities, therefore, market prices are assumed to be good indicators of rationally evaluated economic value.[13] On this basis, the importance of the EMH to the study of financial markets is 'its prediction that, even though all information is not immediately and costlessly available to all participants, the market will act *as if* it were'.[14]

On this basis, it is posited that securities markets are highly efficient in reflecting prices and capturing value – both in relation to individual stocks and to the index holistically – when the following conditions two are satisfied: (i) prices exhibit stability, in the sense that deviations from

---

[10] Sometimes termed 'professionally informed traders'. See Ronald J. Gilson & Reinier H. Kraakman, 'The Mechanisms of Market Efficiency' (1984) 70 VIRGINIA LAW REV. 549 (hereinafter Gilson & Kraakman, 'Mechanisms').

[11] Moreover, as this chapter will demonstrate, there are some market puzzles which undermine even weak-form efficiency.

[12] Stout, 'Mechanisms' 635.

[13] Financial Services Authority, *The Turner Review: A Regulatory Response to the Global Banking Crisis* (2009) (hereinafter FSA, *Turner Review*) 39.

[14] Gilson & Kraakman, 'Mechanisms' 552 (emphasis in original).

an initial value may be predicted within narrow parameters; and (ii) investors make rational choices.[15] With regard to the first condition, prices ought to follow a reasonably stable performance trajectory over time where there is no change in the underlying fundamentals of a particular security; in other words, the default risk associated with well-defined assets can be assessed adequately and the distribution of returns occurs within predictable parameters (this underpins the so-called CAPM, referred to earlier). Modern finance risk management assumes that almost all events occur within a certain range (or 'mean') and that events further from the mean occur less frequently. This is often known as 'Gaussian' or 'bell curve' distribution.[16] Under this theory, the probability of price movements in markets can be used to mitigate risk, and therefore to build portfolios. Gaussian distributions applied to financial markets and used in risk-management tools such as Value at Risk (VaR)[17] and other derivatives effectively assume that certain events are so unlikely to occur that economic models should discount them from ever occurring. The second condition holds that investors are rational in their choices; that is, investors' financial decisions are based upon full assimilation of all available information and do not make systematic mistakes (so-called 'unbounded rationality').[18] Accordingly, rational choice theory assumes that:

> [Everyone] has perfect information about future events … Wages and prices will adjust instantaneously to new conditions, because these conditions will

---

[15] Burton G. Malkiel, 'The Efficient Market Hypothesis and Its Critics' (2003) 17 J. ECON. PERSPECTIVES 59, 62; Eugene F. Fama, 'Efficient Capital Markets: A Review of Theory and Empirical Work' (1970) 25 J. FIN. 383.

[16] Ioannis Karatzas & Steven E. Shreve, *Methods of Mathematical Finance* (Springer, 1998).

[17] 'Value at Risk' measures the potential loss in value of an asset or portfolio over a defined period for a given confidence interval. The components include measures of the probability of default, loss given default, the exposure at default and effective maturity. Operational risk, market risk and credit risk are used to amplify the analysis. Several high-profile collapses due to over-reliance on VaR models have occurred; perhaps the most notable was the 1998 implosion of the hedge fund Long-Term Capital Management. The VaR models it employed indicated that the most it should lose in any one day of trading was $45 million. In one day alone, it lost $550 million. Cumulatively in one month, the fund lost $1.7 billion. See Phillipe Jorion, 'Risk Management Lessons from Long-Term Capital Management' (2000) 6 EUR. FIN. MAN. 277.

[18] Also known as the Rational Expectations Hypothesis, originally developed by John F. Muth, 'Rational Expectations and the Theory of Price Movements' (1961) 29 ECONOMETRICA 315.

> have been anticipated and will already be incorporated in the prices which people charge and expect to pay for their services. No departure from real long-term values is possible even in the short run.[19]

The efficacy of the rational investor model is founded upon the following three core prepositions:

(i) investors are assumed to be rational and therefore value securities rationally;
(ii) where investors are not rational, their trades are random and therefore cancel out the trades of other, irrational, traders; and
(iii) to the extent that some traders are irrational, the effect they have on prices will be arbitraged away by rational investors.

These axioms of modern finance theory dictate that the price of an asset equals its fundamental value based upon the aggregate trades of rational investors: as a consequence, security prices are the products of all available information. As discussed in the previous chapter, this view of market efficiency has provided the basis for the introduction of both corporate governance systems and remuneration systems which rely, to a great degree, on market prices, operating under the implicit assumption that in efficient markets, investors will immediately and accurately incorporate information into the stock price of the relevant firm: 'It follows from the notion that the stock market operates as an efficient market for corporate control that the prices it delivers (i.e. the value of a company's shares) reflect the value of the underlying productive enterprise.'[20]

CONSEQUENCES OF THE USE OF MODERN FINANCE THEORY FOR THE REGULATION OF SECURITIES MARKETS AND CORPORATE GOVERNANCE

Regulatory approaches to managing risk in markets, including corporate governance and compensation systems, are thereby dominated by theories which assume market efficiency, and the EMH is the intellectual foundation upon which is constructed a vast corpus of financial regulatory structures. The logical policy application of the EMH is that

---

[19] Robert Skidelsky, *Keynes: The Return of the Master* (Penguin, 2009) 32.

[20] Sue Konzelmann & Frank Wilkinson, 'Governance, Regulation and Financial Market Instability: The Implications for Policy' (2009) Centre for Business Research, University of Cambridge Working Paper No. 392, 16.

regulation of financial markets or of companies operating within the system is futile as nobody can anticipate an exogenous shock and all currently known liabilities and risks are incorporated into market prices.[21] These assertions lead to several conclusions regarding the role of the market and regulation.[22] Accordingly, modern finance theory

> assert[s] that:
>
> (i) efficient and liquid financial markets deliver major allocative efficiency benefits by making possible a full range of contracts, thus enabling providers and users of funds more effectively to meet their preferences for risk, return and liquidity;
> (ii) markets are sufficiently rational as to justify a strong presumption in favour of market deregulation; and
> (iii) that even if markets are theoretically capable of irrational behaviour, policymakers will never be able to judge when and how far they are irrational with sufficient confidence to justify market intervention.[23]

These principles support the view that the market is, in almost all circumstances, the most appropriate arbiter of corporate conduct and performance. In this way, the aggregate of decisions that are made will be predictable and based on unquestionable rationalism, and will drive the system towards equilibrium. Equilibrium signifies market efficiency and so regulatory intervention in the market is eschewed because it will hinder the process of price discovery and increase transaction costs.[24] Further, there is no room in the efficient market analysis of stock prices for long-term price deviations from the intrinsic value of securities (or 'bubbles'[25]). The rationality of the market determines that any fluctuations from underlying value, where they might occur, will be temporary and very brief.

---

[21] As noted: 'even if markets are theoretically capable of irrational behaviour, policymakers will never be able to judge when and how far they are irrational with sufficient confidence to justify market intervention.' See Financial Services Authority, *The Turner Review: A regulatory response to the global banking crisis* (March 2009) 40 (hereinafter FSA, *Turner Review*) 40.

[22] FSA, *Turner Review* 40.

[23] Ibid.

[24] Robert E. Lucas, 'Econometric Policy Evaluation: A Critique' in Karl Brunner & Allan H. Meltzer (eds), *The Phillips Curve and Labor Markets* (Elsevier, 1976).

[25] Fama has criticised economic methods which seek to explain irrational market phenomena: 'I don't even know what a bubble means. These words have become popular. I don't think they have any meaning … I want people to use the term in a consistent way. For example, I didn't renew my subscription to *The*

On this basis, market forces are expected to create optimal corporate contracts; if the contracts were not optimal, rational agents would renegotiate them until they were. Thus, instead of providing legal rules to govern corporate exchange, the law ought simply to '[complete] open-ended contracts'[26] and rely on market discipline to regulate conduct and governance. This means that the 'essential message is that bargaining, though costly, is likely to be efficient, and that the role of the law is confined to oiling the wheels of corporate self-regulation by avoiding unnecessary costs'.[27] Thus no regulation of any internal corporate relationships – including compensation systems – ought to be permissible: 'US, EU, and … UK [regulatory frameworks are] … largely based on the rational investor model … [This model] assumes that well-informed and educated investors always make optimal resource allocation and wealth maximization decisions, if they are protected from fraud …'.[28] Of course, if securities prices are efficient, and immune from distortions, this position is entirely reasonable (and rational!). In the case of stocks, the market price of shares gives an unbiased value of the expected earnings and cash flow of the relevant corporation. Compensation systems which rely on an objective measure of value such as a stock price, and which may be individually tailored to reward management on the basis of variations in that price, certainly reduce transaction costs. Furthermore, it is clear that the removal of such a metric of performance would create difficulties for organisations in assessing corporate performance based on less 'objective' or less verifiable data.

On the other hand, if securities prices are not always efficient, and modern finance theory does not adequately explain the behaviour of securities markets in all circumstances, it is clear that the EMH should not necessarily be used as a starting point for the design of optimal compensation contracts. For example, asset bubbles (discussed later in

---

Economist because they use the world bubble three times on every page. Any time prices went up and down – I guess that is what they call a bubble. People have become entirely sloppy.' See John Cassidy, 'Rational Irrationality – An Interview with Eugene Fama', *The New Yorker* (New York, 13 January 2010).

[26] Easterbrook & Fischel, *Economic Structure of Corporate Law* 35.

[27] Simon Deakin & Alan Hughes, 'Economic Efficiency and the Proceduralisation of Company Law' (1999) Centre for Business Research University of Cambridge Working Paper No. 133 (hereinafter Deakin & Hughes, 'Economic Efficiency'), 13.

[28] Emilios Avgouleas, 'Reforming Investor Protection Regulation: The Impact of Cognitive Biases' in Michael Faure & Frank Stephen (eds), *Essays in the Law and Economics of Regulation in Honour of Anthony Ogus* (Intersentia, 2008).

this chapter) often presage financial crises and complete price collapses, and yet compensation contracts rarely contain provisions which account for the impact of price distortions on either overall pay levels or the incentives generated by reliance on market prices in assessing executive performance.[29] If one considers the distortions that excessive focus on stock price may induce, it becomes clear that executive compensation plans based on the EMH may provide a flawed model for corporate governance: 'If ... stock prices can depart dramatically from rational estimates of fundamental value, the possibility arises that business strategies that raise share price in the short term can harm firm value and shareholder wealth over the long term.'[30] This naturally reduces the utility of compensation arrangements which are based to some degree on equity market prices.

The recent dissonance to have greeted the EMH following the GFC has important consequences for legal and regulatory structures, in particular for the remuneration systems that subsist in these markets. Instead of prescriptive rules-based regulation, market-driven codes and light-touch regulation of corporate affairs have characterised the approach to most corporate governance requirements at publicly listed companies, summarised in the following way: '[L]egislative design may in principle be used to promote "market" solutions and private contractual orderings which may provide means of overcoming or neutralising market failure without the need for narrowly prescriptive legal control.'[31] However, where people do not behave according to the way certain highly influential economic models predict that they should, public policy ought to be guided by empirical observation and principle, not by the flawed view that certain 'irrational' phenomena do not exist, as 'such an approach would not be consistent with the fundamental goals of creating high performing companies and providing good returns to [investors]'.[32] The next section therefore discusses some of the main flaws of the EMH, which ought to be considered when any corporate governance systems (including compensation contracts) are designed.

---

[29] Of course, many banks now use deferral of compensation to attempt to counter this. See Chapter 6 for discussion.

[30] Stout, 'New Thinking' 15.

[31] Deakin & Hughes, 'Economic Efficiency' 6.

[32] Department of Business, Innovation & Skills, *The Kay Review of UK Equity Markets and Long-Term Decision Making, Final Report* (2012) 4.17 (hereinafter BIS, *Kay Review*).

FLAWS IN THE EMH

(i) Prices Are Not Stable: 'Fat-Tails' and Crashes

Recall the notion that the EMH predicts that market prices exhibit stability when no change in fundamentals is observed (a basic assumption of the CAPM). In practical terms, this should lead to price changes over short intervals being independently and identically distributed. Empirical testing of this assumption reveals it to be flawed. For example, Gaussian distribution models assume that, whilst wild fluctuations from the 'norm' or 'mean' can occur, they are so rare they may be regarded as inconsequential; however, it is clear that acute price movements, experienced with more regularity since the development of sophisticated financial markets, do not reflect this assumption.[33] Whilst Gaussian theory operates efficiently in relation to certain randomness (for example, the height distributions of the human population), financial market prices instead suffer from 'fat-tails': catastrophic events occur far more frequently than standard models predict.[34]

Financial markets, on this basis, may be fractal.[35] A fractal is an object which has a tendency to resemble parts of itself, which is a property of financial markets when viewed across differing time series. These

---

[33] Alan Greenspan, former US Federal Reserve Chairman, writes: 'Probability distributions estimated largely, or exclusively over cycles that do not include periods of panic will underestimate the likelihood of extreme price movements … Furthermore, joint distributions estimate over periods that do not include panics will underestimate correlations between asset returns during panics.' See Alan Greenspan, *The Age of Turbulence: Adventures in a New World* (Penguin, 2007) 507.

[34] Benoit B. Mandelbrot, 'Variation of Certain Speculative Prices' (1963) 36 J. BUS. 394.

[35] Benoit B. Mandelbrot, *The (mis)Behaviour of Markets: A Fractal View of Risk, Ruin and Reward* (3rd edn, Profile, 2008) (hereinafter Mandelbrot, *(mis)Behaviour*). 'A fractal is a geometric shape that can be separated into parts, each of which is a reduced-scale version of the whole. In finance, this concept is not a rootless abstraction but a theoretical reformulation of a down-to-earth bit of market folklore – namely, that movements of a stock or currency all look alike when a market chart is enlarged or reduced so that it fits the same time and price scale. An observer then cannot tell which of the data concern prices that change from week to week, day to day or hour to hour. This quality defines the charts as fractal curves and makes available many powerful tools of mathematical and computer analysis.' See Benoit B. Mandelbrot, 'How Fractals Can Explain What's Wrong with Wall Street', *Scientific American* (15 September 2008), http://www.scientificamerican.com/article.cfm?id=multifractals-explain-wall-street & page=2.

properties, it is posited, are the result of the interactions of agents with high liquidity capacities and differing interpretations of information, principles which are at odds with the EMH: 'This particular mix of local randomness over short time-scales, and global determinism over longer time-scales, is a defining characteristic of "self-similarity", as observed in fractal structures.'[36] The resulting high liquidity and heterogeneous investment time horizons should make markets stable. However, this carries with it the implication that financial markets may become unstable if liquidity dries up or investor time horizons become narrow (homogeneous), and trading is impaired and/or is heavily biased in one direction, or highly short (long) term.[37] As evidence for these implications, extreme events are more common than standard tools such as the CAPM or VaR would suggest, and their effects much more damaging. Research on the Dow Jones industrial average from 1916 to 2003 confirms that financial markets do not conform to Gaussian distribution. If markets were 'efficient' there should have been 58 days during that period in which markets moved more than 3.4 per cent; in fact, there were 1,001. Theory further predicts that swings of more than 4.5 per cent should occur on no more than six days; in fact, these swings occurred 366 times. And finally, standard theory predicts index swings of more than 7 per cent should only occur every 300,000 years; in fact, this occurred on 48 separate days in the observed period.[38]

As evidence for the instability of markets, there is strong evidence that stock markets prices do not behave as predicted by standard theory. The variation in the S&P 500 stock market index between 1970 and 2001 possessed a kurtosis (a statistical measure of how 'peaked' data is relative to a normal or flat distribution) of 43.36.[39] A Gaussian kurtosis would measure 3. It has been demonstrated that in the last 50 years the 10 most extreme days in financial markets account for half of all returns.[40] Accordingly, 'while the occasional and unpredictable large deviations are

---

[36] Nicola Anderson & Joseph Noss, 'The Fractal Markets Hypothesis and its implications for the stability of financial markets' (2013) Bank of England Financial Stability Paper No. 23, 9.

[37] 'The Race to Zero', speech given by Andrew G. Haldane, Executive Director, Financial Stability, Bank of England, at the International Economic Association Sixteenth World Congress, Beijing, 8 July 2011, http://www.bankofengland.co.uk/publications/Documents/speeches/2011/speech509.pdf.

[38] See Mandelbrot, *(mis)Behaviour* 13.

[39] Wim Schoutens, *Levy Processes in Finance: Pricing Financial Derivatives* (Wiley, 2003).

[40] Nassim N. Taleb, *The Black Swan: The Impact of the Highly Improbable* (Penguin, 2007) 276.

rare, they cannot be dismissed as "outliers" because, cumulatively, their impact in the long term is so dramatic'.[41] On this basis, then, the following implications may be drawn concerning market (in)efficiency.

(ii) Stock Price Dependence: Markets Have Memories

So, some of the assumptions used in models designed to predict financial market behaviour are flawed. This leads to a further issue: if the assumptions used to predict market behaviour are flawed, then how do securities markets work in practice? One prediction of the EMH, for example, is that prices ought to move independently of previous price movements; there should be no established relationship between securities prices from one day to the next. This intuitively gave rise to a narrower theory of stock market price movements: the Random Walk Hypothesis (RWH), which claims that stock market prices exhibit no dependence on historical price movements.[42] However, the RWH has been systematically dismantled,[43] particularly the claim of the RWH that stock prices exhibit no dependence on past prices.[44]

Empirical observations confirm that stock prices contain predictable components; between 25 and 45 per cent of the variation of long-term holdings are predictable from past returns.[45] Analysis of weekly stock returns from the S&P 500 from 1962 to 1985 rejects the RWH at all significance levels under both weekly and monthly analysis.[46] The variance for some weekly returns produced errors of up to 30 per cent. Dependence in the short term has been demonstrated in several studies,

---

[41] Benoit B. Mandelbrot & Nassim N. Taleb, 'A Focus on the Exceptions that Prove the Rule' *Financial Times* (London, 23 March 2006).

[42] Paul H. Cootner (ed), *The Random Character of Stock Market Prices* (MIT Press, 1964); See also Louis Bachelier, 'Theorie de la speculation' (1900) 3 ANN. SCI. ECOLE NORM. S. 21; Fama, 'Random Walks'. Indeed, Jensen asserts that the EMH is analogous to the RWH. See Jensen, 'Anomalous Evidence'.

[43] Most notably Andrew Lo & Craig McKinlay, *A Non-Random Walk Down Wall Street* (Princeton UP, 1999) (hereinafter Lo & McKinlay, *A Non-Random Walk*).

[44] The 'January effect' is evidence against the RWH. This term describes the phenomenon in which stock prices in most stock indices demonstrably increase in January more than any other month. See Richard H. Thaler, 'Anomalies: The January Effect' (1987) 1 J. ECON. PERSPECTIVES 197.

[45] Eugene F. Fama and Kenneth R. French, 'Permanent and Temporary Components of Stock Prices' (1988) 96 J. POLIT. ECONOMY 246.

[46] Lo & McKinlay, *A Non-Random Walk* 28.

ascribed to a 'momentum effect' which causes gains in stock prices to precipitate further gains, independent of informational changes.[47] These momentum strategies have been shown to be highly profitable in both US and international equity markets.[48] Accordingly, when analysed in monthly segments, the stocks of 17 countries exhibited short-term dependence.[49] This suggests limits to traditional asset pricing models (such as the CAPM), and provides a persistent pricing anomaly to challenge the RWH:

> The classic Random Walk model makes three claims. First is the so-called martingale condition: that your best guess of tomorrow's price is today's price. Second is a declaration of independence: that tomorrow's price is independent of past prices. Third is a statement of normality: that all the price changes taken together, from small to large, vary in accordance with the mild, bell-curve distribution … [T]hat is two claims too far.[50]

This rejection of the RWH undermines a central plank of the EMH. If, as the RWH claims, past prices have no bearing on future prices, then executive compensation systems need not reflect the effects that market sentiment may have on prices. However, where share prices are demonstrably affected by historical information and stock price memory correlates with some portion of future price changes, investor perceptions of future price trajectories are crucial. In fact, the informational content of financial markets dictates that historical events, institutional memory and the creation of knowledge *must* matter to future market performance[51] and, on this basis '… if investors have heterogeneous expectations, the

---

[47] Benoit B. Mandelbrot, 'Long-run Interdependence in Price Records and Other Economic Time Series' (1970) 38 ECONOMETRICA 122; Narasimhan Jegadeesh & Sheridan Titman, 'Return to Buying Winners and Selling Losers: Implications for Stock Market Efficiency' (1993) 48 J. FIN. 65; John M. Griffin, Xiuqing Ji & J. Spencer Martin, 'Momentum Investing and Business Cycle Risk: Evidence from Pole to Pole' (2003) 58 J. FIN. 2515.

[48] Louis K.C. Chan, Narasimhan Jegadeesh & Josef Lakonishok, 'Momentum Strategies' (1996) 51 J. FIN. 1681; Narasimhan Jegadeesh & Sehridan Titman, 'Profitability of Momentum Strategies: An Evaluation of Alternative Explanations' (2001) 56 J. FIN. 699; Bruce D. Grundy & J. Spencer Martin, 'Understanding the Nature and the Risks and the Sources of the Rewards to Momentum Investing' (2001) 14 REV. FIN. STUD. 29.

[49] Campbell R. Harvey, 'The World Price of Covariance Risk' (1991) 46 J. FIN. 111.

[50] Mandelbrot, *(mis)Behaviour* 247.

[51] Joseph E. Stiglitz, 'Contributions of the Economics of Information' (2000) 115 Q. J. ECON. 1441 (hereinafter Stiglitz, 'Contributions').

market price of a stock may change for a variety of reasons unrelated to any change in the value of the underlying company'.[52] Accordingly, because investor memories are highly short-term, price increases in the recent past will have more significant effects on present prices than more distant price changes. This amplifies short-termism in markets through the price distortions it creates and axiomatically undermines stock-based executive pay, which relies upon market prices to reflect long-run fundamental value. By implication, where investor memory has an effect on stock prices, executive compensation systems ought to reflect the potential for recent price increases to generate further price increases independent of the RWH predictions.

These observations, of course, have serious implications for the use of stock-based compensation plans. As discussed in the previous chapter, stock options are flawed in the sense that they may often reward executives for movements in general market trends rather than through the decisions they take or strategies they embark upon, reducing their utility. The flaws of market models therefore augment this problem; it is conceivable that options are often highly inefficient because, firstly, they are priced using models of doubtful empirical integrity – in the sense that they assume persistent market efficiency – and, secondly, executives capture windfalls which do not result from their actions but from market trends. This lends credence to the contention that the central tenets of market and risk management can be challenged and, by implication, so may the view that prices are subject to rational and self-correcting mechanisms.[53]

(iii) Defining Efficiency: 'Informational' vs. 'Fundamental Value'

The predictions of the EMH do not, then, always result in efficient prices: 'Information is reflected in prices, but not necessarily accurately or completely. There are wide differences in understanding and belief, and different perceptions of a future that can be at best dimly perceived.'[54] However, for the tenets of the EMH to be properly understood

---

[52] Stout, 'Mechanisms' 646.

[53] For example, following the GFC, a survey of 500 risk managers by KPMG in October 2008 that 92% intended to review their risk management practices. See Andrew G. Haldane, 'Why Banks Failed the Stress Test', The basis for a speech given at the Marcus-Evans Conference on Stress-Testing (9–10 February 2009) (hereinafter Haldane, 'Why Banks Failed the Stress Test') 5.

[54] John Kay, 'The Map is Not the Territory: An Essay on the State of Economics' (Institute For New Economic Thinking, 26 September 2011) 7, http://ineteconomics.org/blog/inet/john-kay-map-not-territory-essay-state-economics.

and applied, one must first grapple with what the term 'market efficiency' actually means. Market efficiency may be measured through a number of methods; however, the major distinction between the 'value' placed on the price of securities as encapsulated by market prices is that which determines whether prices fully reflect all available information[55] ('informational efficiency') or whether prices fully reflect the underlying fundamentals of a security ('fundamental value efficiency'). Fundamental value efficiency may be summarised as follows:

> [T]he rapid absorption of information into price, and market prices that accurately reflect economic value … Markets are efficient in the fundamental value sense if stock prices respond to available information not only quickly but *accurately*, so that market prices mirror the best possible estimates, in light of all available information, of the actual economic values of securities in terms of their expected risks and returns.[56]

The neoclassical view of prices of course contends that the informational value of price is absolute; no distinction can be made between informational and fundamental value efficiency.[57] Price efficiency is a foundation of the EMH because in an informationally efficient market, arbitrage profit is impossible: prices reflect value. However, because arbitrage profit is possible in markets, there must be a distinction between fundamental and informational value:[58] the so-called 'Grossman-Stiglitz paradox'.[59] The major impairments to fundamental value efficiency are

---

[55] Information' in this context is 'data that has the capacity to alter one's belief about the world or … one's beliefs about the appropriate price of an asset'. See Gilson & Kraakman, 'Mechanisms' 561.

[56] Stout, 'Mechanisms' 640 (emphasis in original).

[57] Ronald J. Gilson & Reinier H. Kraakman, 'The Mechanisms of Market Efficiency Twenty Years Later: The Hindsight Bias' (2003) 28 J. CORP. LAW 715.

[58] Emilios Avgouleas, *The Mechanics and Regulation of Market Abuse: A Legal and Economic Analysis* (OUP, 2005) 47 (hereinafter Avgouleas, *Mechanics and Regulation*).

[59] As Grossman and Stiglitz note: 'because information is costly, prices cannot perfectly reflect the information which is available, since if it did, those who spent resources to obtain it would receive no compensation'. See Sanford J. Grossman & Joseph E. Stiglitz, 'On the Impossibility of Informationally Efficient Markets' (1990) 70 AM. ECON. REV. 393, 405 (hereinafter Grossman & Stiglitz, 'On the Impossibility'). As noted: 'The implication of the Grossman-Stiglitz paradox is that strong-form efficiency is a rare occurrence, likely to be observed only when all information is freely (hence symmetrically) available. More importantly, the paradox suggests that asymmetric information is probably

asymmetries of information, and obstacles to arbitrage in the market. These issues, by implication, limit the utility of compensation schemes linked to price; reduced price efficiency may mean that the fundamental value of a firm is not reflected in the price of its shares and ergo, may undermine the efficiency of stock-related compensation. The next sections will briefly examine these obstacles.

a. Information asymmetries

Certain markets – particularly stock markets – suffer from imperfect disclosure and asymmetries, which may render them vulnerable to mispricing.[60] Information asymmetries have a significant effect on the efficiency of market prices and in the context of the present discussion are derived from the agency problem between managers and shareholders at large public corporations. These asymmetries exist due to the non-concavity in the value of information;[61] it is often not worthwhile financially for investors to incur the expense associated with information

---

commonplace in markets. This being so, investigations of asset market efficiency should explicitly allow for investors to act on the basis of different information sets.' See Roy E. Bailey, *The Economics of Financial Markets* (CUP, 2005); Sanford J. Grossman & Joseph E. Stiglitz, 'Information and Competitive Price Systems' (1976) 66 AM. ECON. REV. 246.

[60] Information asymmetry in markets has been studied in depth by noted economists; indeed, work on information asymmetry has garnered three Nobel prizes in economics for the relevant researchers. See George A. Akerlof, 'The Market for Lemons: Quality Uncertainty and the Market Mechanism' (1970) 84 Q. J. ECON. 488; A. Michael Spence, 'Job Market Signaling' (1973) 87 Q. J. ECON. 355; Joseph E. Stiglitz & Michael E. Rothschild, 'Equilibrium in Competitive Insurance Markets' (1976) 90 Q. J. ECON. 629.

[61] Roy Radner & Joseph E. Stiglitz, 'A Nonconcavity in the Value of Information' in Marcel Boyer & Richard Khilstrom (eds), *Bayesian Models in Economic Theory* (Elsevier Science, 1984). In relation to financial markets, several analyses by Stiglitz and others confirm that information asymmetries exist and reduce market efficiency. As Stiglitz posits, 'if information were perfect – if all contingencies could have been anticipated – all *important* contingencies … would have been taken care of in the original contract'. See Stiglitz, 'Contributions' 1459 (emphasis in original). Further factors such as reputation mechanisms play a role in driving price away from value. There are costs and rents inherent in losing one's reputation. A 'surplus' is required to generate an incentive to preserve a reputation. If these costs arise and are lost, price *ceteris paribus* cannot equal marginal cost: it is necessary for price to exceed marginal cost in an efficient market. See Carl Shapiro, 'Premiums for High Quality Products as Returns to Reputations' (1983) 98 Q. J. ECON. 658; Benjamin Klein & Keith B. Leffler, 'The Role of Market Forces in Assuring Contractual Performance' (1981) 89 J. POLIT. ECONOMY 615.

gathering, which also leads to a free-rider problem.[62] This principle damages the process of price discovery and is particularly relevant to stock and equity markets, which suffer from structural defects which exacerbate the problems of information reliability transmitted via the channels in those markets. In particular, the dissemination of information may be prevented by managers who wish to preserve informational advantages in order to benefit themselves which, as noted in the previous chapter, damage the price formation process. Moreover, in large corporations with dispersed ownership structures, smaller shareholders lack the incentives or wherewithal to actively monitor managers and exert any meaningful discipline on them.[63]

Securities market financing analysis confirms that this view holds. The use of debt financing rather than equity financing in capital markets by the majority of firms demonstrates that market prices do not fully reflect information: asymmetries persist in stock markets because disclosure regarding firm value is not completely transparent.[64] For example, the relative reluctance to raise finance through equity capital in firms where insiders have more information on the state of a firm than outsiders, may be attributable to the desire of management to prevent sending signals to the market that, on average, shares are overpriced.[65] In diverse and liquid capital markets, the method of firm financing should (in the absence of tax considerations and bankruptcy costs) be irrelevant, yet most firms choose to raise capital through debt. This is because the issuance of equity transmits a signal that the managers/owners believe that the market has overvalued the shares. Any attempt to raise equity capital will therefore meet a market response which lowers price, thus harming shareholder interests, which both reduces the value of managers' options and damages their reputations.[66]

---

62 Oliver D. Hart, *Firms, Contracts, and Financial Structure* (OUP, 1995); Jack Hirshleifer & John G. Riley, *The Analytics of Uncertainty and Information* (CUP, 1992); Drew Fudenberg & Jean Tirole, *Game Theory* (MIT Press, 1991).

63 Emilios Avgouleas & Jay Cullen, 'Market Discipline and EU Corporate Governance Reform in the Banking Sector: Merits, Fallacies, and Cognitive Boundaries' (2014) 41 J. LAW & SOCIETY 28.

64 George J. Stigler, 'Imperfections in the Capital Market' (1967) 75 J. POLIT. ECONOMY 287.

65 See Colin Mayer, 'Financial Systems, Corporate Finance and Economic Development' in R. Glenn Hubbard (ed), *Asymmetric Information, Corporate Finance and Investment* (University of Chicago Press, 1990).

66 Francis Modigliani and Merton H. Miller, 'The Cost of Capital, Corporate Finance and the Theory of Investment' (1958) 48 AM. ECON. REV. 251. For a rejoinder to this view, see Anat R. Admati, Peter M. DeMarzo, Martin F. Hellwig

These effects have been tested empirically: several studies demonstrate that a firm's market value drops when it announces a stock issue, but that an announcement of debt financing results in no change in value.[67] This has been termed 'the entrenchment choice' and explains, at least partially, the preference for debt over equity financing in preserving managerial tenure.[68] One of the prime motivations for CEO removal is corporate financial distress: CEOs who can reduce the risk of entering bankruptcy become more entrenched than CEOs whose firms suffer financial hardship.[69] Capital structure decisions are therefore often motivated by the desire of managers to preserve their positions and it is this that prevents information channels from operating at maximum efficiency. This has the effect of constraining firms' behaviour[70] due to the increased threat of bankruptcy carried by debt financing.[71] A consequence that follows from this is that inefficient management may be kept in place at companies because they have propagated informational gaps which the disciplining market for corporate control is unable to overcome. This provides significant incentives for management to increase asymmetry of information in financial markets and, in doing so, reduces the efficiency of market prices. They benefit from this in a dual capacity: firstly, they are able to restrict the information flow to markets and thereby benefit from inefficient price levels where their compensation is linked to stock prices; and secondly, they are able to entrench themselves at firms by reducing the threat of market discipline.

& Paul Pfleiderer, 'Fallacies, Irrelevant Facts, and Myths in the Discussion of Capital Regulation: Why Bank Equity is *Not* Expensive' (2010) Rock Center for Corporate Governance at Stanford University Working Paper No. 86.

[67] Ricardo N. Bebczuk, *Asymmetric Information in Financial Markets* (CUP, 2003) 48.

[68] Walter Novaes & Luigi Zingales, 'Capital Structure Choice When Managers Are in Control: Entrenchment Versus Efficiency' (1995) 76 J. BUS. 49.

[69] A study of 434 US firms over an eight-year period has confirmed that firms with entrenched CEOs on average utilise a sub-optimal mix of debt and equity financing in their capital structures. See Phillip G. Berger, Eli Ofek & David L. Yermack, 'Managerial Entrenchment and Capital Structure Decisions' (1997) 52 J. FIN. 1411.

[70] Bruce C. Greenwald and Joseph E. Stiglitz, 'Financial Market Imperfections and Business Cycles' (1993) 108 Q. J. ECON. 77.

[71] Sanford J. Grossman & Oliver D. Hart, 'Corporate Financial Structure and Managerial Incentives' in John McCall (ed), *The Economics of Information and Uncertainty* (UMI, 1982) 108–109.

b. Limits to arbitrage

The obstacles to information disclosure just outlined are compounded by structural imperfections of the financial market which undermine attempts at price arbitrage. Arbitrage is the main method through which the EMH is validated; according to the EMH even where prices depart from value in the very short term, they will be returned to their fundamental value almost instantaneously:

> Where, because of the costs of information acquisition, prices exhibit signs of inefficiency and depart from 'reasonable value estimates' ... then groups of sophisticated traders acting as rational utility maximizers, so-called 'arbitrageurs', spot the price differences and enter the market trying to exploit the efficiency loophole. Their arbitrage activity allows this group of traders to make profits until, because of their trades, prices are brought into line with the 'fundamental' or 'reasonable value' equilibrium and the efficiency 'hole' is closed.[72]

One of the most effective methods through which prices are brought to efficient levels is short selling.[73] However, short selling is hindered by three main factors:[74] cost; legal and structural obstacles;[75] and the imposition of regulatory limits to short selling of financial securities, particularly following the GFC.[76] Further, arbitrageurs generally speculate with other people's money. Fund managers attract investment and

---

[72] Avgouleas, *Mechanics and Regulation* 47.

[73] Short selling is the term used to describe the buying of securities when an investor believes them to be trading at higher levels than their efficient price, i.e. they are overvalued. This is achieved through a particular security being loaned to an arbitrageur by the owners of that security with the arbitrageur returning identical assets back to the lender at a later date. If the price of the security drops in the interim, the arbitrageur profits by the amount that the security has dropped by. Short sales are therefore essentially a gamble that the price of a security will drop.

[74] For a thorough discussion, see Robert J. Shiller, 'From Efficient Market Theory to Behavioral Finance' (2003) 17 J. ECON. PERSPECTIVES 83 (hereinafter Shiller, 'From Efficient Market Theory').

[75] In the US, for example, as of 2003, approximately only 3,900 of around 9,000 registered financial companies were permitted by their constitutions to engage in short selling. See Staff Report to the United States Securities and Exchange Commission 41, *Implications of the Growth of Hedge Funds* (September 2003) 108. See Pedro A.C. Saffi & Kari Sigurdson, 'Price Efficiency and Short Selling' (2008) IESE Business School University of Navarra Working Paper No. 748, 5.

[76] For example, see Regulation (EU) No. 236/2012 of the European Parliament and of the Council of 14 March 2012 on short selling and certain aspects of

generate management fees based on their short-term performance.[77] If a price discrepancy that an arbitrageur spots does not close quickly, the arbitrageur's financial sponsors will lose money. Those people may therefore withdraw funds based on the apparent poor performance of the arbitrage strategy, meaning that the arbitrageur cannot keep funds committed to closing the efficiency hole, which therefore persists.[78] Naturally, this necessarily makes the trading strategies of many financial market traders highly short-term.

In a further limitation to arbitrage, shorting stocks operates as an arbitrage strategy that subsists to correct mispricing where stocks have become *overvalued*. However, where stocks are *undervalued* arbitrageurs in search of profit will be forced to buy undervalued stocks until price and fundamental value converge. This is a much more expensive process and 'if arbitrage activity fails to correct a precipitous price fall caused by short selling, the majority of market actors may feel compelled to imitate short sellers' trades, adding further downward pressure on prices'.[79] Even where a money manager recognises that a security is overvalued they will not realize a gain on the asset unless a majority of their peers also hold the same view and begin to sell the relevant shares. Where an overvaluation persists, an investment manager who sells his/her position in a market may, in the short term, appear to be underperforming his/her rivals.[80] In this situation, an arbitrageur who spots a gap between fundamental value and price may even be bankrupted before the resulting market correction takes place.

---

credit default swaps, which gives powers to competent authorities to suspend short selling or limit transactions when the price of various instruments (including shares, sovereign and corporate bonds, and exchange traded funds) fall by set percentage amounts from the previous day's closing price; for similar measures in the US, see Securities and Exchange Commission 17 CFR Parts 200 And 242 Release No. 34-60388, Amendments to Regulation SHO, Final Rule, July 31, 2009.

[77] The horizon for performance measurement is generally quarterly periods.

[78] Andrei Shleifer & Robert W. Vishny, 'The Limits of Arbitrage' (1997) 52 J. FIN. 35 (hereinafter Shleifer & Vishny, 'Limits of Arbitrage').

[79] Emilios Avgouleas, 'A New Framework for the Global Regulation of Short Sales: Why Prohibition is Inefficient and Disclosure Insufficient' (2010) 15 STANFORD J. LAW BUS. & FIN. 376, 395.

[80] Paul A. Gompers & Andrew Metrick, 'Institutional Investors and Equity Prices' (2001) 116 Q. J. ECON. 229; Russ R. Wermers, 'Mutual Fund Herding and the Impact on Stock Prices' (1999) 54 J. FIN. 58; David S. Scharfstein & Jeremy C. Stein, 'Herd Behavior and Investment' (1990) 80 AM. ECON. REV. 465.

There are further reasons why arbitrage may be ineffective in correcting mispricing. As the EMH posits that all investors are rational, all arbitrageurs pursue investment strategies in order to maximise utility. The failure of arbitrage in some instances may be attributable to the fact that there may also be 'quasi-rational' traders in the marketplace, often referred to as 'noise traders'. These noise traders are those who 'are not fully rational and [whose] demand for risky assets is affected by their beliefs or sentiments that are not fully justified by fundamental news'.[81] They are therefore prone to systematic biases inferable to irrational reactions to changes or expectations which are not fully justified by the relevant information. Where the trades of noise traders are uncorrelated, they cancel each other out and the arbitrage mechanism is unaffected. However, where investor sentiment propels enough noise traders to engage in the same trading strategies, they may move markets. The market movement will be uncorrelated to changes in fundamentals to some degree because those traders that are driving the movements are not fully rational.[82]

SUMMARY OF FLAWS IN THE EMH

Researchers in financial economics have therefore provided convincing evidence that financial market pricing does not conform to the predictions of the EMH. Empirical observations of real-world markets do not always reflect the EMH's claims, especially concerning the stability of prices, which may move away from fundamental value on a sustained basis. Moreover, the market contains structural imperfections which may prevent the dissemination and/or incorporation of information into prices. Whilst weak-form efficiency is largely uncontroversial in orthodox literature,[83] it is clear that due to the embedded structural imperfections outlined and short-termism (often ascribable to compensation incentives) the EMH fails to explain market behaviour in all circumstances, especially as (even in its weak form) it discounts the possibility that prices

---

81 Andrei Shleifer & Lawrence H. Summers, 'The Noise Trader Approach to Finance' (1990) 4 J. ECON. PERSPECTIVES 19; see also J. Bradford De Long, Andrei Shleifer, Lawrence H. Summers & Robert J. Waldmann, 'The Size and Incidence of the Losses from Noise Trading' (1989) NBER Working Paper No. 2875.

82 Shleifer & Vishny, 'Limits of Arbitrage'.

83 BIS, *Kay Review* 4.1.

may not equal fundamental value, therefore discounting the characterisation of sustained asset price increases as 'bubbles' or collapses in asset prices as 'crashes'.

The problems associated with efficient markets arguably undermine the use of any managerial compensation schemes which are based to a large degree on stock prices (in particular, because some price distortions may be ascribed to the role of incentives in remuneration contracts). They further suggest that any compensation scheme which links pay to performance ought to assess a stock price over a medium- to long-term horizon, allowing potential price distortions to fall away.[84] The repeated failures of modern finance theory – and especially of the EMH – to completely explain market behaviour arguably demands an alternative view of the operation of securities markets. To refute the position of the EMH, outlined above, this chapter will now move to consider behavioural finance theory, which in some cases may provide more complete explanations for the basis of individual investor behaviour and the consequent occasional price distortions in financial markets.

BEHAVIOURAL FINANCE

Behavioural finance theory uses principles drawn from a range of other disciplines including psychology and sociology to explain the effect of investor behaviour on aggregate pricing (and consequent swings in asset prices which are quite frequently observed in markets) and it is perhaps the most serious rival to the EMH to emerge in recent years.[85] Behavioural finance focuses largely on the shortcomings of the second plank of the EMH (the rational investor model) to explain observations refuting the first plank (stable market prices).

The rational investor model suggests that investors have an unlimited ability to process information to account for risk within their portfolios.

---

[84] This form of deferral of compensation has, of course, been a major theme of reforms to bankers' compensation packages following the GFC.

[85] Behavioural economics may be traced back to the work of Herbert Simon (who received a Nobel Prize for his work in this field). See Herbert A. Simon, 'A Behavioral Model of Rational Choice' (1955) 69 Q. J. ECON. 99; Herbert A. Simon, 'Rational Choice and the Structure of the Environment' in Herbert A. Simon, *Models of Man: Social and Rational* (John Wiley, 1957) 261, 271; Herbert A. Simon, 'Rationality as Process and Product of Thought' (1978) 68 AM. ECON. REV. 1.

As noted by Avgouleas: '[a]rguably, most investors' computational capacity and trading behaviour does not conform to this model'.[86] Instead, investors ought to be classed as 'boundedly rational' agents who make frequent cognitive errors: humans have 'limited computational skills and seriously flawed memories'.[87] On this basis behavioural economists employ Behavioural Decision Theory (BDT) to explain certain observed market phenomena which do not conform to rational choice theory and are instead ascribed to cognitive biases. In summary:

> [The] view of the markets as an agglomeration of rational investors, who make optimal resource allocation and wealth maximisation decisions, when provided with sufficient information, appropriately structured economic incentives and sensible regulations, is refuted by recent empirical and experimental research … [T]his research … shows financial markets to be complex evolutionary and dynamic systems encompassing both rational and irrational behaviour.[88]

(i) Heuristics and 'Rules of Thumb'

The deepest insights of behavioural finance concern the importance of the inherent and acquired biases which may influence people's decision making.[89] BDT demonstrates that these influences partially govern the way in which investment decisions are made, in contrast to the rational investor model, which assumes unbounded rationality. Market actors rely on a limited number of principles which reduce the complex tasks of

---

[86] Emilios Avgouleas, 'Cognitive Biases and Investor Protection Regulation: An Evolutionary Approach' (2006) http://ssrn.com/abstract=1133214 (hereinafter Avgouleas, 'Cognitive Biases').

[87] Christine Jolls, Cass R. Sunstein & Richard Thaler, 'A Behavioral Approach to Law and Economics' (1998) 50 STANFORD LAW REV. 1471, 1477 (hereinafter Jolls et al, 'A Behavioral Approach').

[88] Emilios Avgouleas, 'The Global Financial Crisis, Behavioural Finance and Financial Regulation: In Search of a New Orthodoxy' (2009) 9 J. CORP. LAW STUD. 23, 28 (hereinafter Avgouleas, 'Global Financial Crisis'). For an 'irrational' reaction to information, consider the 2007 bank run on Northern Rock. Following the initial run on Northern Rock, the Financial Services Compensation scheme extended depositor cover to £35,000 in the event of bank failure; this failed to stop depositors from withdrawing their funds, even where they had less than £35,000 in the bank. For further discussion see House of Commons Treasury Committee, Fifth Report of Session 2007–08, *The Run on the Rock* (January 2008).

[89] Amos Tversky & Daniel Kahneman, 'Judgement under Uncertainty: Heuristics and Biases' (1974) 185 SCIENCE 1124 (hereinafter Tversky & Kahneman, 'Judgment under Uncertainty').

calculating probabilities and predicting values to simpler judgmental operations.[90] These are termed 'heuristics' or 'rules of thumb', which are intuitive judgments or choices, rather than deliberate reasoning.[91] Generally, these heuristics are quite useful, and assist in economising of time and facilitating *accessibility* – the readiness with which mental contents may be recalled:[92] 'people are not used to thinking hard, and are more often content to trust a plausible judgment that quickly comes to mind'.[93] However, they may occasionally lead to cognitive biases which result in '(i) systematic errors in estimates of known quantities and statistical facts; and (ii) systematic departures of intuitive judgments from the principles of probability theory'.[94] Heuristics may also help to explain the tendency of people to oversimplify issues when confronted with complex sets of data, thereby contradicting some of the key assumptions of the rational investor model, which assumes limitless informational interpretive capacity.[95]

These heuristics may be categorised into three broad sets: 'representativeness', 'availability' and 'anchoring'.[96] The representative heuristic prevents people from correctly weighting probabilities when making judgments. Human predictions are influenced to compare the perceived outcome of a particular event via comparison with the closest match to past patterns, without paying sufficient regard to the observed probability of matching the pattern. It is often helpful in reducing the complexity of

---

[90] Ibid.

[91] 'The impossibility of invariance raises significant doubts about the descriptive realism of rational-choice models.' See Daniel Kahneman, 'Maps of Bounded Rationality: Psychology for Behavioral Economics' (2003) 93 AM. ECON. REV. 1449, 1459.

[92] E. Tory Higgins, 'Knowledge Activation: Accessibility, Applicability and Salience' in E. Tory Higgins & Arien W. Kruglanski (eds), *Social Psychology: Handbook of Basic Principles* (Guildford Press, 1996).

[93] Daniel Kahneman, 'Maps of Bounded Rationality: Psychology for Behavioral Economics' (2003) 93 AM. ECON. REV. 1449, 1450.

[94] Avgouleas, 'Global Financial Crisis' 31.

[95] 'While … heuristics are useful on average … they lead to errors in particular circumstances. This means that someone using such a rule of thumb may be behaving rationally in the sense of economizing on thinking time, but such a person will nonetheless make forecasts that are different from those that emerge from the standard rational-choice model … Just as unbiased forecasting is not a good description of actual human behavior, expected utility theory is not a good description of actual decision making. While the axioms of expected utility theory characterize rational choice, actual choices diverge in important ways from this model.' See Jolls et al, 'A Behavioral Approach' 1477–78.

[96] Tversky & Kahneman, 'Judgment under Uncertainty' 1124–30.

decision making but may lead to severe biases. People place far greater relative weight to outcomes with statistically small probabilities. For example, people are poorly calibrated when calculating probabilities: events they believe will occur with certainty actually occur only around 80 per cent of the time, and events they deem impossible occur approximately 20 per cent of the time.[97] The representative heuristic may affect the judgment of people in many different fashions; for example, the representativeness heuristic leads to the following, non-exhaustive list of symptoms: people are insensitive to the prior probability of outcomes;[98] fail to judge probabilities on the basis of sample size;[99] misconceive the role of chance;[100] are insensitive to predictability;[101] attribute too much weight to certain descriptors ('the illusion of validity');[102] or misconceive the power of regression.[103]

The availability heuristic limits the calculation of probability in judgment; under this heuristic, people judge the probability of an event by the ease with which they can recall other instances of the same or similar events occurring. As with representativeness, availability is often a useful tool with which to assist in decision making (it is useful to assess the frequency of events because if an event is common it will normally be easier to recall); however, this may lead to a severe underestimation of the probability of particular events from occurring:

---

[97] Nicholas Barberis & Richard Thaler, 'A Survey of Behavioral Finance' in George M. Constantinides, Milton Harris & Rene M. Stulz, *Handbook of the Economics of Finance* (Elsevier, 2003) 1063 (hereinafter Barberis & Thaler, 'A Survey').

[98] People ignore the prior probability of outcomes in their estimation of future probabilities.

[99] Sample size will affect probability, although most people will recognise this.

[100] People expect that a process comprised of a random sequence of events will represent the essential characteristics of that process, irrespective of the length of that sequence.

[101] People fail to take into account the way in which a statement or description is posited in their estimation of probability; they do not consider that the description itself may be inaccurate.

[102] People often predict by using the outcome (for example, an occupation) that is most representative of an input (for example, a description of a person). The greater the match (or representativeness) between the outcome and the input, the greater the confidence they will have in their prediction.

[103] People fail to recognise the phenomenon of 'regression towards the mean'; that is, if the measurement of a variable is at first extreme, there is a high probability that the next measurement will be closer to the average.

> Lifelong experience has taught us that … instances of large classes are recalled better and faster than instances of less frequent classes; that likely occurrences are easier to imagine than unlikely ones; and that the associative connections between events are strengthened when the events frequently co-occur … [T]his valuable estimation procedure results in systematic errors.[104]

Anchoring refers to the process via which people make estimates by starting at a particular initial value that is adjusted to yield the final answer. In most cases, any adjustment made to the initial starting point is insufficient – the final answer remains heavily biased towards the initial estimate. Furthermore, anchoring contributes to biases in the assessment of distinctive and conjunctive events; people tend to overestimate the probability of conjunctive events and underestimate that of disjunctive events.[105]

(ii) Overconfidence and Herding

In the sphere of BDT, 'perhaps the most robust finding in the psychology of judgment is that people are overconfident'.[106] Cognitive research demonstrates that individuals possess a profound bias towards optimism in predicting future events.[107] The levels of confidence people ascribe to their predictions are, in general, far too high. Further, people have 'unrealistically rosy views of their abilities and prospects'.[108] Whilst individuals are, in general, possessed of remarkable overconfidence in their abilities, they also attribute too much weight to experiences which confirm their abilities to themselves, whilst systematically ignoring instances which should reduce the measurement of their abilities; so-called cognitive dissonance.[109] Cognitive dissonance in the context of

---

[104] Tversky & Kahneman, 'Judgment under Uncertainty' 1128.

[105] Ibid.

[106] Werner F.M. De Bondt & Richard H. Thaler, 'Financial Decision Making in Markets and Firms: A Behavioral Perspective' in Robert A. Jarrow, Vojislav Maksimovic & William T. Ziemba (eds), *Handbook in Operations Research and Management Science: Finance* (Elsevier, 1995) (hereinafter De Bondt & Thaler, 'Financial Decision Making').

[107] Neil D. Weinstein, 'Unrealistic Optimism about Future Life Events' (1980) 39 J. PERSONALITY & SOCIAL PSYCH. 806.

[108] Barberis and Thaler, 'A Survey' 1064.

[109] The term refers to the psychological condition which arises when an individual holds two conflicting cognitions resulting in mental conflict. This conflict will drive the subject to attempt to modify existing beliefs to reduce the dissonance between the cognitions. Thus, for example, where an investor loses a

finance dictates that when an investor receives confirming public information (which would support his/her investment) it affects his/her confidence levels in a positive manner; however, if the same investment is greeted with disconfirming information, the negative effect on his/her confidence level is comparatively less pronounced.[110] Conversely, agents have a profound propensity to underestimate the probability of adverse outcomes,[111] often termed 'disaster myopia'; this leads agents to seriously underestimate the risks facing both individual institutions and the system as a whole.[112]

Overconfidence has been shown to affect many sorts of finance professionals, including investment bankers[113] and securities analysts.[114] The Enron collapse, discussed briefly in the previous chapter, is instructive in this context. Enron's gross profit margins, in contrast to its revenues, declined from 21.2 per cent in 1996 to 6.2 per cent in 2000, despite its reported earnings increasing by 750 per cent over the same

---

lot of money on an investment, the cognitive dissonance that greets him via the conflicting emotions resulting from the loss (feelings of foolhardiness, guilt etc on the one hand and the investor's image of himself as a smart, intelligent person on the other) might convince him to rationalise the loss as being due to factors beyond his control, for example bad luck.

[110] See Shelley E. Taylor & Jonathon D. Brown, 'Illusion and Well-being: A Social Psychological Perspective on Mental Health' (1988) 103 PSYCH. BULL. 193; Baruch Fischoff, 'For Those Condemned to Study the Past: Heuristics and Biases in Hindsight' in Daniel Kahneman, Paul Slovic & Amos Tversky (eds), *Judgment under Uncertainty: Heuristics and biases* (CUP, 1982); Ellen J. Langer & Jane Roth, 'Heads I Win, Tails It's Chance: The Illusion of Control as a Function of the Sequence of Outcomes in a Purely Chance Task' (1975) 32 J. PERSONALITY & SOCIAL PSYCH. 951; Dale T. Miller & Michael Ross, 'Self-serving Bias in Attribution of Causality: Fact or Fiction?' (1975) 82 PSYCH. BULL. 213; Daryl J. Bem, 'An Experimental Analysis of Self-persuasion' (1965) 1 J. EXPERIMENTAL PSYCH. 199. For an overview of these theories, see Rowland Bismarck & Fernando Pasaribu, 'About Stock Bubbles' (2009) Econometric Research Institute Working Paper.

[111] See Haldane, 'Why Banks Failed the Stress Test'.

[112] For discussions of disaster myopia relating to financial markets see Jack M. Guttentag & Richard J. Herring, *Disaster Myopia in International Banking* (Princeton University Essays in International Finance, 1986). See also Richard J. Herring, 'Credit Risk and Financial Instability' (1999) 15 OX. REV. ECON. POL. 63.

[113] C.A.S. Stael von Holstein, 'Probabilistic Forecasting: An Experiment Related to the Stock Market' (1972) 8 ORGAN. BEHAVIOR & HUMAN PERF. 139.

[114] De Bondt & Thaler, 'Financial Decision Making'.

period.[115] However, in spite of the litany of red flags concerning Enron's financing and conflicts of interest, even by October 2001, shortly before its collapse, 16 out of 17 Wall Street analysts covering Enron maintained either 'buy' or 'strong buy' recommendations on Enron stock.[116] Indeed, just six months prior to its collapse, Enron's market capitalisation remained at over $35 billion,[117] despite clear signs that the stock was overvalued.[118] In keeping with the 'optimism narrative' concerning technology company stocks in the early twentieth century, large fund managers were left holding approximately 20 per cent of outstanding stocks when the corporation collapsed.[119] Thus, where overconfidence operates, stock prices may fail to react to negative news to a corresponding degree because available information is not accurately impounded into prices.[120]

A hugely significant consequence of overconfidence in relation to finance and investment is that it negatively influences the ability of market participants to correctly distinguish between the potential length of the short run and the long run.[121] Therefore, where an institution or investor appears to be gaining abnormally large profits in the short term, other investors will usually attribute greater probability to those high profits continuing than is warranted by financial data. This may produce

---

115 Enron Annual Report, 2000; Enron Annual Report, 1996.

116 See 'Statement of Frank Torres, Legislative Counsel, Consumers Union, Before the United States Senate Committee on Governmental Affairs, on the Collapse of Enron: The Role Analysts Played and the Conflicts They Face', 27 February 2002, 6. 2002 WL 2011028.

117 Steven L. Schwarcz, 'Enron and the Use and Abuse of Special Purpose Entities in Corporate Structures' (2002) 70 UNIV. CINCINNATI LAW REV. 1309.

118 Paul M. Healy & Krishna G. Palepu, 'The Fall of Enron' (2003) 17 J. ECON. PERSPECTIVES 3.

119 An analyst noted in December 2001: 'Enron was seen as a new-economy play because it was so revolutionary, and the bulk of its business was coming through Enron Online and it talked about getting into broadband. It was seen as an aggressive growth stock by a lot of managers.' See Kathleen Pender, 'Mutual Funds Hurt by Enron's Fall/Mutual Funds Hit Hard', *SFGate* (4 December 2001), http://www.sfgate.com/business/networth/article/Mutual-funds-hurt-by-Enron-s-fall-Mutual-funds-2847031.php.

120 The 'overconfidence' factor influencing stock prices may be marginalised over time as the market recognises more relevant information; however, its effects may remain pervasive.

121 Narasimhan Jegadeesh & Sheridan Titman, 'Returns to Buying Winners and Selling Losers: Implications for Stock Market Efficiency' (1993) 48 J. FIN. 65 (hereinafter Jegadeesh & Titman, 'Returns to Buying Winners').

the result that '[i]n a rising stock market or any other asset market … individuals embrace unsustainable beliefs that the price rises will continue indefinitely'.[122] These biases often lead to overconfidence, fed by the subjective underestimation of particular probabilities generated by other heuristics,[123] a process often referred to as a 'feedback loop': '[P]ositive feedback reinforces, accelerates, or amplifies whatever is happening, whether it is a virtuous cycle or downward spiral. Systems with positive feedback can thus exhibit exponential growth, exponential collapse, or oscillations with increasing amplitude.'[124] In financial markets, positive feedback loops occur when an initial increase in prices due to precipitating factors yields ever increasing price inflation: a self-repeating cycle develops, driven by investor demand. They may be propelled by one of two factors (or a combination of both): adaptive expectations,[125] which are driven by the notion that past price increases will generate further price increases, and/or greater investor confidence, which occurs in response to past price increases.[126] Feedback effects decline in time following the initial precipitating factors; in other words, the effects are felt most strongly in the periods immediately following the high returns which produced the altered perceptions of stocks independently of future potential performance.[127] Of course, feedback loops may also produce negative results: as investor confidence wanes, stock and security prices may be driven far away from previous values and

[122] Avgouleas, 'Global Financial Crisis' 33.

[123] Tversky & Kahneman, 'Judgment under Uncertainty' 1129.

[124] Eric D. Beinhocker, *The Origin of Wealth: Evolution, Complexity and the Radical Remaking of Economics* (Random House, 2007) 101.

[125] Andrei Shleifer & Robert Vishny, 'A Model of Investor Sentiment' (1998) 49 J. FIN. ECON. 307.

[126] John Y. Campbell & John H. Cochrane, 'By Force of Habit: A Consumption-Based Explanation of Aggregate Stock Market Behaviour' (1999) 107 J. POLIT. ECON. 205.

[127] This is also partly the basis for Hyman Minsky's theories on the financial system, which will be analysed in the following chapter. Other varieties of feedback include price-GDP-price loops, which are manifested in higher stock and security prices due to the so-called 'wealth-effect'; as people 'feel' more prosperous, increased consumer spending raises general price levels in the economy. See Karl E. Case, John M. Quigley & Robert J. Shiller, 'Comparing Wealth Effects: The Stock Market vs. the Housing Market' (2005) NBER Working Paper No. 8606.

downward pressure on prices may cause rapid price deflation, driven by 'Knightian uncertainty' (the fear of risks which cannot be computed).[128]

Evidence derived from research on the use of heuristics by investors supports feedback theories. For example, the representativeness heuristic might lead subjects 'to match stock price patterns into salient categories such as dramatic and persistent price trends, thus leading to feedback dynamics, even if these categories may be rarely seen in fundamental underlying factors'.[129] As noted, the availability heuristic holds that people make judgments about the probability of an event occurring by recalling recent instances of its occurrence. This, of course, involves a focus on short-term memories as longer-term memories are recalled less easily. Thus, where a stock market has experienced strong returns for a protracted period of time and the memory of these returns is recent, investors will almost certainly overestimate the likelihood of such extraordinary gains persisting – at least in the short term: the so-called 'status-quo' bias, or 'persistence' bias, which induces investors to believe that what has happened recently will continue to happen.[130] Accordingly, as markets soar in price, investors operating under heuristics conclude that strong returns will proceed exponentially.[131]

These heuristics may cause investors to act collectively and begin to mimic the investment decisions of one another, a process known as 'herding'. Investors are more likely to buy (sell) if others are buying (selling).[132] This is because others' behaviour may presumably be based upon better information regarding the future of the market.[133] Complex judgments that investors must arrive at are necessarily influenced by the

---

128 This was originally proposed in Frank H. Knight, *Risk, Uncertainty and Profit* (Houghton Mifflin, 1921).

129 Shiller, 'From Efficient Market Theory' 18.

130 Avgouleas, *Mechanics and Regulation* 66.

131 Coffee, 'Gatekeeper Failure' 325.

132 The rationale for herding has been summarised thus: 'Investors like to buy what others are buying, sell what others are selling and own what others own.' See Avinash Persaud, 'Sending the Herd Off the Cliff Edge: The Disturbing Interaction Between Herding and Market-sensitive Risk Management Practices' (2000) 1 WORLD ECON. 15.

133 This is known as an 'informational cascade', which occurs 'when it is optimal for an individual, having observed the actions of those ahead of him, to follow the behavior of the preceding individual without regard to his own information'. See Sushil Bikhchandani, David Hirshleifer & Ivo Welch, 'A Theory of Fads, Fashion, Custom and Cultural Change as Informational Cascades' (1992) 100 J. POLIT. ECON. 992, 994.

plausible judgments of others.[134] From this, market actors rely on the actions of others based on the fact that they believe those others to have superior information which they themselves do not. Even where this belief is empirically false, self-reinforcing contagion may ensue: '[P]eople are rationally choosing not to, as they see it, waste their time and effort in exercising their judgment about the market … Ultimately, all such information cascade theories *are theories of the failure of information about true fundamental value to be disseminated and evaluated.*'[135] Even completely rational individuals may engage in herd behaviour when they rely on the judgments of others;[136] whilst this may be individually rational, in the sense that 'following the crowd' may sometimes be a rational strategy, it has the potential to produce group behaviour which is irrational.[137] This may result in a significant proportion of market actors 'following the crowd', relying not on information that they have, but on the signal sent to them by other actors' decisions, if not to beat the market, then at least to match it.[138] Thus, the earliest actions in a market may have

---

[134] Robert J. Shiller, 'Bubbles, Human Judgment, and Expert Opinion' (2002) FIN. AN. J. 18 (hereinafter Shiller, 'Bubbles').

[135] Shiller, *Irrational Exuberance* (2nd edn, Princeton University Press, 2005) 160 (emphasis in original) (hereinafter Shiller, *Irrational Exuberance*).

[136] Indeed, it may itself be rational to observe the activities of others in coming to an investment decision. See, for example, the famous analogy between beauty contests and financial forecasting proffered by John Maynard Keynes. In short, Keynes described the actions of rational agents in a stock market in terms of the judges of a fictional beauty contest, in which the judges are asked to select a set of six faces from photographs of women that they deem to be 'the most beautiful'. Keynes observed that the best strategy to win the prize would not be for the individual judge to choose the six faces that he deemed most beautiful, but to try to deduce what the majority perception of 'beauty' is and make a selection based upon that. As Keynes himself pointed out: 'It is not a case of choosing those [faces] that, to the best of one's judgment, are really the prettiest, nor even those that average opinion genuinely thinks the prettiest. We have reached the third degree where we devote our intelligences to anticipating what average opinion expects the average opinion to be.' See John M. Keynes, *The General Theory of Employment, Interest and Money* (Palgrave Macmillan, 1936) (hereinafter Keynes, *The General Theory*) 155–56.

[137] Abhijit V. Banerjee, 'A Simple Model of Herd Behavior' (1992) 107 Q. J. ECON. 797.

[138] See the seminal work of Solomon Asch, *Social Psychology* (Prentice Hall, 1952); see also Morton Deutsch & Harold B. Gerard, 'A Study of Normative and Informational Social Influences upon Individual Judgment' (1955) 51 J. ABNORMAL SOCIAL PSYCH. 629.

a disproportionate effect on the judgments made by successive agents.[139] Investors are necessarily uninterested in the long-term performance of securities because they intend to sell at a later, unspecified date, but their trades impair the efficiency of the market and reveal less data concerning assets' long-term values.[140] Overvaluations of assets therefore may occur because of significant amplifying reactions of speculators on deviations from fundamentals,[141] which may be a reason why one may observe misalignments between the price of securities and their long-run value.[142] The power of herding is demonstrated by research which confirms that investors will herd even when they know that their peers are not fully informed.[143] Furthermore, reputational constraints in relation to professional investment advisers and fund managers also play a role.[144] As discussed earlier in the context of arbitrage, the first aim of any investment adviser is to outperform his peers. This may be an inducement to herd:[145] 'those who are cautious and prudent will be outperformed by those who recklessly predict extraordinary returns'.[146] The effect on prices may be sustained and severe. Where herd behaviour takes hold, information stops flowing to the market and dislocation between prices and values may ensue.

---

139 This is known as 'mutual mimetic investor contagion', which is 'concerned with short-term behaviour where agents do not really have time to interpret news and may spontaneously follow other market participants'. See Richard Topol, 'Bubbles and Volatility of Stock Prices: Effect of Mimetic Contagion' (1991) 101 ECON. J. 786, 787 note 1; see also Andre Orlean, 'Mimetic Contagion and Speculative Bubbles' (1989) 27 THEORY & DECISION 63.

140 Kenneth A. Froot, David S. Scharfstein & Jeremy C. Stein, 'Herd on the Street: Informational Inefficiencies in a Market with Short-term Speculation' (1992) 47 J. FIN. 1461; Kenneth A. Froot & Maurice Obstfeld, 'Intrinsic Bubbles: The Case of Stock Prices' (1991) 81 AM. ECON. REV. 1189.

141 Thomas Lux, 'Herd Behaviour, Bubbles and Crashes' (1995) 105 ECON. J. 881.

142 Marco Cipriani & Antonio Guarino, 'Herd Behavior and Contagion in Financial Markets' (2008) 8 B.E. J. THEORETICAL ECON. Article 24, 1.

143 Richard Topol, 'Bubbles and Volatility of Stock Prices: Effect of Mimetic Contagion' (1991) 101 ECON. J. 786.

144 Avgouleas, *Mechanics and Regulation* 68.

145 Judith Chevalier & Glenn Ellison, 'Career Concerns of Mutual Fund Managers' (1999) 114 Q. J. ECON. 389 (hereinafter Chevalier & Ellison, 'Career Concerns').

146 Avgouleas, *Mechanics and Regulation* 69.

(iii) Asset Bubbles

The pervasive influences of behavioural influences on 'real-world' markets are manifested in the most pertinent market puzzle which presents itself in relation to the application of the EMH to financial and securities markets analysis: the asset bubble phenomenon. The heuristics and biases discussed previously occasionally act in concert to produce a pervading sense of optimism which may result in speculation on a grand scale. If this speculation continues, an asset bubble may develop – in other words, a deviation of the market price from its true or fundamental value. Asset bubbles are a ubiquitous phenomenon in modern capitalist development;[147] they may afflict any market, although stock market bubbles (along with housing bubbles) appear to be the most discussed, perhaps because of the perceived damage caused to the economy by their deflation, and the proximity of the general public to those markets.[148] As was noted earlier in this chapter, neoclassical economic theory holds that an asset bubble is an impossibility: that market prices always convey fundamental value. Securities market bubbles, the effects of which may be described as 'mass hysteria [which leads to] an occasional deviation from rational behaviour',[149] are the most obvious challenge to the EMH, because they appear so frequently, and often seem to be based on a form of irrational speculation.

In his seminal work, Shiller defines the market frenzy which leads to bubbles (often referred to as 'irrational exuberance'[150]) thus: 'The psychological basis of a speculative bubble ... [is] ... a situation in which news of price increases spurs investor enthusiasm, which spreads by psychological contagion from person to person.'[151] His analysis concludes that markets in general are susceptible to inflationary pressures attributable to psychological factors and investor perceptions rather than the economic factors underpinning prices. Bubbles are usually propelled

---

[147] The history of financial market bubbles has been masterfully charted by the late economic historian Professor Kindleberger. See Charles P. Kindleberger & Robert Z. Aliber, *Manias, Panics and Crashes: A History of Financial Crises* (6th edn, Palgrave Macmillan, 2011) (hereinafter Kindleberger & Aliber, *Manias, Panics and Crashes*).

[148] Marcel Kahan, 'Securities Laws and the Social Costs of "Inaccurate" Stock Prices' (1992) 41 DUKE LAW J. 989.

[149] Kindleberger & Aliber, *Manias, Panics and Crashes* 26–27.

[150] A term first coined by Alan Greenspan, 'The Challenge of Central Banking in a Democratic Society', speech before the American Enterprise Institute for Public Policy, Washington DC, December 5, 1996.

[151] Shiller, *Irrational Exuberance* 2.

by 'new-era' thinking, a frame of reference which drives people to believe that future market prospects are 'brighter or less uncertain'[152] than in past periods. Stock market prices therefore – to some degree at least – are driven by the prevailing economic and financial climate: in bull markets investors are psychologically more inclined to expect further market gains, whereas in bear markets expectations of future market strength are lowered.[153] Research confirms that this form of thinking may affect stock analysis, and lead to price departures from value.[154] Accordingly, asset bubbles are arguably driven by the heuristics previously discussed, especially overconfidence.

The process of stock overvaluation is linear: enthusiasm for particular stocks leads to short- or medium-term increases in the price of those stocks. These increases cannot usually be justified objectively from available economic data. Instead, momentum effects and near-term memories of strong performance lead to an increase in prices, which attracts further investment: 'The high demand for [an] asset is generated by the public's memory of high past returns and the optimism the high returns generate for the future.'[155] This enthusiasm for those stocks in effect becomes a self-reinforcing cycle; as other market participants are drawn to invest by the returns available, stock prices may become further divorced from the value that would be evidenced based upon the measure of stocks' fundamental worth, processes which are naturally reflexive.[156] In fact, Shiller compares asset bubbles in financial markets to those

---

152 Ibid. 96.

153 Renowned financier George Soros performs a similar analysis to the stock market crash of 1987. He argues that markets demonstrate 'reflexivity' – that financial markets cannot reach equilibrium because of their participants' biases. See George Soros, *The Alchemy of Finance* (2nd edn, John Wiley & Sons, 1994); George Soros, *The Crisis of Global Capitalism: Open Society Endangered* (Public Affairs, 1998). See also Shiller, *Irrational Exuberance* 59–64.

154 Maosen Zhong, Ali F. Darrat & Dwight C. Anderson, 'Do US Stock Prices Deviate From Their Fundamental Values? Some New Evidence' (2003) 27 J. BANKING & FIN. 673.

155 Shiller, 'Bubbles'; Kenneth L. Fisher and Meir Statman, 'Blowing Bubbles' (2002) 3 J. PSYCH. FIN. MAR. 53.

156 Shiller uses the price–earnings ratio ('P/E') to demonstrate this phenomenon. Shiller's P/E index chart is available at http://www.econ.yale.edu/~shiller/data.htm.

exhibited in Ponzi schemes,[157] describing such speculative bubbles as 'naturally occurring Ponzi processes'.[158]

Accordingly, this pattern is redolent of two of the manifestations of investor behaviour just discussed, each of which has been shown to contribute to distortions in pricing: feedback loops and herding. Herding and feedback loops are amplification mechanisms, which amplify extant forces present in securities markets. The feedback loop sustains the optimistic beliefs about market prices and their future trajectory, whilst the prices themselves are given credence by herding by investors into rising markets. Accordingly, overconfidence may also explain why asset bubbles inflate and continue to persist. Where agents possess heterogeneous beliefs concerning the future path of asset markets, a preponderance of confidence amongst those agents will lead to increased asset prices, even where this confidence may be misplaced.[159] On this basis, market prices may fail to reflect fundamental value if the aggregate information on a stock or market is spread amongst investors.[160] These issues may be compounded by the knowledge that predicting losses may be catastrophic for long-term investment and/or job security for agents who control large volumes of finance, especially fund managers. Thus, in securities market bubbles, outward optimism (even where this optimism may not reflect fully the opinion of the fund manager) 'amounts less to a heuristic bias than a competitive necessity',[161] a position

---

[157] Ponzi schemes are fraudulent investment schemes which promise large rewards through investment. However, no investment of subscriber funds is actually made. Instead, initial investors are paid 'returns' from the later subscriptions of other people who are drawn to the scheme by reports of abnormal financial performance. This process continues until no new investment can be procured (for example, owing to a lack of investors, the discovery of the scheme etc), and the scheme collapses.

[158] Shiller, *Irrational Exuberance* 78. Although Shiller acknowledges that in most speculative bubbles there is no fraud involved, he contends that they are similar to Ponzi schemes in that investors are drawn to them by tales of large returns. Investors often make these investments based on the perceived returns on offer without performing proper due diligence on the investment itself.

[159] José A. Scheinkman & Wei Xiong, 'Overconfidence and Speculative Bubbles' (2003) 111 J. POLIT. ECONOMY 1183.

[160] Markus K. Brunnermeier, *Asset Pricing under Asymmetric Information: Bubbles, Crashes, Technical Analysis, and Herding* (OUP, 2001) (hereinafter Brunnermeier, *Asset Pricing under Asymmetric Information*).

[161] Ibid.

confirmed by analysis of fund manager investing behaviour.[162] This provides a convincing explanation of why bubbles may be a 'rational' phenomenon, on the basis that herding and other manifestations of 'following the crowd' may be a rational investment strategy, particularly for bankers and other finance professionals.[163]

On this basis, other analyses attempt to explain securities market bubbles as manifestations of rational profit maximisation efforts by risk-averse traders.[164] In this synthesis, investors are categorised as 'smart and informed', or 'irrational and uninformed'. It is structural imperfections which prevent the 'smart and informed' investors from fully arbitraging the market, and making money at the expense of uninformed traders who in normal circumstances, presumably, would be forced to exit the market due to heavy losses. 'Smart' investors, who know that the securities concerned are overvalued, are aware that their purchases will generate positive feedback effects and encourage others to herd. As prices

---

[162] Paul M. Healy & Krishna Palepu, 'Governance and Intermediation Problems in Capital Markets: Evidence from the Fall of Enron' (2002) NBER Working Paper No. 02-27, 26, observing that a fund manager who believes that a stock is overvalued but fails to act on this (and instead follows the crowd) will neither be rewarded for foreseeing the problem nor penalized for herding, because their peers made the same error; Stephen M. Bainbridge, 'Mandatory Disclosure: A Behavioral Analysis' (2000) 68 UNIV. CINCINNATI LAW REV. 1023, 1038 (observing how herding strategies may still garner a reputational pay-off for a fund manager, even where that behaviour ultimately results in losses, and arguing that fund managers who comply with 'conventional wisdom' concerning particular stocks or industries suffer reduced adverse reputational consequences in the face of losses than would be expected.

[163] On this, note the observation of Keynes: 'A sound banker, alas! Is not one who foresees danger and avoids it, but one who, when he is ruined, is ruined in a conventional and orthodox way along with his fellows, so that no one can really blame him.' See John Maynard Keynes, *Essays in Persuasion*, 'The Consequences to the Banks of the Collapse of Money Values' (Macmillan, 1931) 180. See also Viral V. Acharya & Tanju Yorulmazer, 'Information Contagion and Bank Herding' (2008) 40 J. MONEY, CREDIT & BANKING 215–31.

[164] For rational bubble models, see Paul De Grauwe & Marianna Grimaldi, 'Bubbles and Crashes in a Behavioural Finance Model' (2006) Central Bank of Sweden Working Paper No. 164; Dilip Abreu & Markus K. Brunnermeier, 'Bubbles and Crashes' (2003) 71 ECONOMETRICA 173; Bradford J. Delong, Andrei Shleifer, Lawrence H. Summers & Robert J. Waldman, 'Positive Feedback Investment Strategies and Destabilising Rational Speculation' (1990) 45 J. FIN. 375; Robert P. Flood & Robert J. Hodrick, 'On Testing for Speculative Bubbles' (1990) 4 J. ECON. PERSPECTIVES 85; Jeffrey A. Frankel & Kenneth A. Froot, 'Understanding the U.S. Dollar in the Eighties: The Expectations of Chartists and Fundamentalists' (1987) NBER Working Paper R0957.

rise, the positive feedback loop will beget further rises. The 'smart' money knows that prices will eventually collapse but they are prepared to get out of the market at the 'right' time and leave the 'uninformed' traders with the losses. Once the number of smart investors reaches a critical mass and enough of them realise that a bubble is in existence, their combined trades burst the bubble and prices return to pre-bubble levels.[165]

ADAPTIVE MARKETS AND COMPLEXITY

Recent research into financial market dynamics has amplified the contributions of behavioural finance, including work in the fields of complexity theory, systems theory and evolutionary dynamics, which offer further insights into the mechanisms that give rise to price discovery. These theories also attempt to explain how asset bubbles and instability are likely to arise in financial markets as the result of natural processes based on the inherent traits of the financial system, including its complexity and interconnectedness. In this way, attempts have been made to synthesise the findings of the EMH with behavioural finance, a notable example being the Adaptive Markets Hypothesis (AMH).[166] This theory is also heavily influenced by the findings of evolutionary psychology and posits that the principles of competition, reproduction and natural selection, often applied to social interactions and natural ecosystems, may also be applied to financial and economic markets. Financial markets under this view are complex and evolutionary, comprised of many forms of agent of differing levels of sophistication and risk-tolerance, interacting in mutually reinforcing ways. Like behavioural finance the AMH posits that investors are boundedly rational, and they will therefore use heuristics to

---

[165] Whilst on the surface, the central thread of these theories appears convincing, the models' strict adherence to the rigours of modern finance theory ignores many of the criticisms levelled at standard financial theory detailed earlier in this chapter. By framing these models in terms of rational choice, supporters of rational bubble theories ignore the significance of imperfect information and/or heuristic biases, which imply that irrational behaviour cannot be modelled adequately with predetermined mechanistic precepts. For a summary of rejoinders to rational bubble models, see Roman Frydman & Michael D. Goldberg, *Beyond Mechanical Markets: Asset Price Swings, Risk and the Role of the State* (Princeton UP, 2011).

[166] Andrew Lo, 'The Adaptive Markets Hypothesis: Market Efficiency From an Evolutionary Perspective' (2004) J. PORTFOLIO MAN., 30th Anniversary Issue 15.

guide their decision making in the face of uncertainty. Where the AMH arguably extends the behavioural finance analysis is in its prediction that investors will continue to adapt those heuristics according to past experiences, which will allow the system to eventually reach near-equilibrium. As in biological systems, those agents which fail to adapt will die out, and those agents with the best strategies for survival will continue in existence. There are therefore certain strategies which will pay off in some environments, but will fail in others. This will lead the system naturally towards equilibrium, although equilibrium itself is unlikely to be reached due to the inherent biases of market participants which may be impossible to overcome even through adaptive learning. On this basis, financial markets may not trend towards maximal efficiency, and instead exhibit complex market dynamics which emphasise the importance of survival over optimal financial returns, resulting in 'cycles as well as trends, and panics, manias, bubbles, crashes, and other phenomena that are routinely witnessed in natural market ecologies'.[167]

The role for regulation in this context is twofold. Firstly, regulations should be used to ensure greater transparency within the financial system to ensure that risk is borne by the appropriate parties, and to ensure that those parties understand the risks that they face. Accordingly, both increased information provision in markets and greater education of market participants are required to reduce the likelihood of market failure. Under this view market solutions remain preferable to government intervention, which is likely to be costly and inefficient. Secondly, regulation may be used to counter the effects of certain human behaviours which are driven by emotion, rather than logic. The aim of this regulation should be to limit the effects of certain non-adaptive behaviours to lead to patterns which cause damage to the economic system. These behaviours – most notably overconfidence, greed and fear – are dynamic factors in all corporate organisations and markets, although they are perhaps most obvious prior to the emergence of, during and post episodes of financial instability. Greed and overconfidence during times of prosperity tend to lead businesses to overextend their activities, which in the case of financial institutions, is manifested in larger loan volumes and lower regulatory demands for margins of safety. Fear is evidenced during and following financial crashes, when businesses contract investment and hoard finance which, in the case of financial institutions, may have catastrophic knock-on consequences for the real economy. However, the complexity of financial markets means that any regulations must not

[167] Ibid. 24.

be overly prescriptive, and must be responsive to the flexibility and dynamism of modern finance.[168]

Theories which tread similar ground – complexity theory in particular – have also been used to explain the workings of the financial system.[169] A 'complex system' is formally understood as an agglomeration of many interdependent smaller parts that interact with one other through competitive, non-linear collaboration, and lead to emergent, self-organised behaviour. 'Emergence' in this context refers to the fact that complexity may arise naturally from a multiplicity of relatively simple interactions. Complexity theorists posit – as does the AMH – that the financial system has all the properties of a complex, evolutionary system. Some of these properties include the following:

(i) The system may spend long periods of time far from equilibrium, even when equilibrium in principle exists.
(ii) The system may have multiple equilibria, any of which may be unstable.
(iii) The system cannot be strictly optimized in real-time.
(iv) Feedback, cascades and extreme events are common.
(v) The system exhibits self-organised dynamics and is therefore hard to control in a centralized or top-down way.
(vi) The system may have emergent properties, i.e. properties that cannot be understood from the properties of the system components, but rather from the interactions between them.
(vii) The system behaviour is often counter-intuitive and hard to predict (not simply due to randomness).

---

[168] For example, Lo notes: 'The complexity of financial markets is straining the capacity of regulators to keep up with its innovations, many of which were not contemplated when the existing regulatory bodies were first formed. New regulations should be adaptive and focused on financial functions rather than institutions, making them more flexible and dynamic. An example of an adaptive regulation is a requirement to standardize an OTC contract and create an organized exchange for it (with standardized contracts, a clearing corporation, and daily market-to-market and settlement) whenever its size – as measured by open interest, trading volume, or notional exposure – exceeds a certain threshold. The CDS market should be among the first to be transformed into an exchange.' See Andrew Lo, 'Regulatory Reform in the Wake of the Financial Crisis of 2007–2008' (2009) 1 J. FIN. ECON. POL. 4, 6.

[169] Most of this work is modelled after the seminal contribution to complexity of Herbert A. Simon in 'The Architecture of Complexity' (1962) 106 PROC. AM. PHILOSOPHICAL SOCIETY 467.

(viii) Stakeholders (and even countries) will often fail to behave as they prefer or as they should, because they cannot act independently.[170]

The financial system comprises traders (agents) of varying financial resources, and the transacting rules (regulations and laws) of the relevant market. Through a series of interactions, the agents attempt to achieve maximum profit (at each other's expense) by trading in financial assets, in a highly competitive and non-linear way. The results of those interactions, including bubbles, crashes, collapses and manias, resemble prototypical phenomena characteristic of dynamic and complex systems. These are manifestations of typical non-linear processes, and their combined effects may be strongly amplified by the internal dynamics of the system, termed autocatalysis (similar to the feedback loops discussed earlier). Naturally, this means that the financial system cannot remain in equilibrium for prolonged periods, nor can regulators accurately predict its behaviour. Accordingly, the best way to understand financial crises is as (non-linear) unpredictable emergent phenomena, generated endogenously by the interactions between systemic constituents.

Complexity theory has been given further support by the development of 'network theory', which investigates the properties of networks where the stability of each constituent is a function of its linkages with other constituents.[171] In the context of the financial system, network theory regards the financial system as an intricate lattice of 'nodes', which through evolutionary steps has become increasingly interconnected through links between individuals and institutions.[172] The complexity and depth of the financial network have frequently been cited as indicating that risk is more efficiently allocated, thereby reducing systemic vulnerability. However, its complexity may also mask the mutual dependency and homogeneity of its constituent parts, features which may also make the system fragile. The nodes of the financial system, whose numbers and individual size have increased massively since the advent of complex financial engineering, lead to both opacity and a much higher degree of

---

170 Dirk Helbing & Alan Kirman, 'Rethinking Economics Using Complexity Theory' (2013) 7–8, http://papers.ssrn.com/sol3/papers.cfm?abstract_id=2292370.

171 David L. Levy, 'Applications and Limitations of Complexity Theory in Organization Theory and Strategy' in Jack Rabin & Gerald J. Miller (eds), *Handbook of Strategic Management* (2nd edn, CRC Press, 2000) 67, 68 (hereinafter Levy, 'Applications of Complexity Theory').

172 Andrew G. Haldane, 'Rethinking the Financial Network', Speech given at the Financial Student Association, Amsterdam, 28 April 2009, http://www.bankofengland.co.uk/archive/Documents/historicpubs/speeches/2009/speech386.pdf.

interconnectedness. In the case of larger losses, the proximity and multiple linkages of nodes within the network allow those losses to be passed between nodes extremely quickly, often with catastrophic consequences for systemic stability. Contagion risk is therefore multiplied as shocks are transmitted much more rapidly, issues which are more pronounced where the trading and investment of nodes is homogeneous (a pattern which, in the case of the Anglo-American financial system, has become markedly more prevalent). The lack of diversification amongst those nodes makes individual shocks more likely to cause widespread systemic damage. Collectively, these factors make cascade or domino effects much more likely, through large network interdependencies and homogeneous nodal trading directions, combined with overarching uncertainty in chains of claims generated by financial innovations, opacity and complexity. Feedback effects experienced under periods of stress (or market panic) exacerbate these problems, as nodes in the network are unable to assess counterparty risk. In these periods of stress the result is mass hoarding of liquidity, firesales and asset price crashes. The shortening of the network chain in the modern financial system brought about by advances in information and communication technology, and the frenetic pace of global financial transactions simply makes the effects of these crises more devastating when they do arise.[173]

The benefits of these views concerning the operation of financial markets are that they may provide a more appropriate lens through which to formulate legislation than when viewed through modern finance theory. Each expands upon the key insights from behavioural finance and associated disciplines to offer a more nuanced view of investor behaviour and the performance of the financial system. Significantly, each provides a theoretical basis for greater regulation of financial markets in order to temper some the natural tendencies of financial markets to experience crisis. As noted by Schwarcz, legislation has a role in addressing market failures, but the complexity and rapid evolution of financial markets mean that prescriptive rules based on arguably outdated models (including modern finance theory) often lag behind market developments. Complexity theory and its associated offshoots allow regulators to understand that as financial markets are chaotic and evolving systems, their failure is virtually inevitable. The focus should therefore not be on

---

173 Ibid.

preventing failure, but on reducing its effects, especially through minimising contagion risk and short-circuiting systemic risk-inducing channels in the event of market panic.[174]

LIMITATIONS TO HETERODOX MODELS OF INVESTOR BEHAVIOUR

There have therefore been a number of fresh attempts beyond the traditional challenge mounted by behavioural finance to refute the EMH, which purport to explain both the behaviour of financial markets and the financial system itself. Whilst these theories (particularly the AMH) express some very novel and plausible views concerning phenomena which blight both the EMH and its application to financial system performance, they themselves suffer from some defects. Because orthodox models cast agents as rational decision makers, irrationality and other behavioural limitations are necessarily assumed away. Whilst, as explained, these assumptions undoubtedly lead to imperfect legislative design, they give regulators a universal investor model around which rules and principles may be constructed (even if those models only account for investor behaviour at certain points in time). On the basis that behavioural finance and other heterodox theories posit that investors may be driven by several forms of competing influences and sentiments, thus resulting in unpredictable investment behaviour, designing a system of regulation which adhered to the tenets of these theories – even if it were possible – would produce a patchwork of uncertainty.

Accordingly, in the case of behavioural finance, whilst it certainly does provide some far-reaching insights into investor behaviour – which has serious implications for the integrity of the EMH – its power as a predictive tool is naturally limited. Of course, as an analytical tool, behaviourism may explain why financial market phenomena such as asset bubbles occur, but it is difficult for regulators and others to use models about human behaviour to positively predict *ex ante* how markets may react to particular events, especially as behavioural finance scholarship tends to focus on what people 'won't do', as opposed to what they 'will do'. Behavioural finance provides some convincing explanations for investor 'irrationality' in certain predefined situations, but it is clear that in many circumstances investors do act rationally, and that deviations

---

[174] Steven L. Schwarcz, 'Regulating Complexity in Financial Markets' (2009) 87 WASH. LAW REV. 211, 215.

from 'normal' behaviour, whilst sometimes being irrational, are not ubiquitous; many of the anomalies cited by behavioural finance scholars are often concerned with rather narrow market phenomena, which are often caused as much by structural imperfections and information asymmetries (market failures) as investor behaviour.[175]

As noted, in focusing on the capacity of individual failures of rationality to produce optimal decision making, behavioural finance offers some convincing narratives concerning individual investor irrationality, but precisely because of this, it offers contradictory implications; for example, are investors likely to be risk-averse or overconfident? Behavioural finance often fails to answer these questions precisely because it is designed to highlight instances in which people fail to comply with the rational investor model, rather than itself generating a normative model of behaviour. Accordingly, empirical research does not provide evidence that people are consistently biased in a particular direction, which naturally makes it extremely difficult to engage in predictive modelling. For example, individuals will often invest in mutual funds which have had strong recent returns,[176] yet are more likely to sell stocks which have performed well, and hold on to stocks that have

---

[175] Some of these 'narrow' market anomalies include: (i) the Royal-Dutch Shell paradox, where Shell Transport and Royal Dutch Petroleum's shares trade at varying discounts to one another despite comprising the same share capital (see Avgouleas, *Mechanics and Regulation*; Kenneth A. Froot and Emil Dabora, 'How Are Stock Prices Affected by the Location of Trade?' (1999) 53 J. FIN. ECON. 189); (ii) the closed-end fund puzzle which demonstrates that the share prices of these funds trade at a discount of approximately 10% (see Barberis and Thaler, 'A Survey' 109697; Charles M.C. Lee, Andrei Shleifer & Richard H. Thaler, 'Investor Sentiment and the Closed-end Fund Puzzle' (1991) 46 J. FIN. 75); (iii) the equity premium (see Narayana R. Kocherkalota, 'The Equity Premium: It's Still a Puzzle' (1996) 34 J. ECON. LIT. 42; Shlomo Benartzi & Richard H. Thaler, 'Myopic Loss Aversion and the Equity Premium Puzzle' (1995) 110 Q. J. ECON. 73; Rajnish Mehra & Edward C. Prescott, 'The Equity Premium: A Puzzle' (1985) 15 J. MONETARY ECON. 145); (iv) excessive volatility (see Robert J. Shiller, 'Do Stock Prices Move Too Much to Be Justified by Subsequent Changes in Dividends?' (1981) 71 AM. ECON. REV. 421; Stephen F. LeRoy & Richard D. Porter, 'The Present-value Relation: Tests Based on Implied Invariance Bounds' (1981) 49 ECONOMETRICA 555); and (v) excess trading volumes (see Terrance Odean & Brad M. Barber, 'Trading is Hazardous to Your Wealth: The Common Stock Investment Performance of Individual Investors' (2000) 55 J. FIN. 773).

[176] Chevalier & Ellison, 'Career Concerns'; Erik R. Sirri & Peter Tufano, 'Costly Search and Mutual Fund Flows' (1998) 53 J. FIN. 1589.

performed badly.[177] These contradictory behaviours merely exemplify the difficulties inherent in constructing a testable and predictive theory based on the concept of irrationality, and on this basis it remains extremely difficult to explain how individual acts and/or decisions produce aggregate results.

Similarly, the AMH and complexity (network) theories present highly similar dilemmas; namely, in arguing that predicting systemic behaviour is virtually impossible, designing a system of regulation based on these theories which can be used to lessen the effects of financial market swings is commensurately complex. On the basis that one of the key problems associated with financial systems failures in recent years has been the advent of ever more complex and innovative products and risk models, it would appear paradoxical if the solution to reducing risk were to be found in the highly sophisticated and rigorous mathematical modelling characteristic of complexity theory. Modelling financial systems based on the parameters of complexity theory, which are normally applied to physical systems, raises a set of unique challenges. Whilst many of the processes witnessed in financial markets resemble patterns visible in other non-linear systems, it is difficult to conclusively ascribe those phenomena to complexity, or network effects, rather than simple randomness.[178] If a system exhibits randomness, rather than chaos, any forces pushing that system away from equilibrium is necessarily exogenous, and therefore complexity (chaos) theory cannot be used as a basis on which to regulate it. Furthermore, in a system such as the financial system, which is highly dependent on other forces for its aggregate behaviour – including political, legal, social and financial considerations – and where outcomes reflect extremely complex underlying relationships, applying complexity theory represents arguably *too* simple a rubric in accounting for system behaviour. On this basis, the search for a simple mathematical engine to explain (non-natural) systemic behaviour through complexity theory (and through network theory, which may also be too simplifying) is probably futile.[179]

These considerations perhaps reflect the most significant limitation to applying complexity theory to the operation of financial markets: human

---

177 Hersh Shefrin & Meir Statman, 'The Disposition to Sell Winners Too Early and Ride Losers Too Long: Theory and Evidence' (1985) 40 J. FIN. 777; Terrance Odean, 'Are Investors Reluctant to Realize Their Losses?' (1998) 53 J. FIN. 1775.

178 David A. Hsieh, 'Chaos and Nonlinear Dynamics: Application to Financial Markets' (1991) 46 J. FIN. 1839.

179 Levy, 'Applications of Complexity Theory'.

agency. Physical systems are defined by constant and non-malleable 'natural' laws, whereas social systems, including financial markets (as we have seen) are subject to interference by humans, whose behaviour may be unpredictable both at the individual and at the aggregate levels. Human agency has the capacity to alter *all* aspects of financial market operation, most relevantly the laws and regulations which restrict conduct in particular ways, and thereby reduce (or increase) the potential for chaotic patterns to emerge. Especially in the case of financial markets, complexity theory cannot model the influences exerted by individual actors within the financial system who engage in rent seeking and manipulation of existing regulations (even creating 'false' or hidden markets in the process) to further their individual interests.[180] These findings are not truly consistent with a 'genuine evolution' of the financial system. Complexity theory and the AMH, alongside behavioural finance, certainly have roles to play in explaining how the financial system may operate, but the 'exogenous' activity of human participants, whose activities influence the development of the financial system at all stages of the evolutionary process, cannot be entirely reconciled with the property of 'emergence', which is a necessary feature of complex systems. Instead of the modern financial system evolving or emerging as a natural ecosystem might evolve or emerge, rather the financial system was the crucible in which bankers and other finance professionals pushed the limits of financial innovation, complexity and credit creation and, in doing so, forged the conditions necessary for crisis. As forcefully outlined by Avgouleas:

> In doing so, bankers were motivated by narrow self-interest (greed), although in some cases they were also 'gambling' the bank … what we have experienced is more or less the product of a totally man-made financial

---

[180] Many financial products were deliberately designed to be complex and opaque. A characteristic example is the Goldman Sachs 'ABACUS' scheme which became the subject of an SEC complaint that was subsequently the object of a settlement by the investment bank. The most striking feature of the scheme was the extreme complexity of the transactions involved and the (allegedly) deliberate clouding of their true purpose by the parties concerned. See 'Who's, Why's & How's of Allegations vs. Goldman' NYDailynews.com, 20 April 2010, http://www.nydailynews.com/money/2010/. On this theme, renowned economist John Kenneth Galbraith notes: 'The world of finance hails the invention of the wheel over and over again, often in a slightly more unstable version [allowing credit levels to become] dangerously out of scale in relation to the underlying means of payment.' See John K. Galbraith, *A Short History of Financial Euphoria* (Penguin Business, 1994) 19, 20.

revolution founded on political decisions and technological breakthroughs, which was pushed to its limits due to rent-seeking.[181]

CONCLUSION

Based on these observations, it is highly likely that whilst the EMH cannot survive as a stand-alone theory in explaining price behaviour in financial markets, behavioural finance, complexity theory and others will fail to completely fill the void left by its demise.[182] Moreover, whilst the EMH may not hold in all situations, in the absence of a competing valid theory to explain financial market operation, it may be futile to dismantle existing regulatory structures.

On this basis, the following chapter will discuss a further riposte to modern finance theory and its various rivals in explaining financial market and system behaviour – the Financial Instability Hypothesis (FIH) – which provides a theory to explain the proposition that market prices may not always necessarily reflect fundamental value, particularly through the operation and influence of the financial system. I will argue in this chapter that in combining some key insights from each of the theories discussed previously, the FIH provides the most coherent and comprehensive explanation for the way in which the banking system affects the market pricing mechanism, through instigating instability in the financial system, which is the main channel for stock market and capital finance. Under this view, the incentives prevalent within the banking system are of cardinal importance because of the significant influence they exert over bank behaviour – chief amongst them, compensation systems. This will provide a basis for a critical analysis of the causes of the GFC, and an assessment of the validity of subsequent reforms to incentive structures at financial institutions.

---

181 Emilios Avgouleas, *Governance Of Global Financial Markets: The Law, The Economics, The Politics* (CUP, 2012) 148–49.

182 Ibid. 62.

4. Minsky and the Financial Instability Hypothesis: implications for market efficiency

INTRODUCTORY REMARKS

The previous chapter explained the inherent problems associated with the traditional interpretation of financial market and financial system behaviour. The theories that underpin current regulation of securities markets reflect the view that capitalist systems are 'equilibrium seeking' and business cycles and asset swings are the product of exogenous shocks to market processes. The logical policy extension to this position is that regulation of financial markets or of companies operating within the system is futile as all currently known liabilities and risks are incorporated into market prices and nobody can anticipate an exogenous shock.

However, on the basis of the discussions in the previous chapter concerning market inefficiency, it is clear that there are serious theoretical and empirical challenges to the EMH. Studies, particularly by behavioural finance scholars, have identified several market phenomena which are inconsistent with the EMH. Some of these are rather idiosyncratic, and may only undermine market efficiency in certain, limited circumstances. However, many are pervasive in financial markets, and may cause catastrophic damage if left unchecked, particularly bubbles in securities and asset markets. Further, the structural obstacles to the correction of mispricing are significant. When arbitraging a market is too costly – or impossible – to perform, significant mis-valuations may persist for protracted periods. However as noted in the previous chapter, behavioural finance and complexity theories themselves suffer from practical limitations and, by their very nature, are not adept at providing regulators with a basis for designing regulatory systems.[1] In the absence

[1] 'The absence of … a unified explanation of market efficiency presents a serious problem for those judges, lawyers and regulators who would rely upon the [EMH] as the basis for judicial or regulatory policy making.' See Gilson & Kraakman, 'Mechanisms' 553.

of a credible alternative, the EMH has continued to dominate intellectual and policy-making circles and shaped the architecture regulating Anglo-American financial markets since the 1970s.[2] Moreover, this is, as noted in Chapter 2, true of both corporate governance regimes and, in particular, compensation schemes.

Whilst the EMH, Behavioural Finance, and other associated theories suffer limitations in explaining financial system behaviour, there is a credible alternative: the Financial Instability Hypothesis (FIH), conceived of by the late post-Keynesian economist, Hyman Minsky.[3] The FIH provides, amongst other things, a concise explanation for financial instability as the result of endogenous processes and accordingly, booms and busts are considered to be an inherent aspect of the system.[4] The FIH analysis frames the dynamism of the capitalist economy in terms of speculative excess followed by contraction and recession. It focuses particularly on the potential for asset prices to become inflated during 'euphoric'[5] periods leading to distortions in asset markets and increased systemic fragility through destabilising accruals of leverage within the financial system, as financial institutions extend credit and engage in financial innovation to undertake expansion. On this basis, the FIH provides an explanation of how prevailing investor behaviour and the commensurate adoption of progressively more fragile financial regimes may drive markets away from fundamental value, lead to asset bubbles

---

[2] Easterbrook & Fischel, *Economic Structure of Corporate Law*.

[3] Hyman P. Minsky, 'The Financial Instability Hypothesis' (1992) Levy Economics Institute of Bard College Working Paper 74, 2 (hereinafter Minsky, 'The FIH'); Hyman P. Minsky, 'The Financial Instability Hypothesis' in Charles P. Kindleberger & Jean-Pierre Laffargue (eds), *Financial Crises: Theory, History, and Policy* (CUP, 1982) 37.

[4] 'Such an economy is inherently flawed, because it is intractably cyclical … each of a succession of cyclical states is transitory in the sense that relations are built up which transform the way in which the economy will behave.' See Hyman P. Minsky, *John Maynard Keynes* (Columbia University Press, 1975) 57 (hereinafter Minsky, *John Maynard Keynes*).

[5] Minsky defines euphoria as when 'gross profits in the present-value calculations that had reflected expected recessions are replaced by those that reflect continuing expansion. Simultaneously there is less uncertainty about the future behavior of the economy.' See Hyman P. Minsky, 'Financial Instability Revisited: The Economics of Disaster', Policy Paper prepared for the Steering Committee for the Fundamental Reappraisal of the Discount Mechanism Appointed by the Board of Governors of the Federal Reserve System (January 1970) (hereinafter Minsky, 'Financial Instability Revisited') 8.

and thereby undermine the market pricing mechanism. Moreover, particularly in the context of the financial system, the FIH explains in two propositions how financialised economies are prone to crisis, and market pricing cannot be efficient. Firstly, the FIH states that there are two forms of financing regime – one which is consistent with stability, and one which subjects the economy to instability. Secondly, over protracted periods even 'stability is destabilising', and stable economies will become progressively more unstable due to endogenous processes which are 'an inherent and inescapable flaw of capitalism'.[6] On this basis, the conclusions of the FIH have profound implications for the use of equity-based compensation incentives, because a natural consequence of financial instability is distress amongst financial institutions, which has ramifications for their market value.

This chapter will begin by synthesising the research in the areas of behavioural finance, the AMH, and complexity theory with the principles of the FIH, to provide a basis for the conjecture that financial market pricing may be driven by forms of investor behaviour which do not conform to the assumptions of modern finance theory. Whilst there are differences in the implications of each set of theories – especially because the FIH does not assume investor 'irrationality' per se – there are also undoubted complementarities between them, in that each rejects the assumptions of the rational investor model and posits that the behaviour of agents within a system is not independent of system performance. The chapter will also demonstrate how Minsky's theories explain the financial cycle, and how inherent dynamics in financialised systems may lead to asset bubbles and drive instability, particularly through leverage and excessive debt. This will set the scene for a discussion of the GFC in the following chapter, which arguably exhibited the FIH taxonomy, and has been dubbed by many 'the Minsky moment'.[7]

---

[6] Words of Hyman Minsky cited in Stephen Mihm, 'Why Capitalism Fails', *Boston Globe* (Boston, 14 September 2009).

[7] For a flavour, see Paul McCulley, 'The Shadow Banking System and Hyman Minsky's Economic Journey' in Larry Siegel (ed), *Insights into the Global Financial Crisis* (Research Foundation of CFA Institute Publications, 2009) (hereinafter McCulley, 'Shadow Banking and Hyman Minsky'); John Cassidy, 'The Minsky moment', *The New Yorker* (New York, 4 February 2008); Charles Whalen, 'Understanding the Credit Crunch as a Minsky Moment' (2008) CHALLENGE 91.

MINSKY AND UNCERTAINTY IN EXPECTATION FORMATION

Minsky, whilst holding views in opposition to modern finance theory, was undoubtedly not a behavioural finance scholar, and he did not adopt a formal behaviourist model to his crisis theory, in particular because 'the financial instability hypothesis [and his other work] was formulated before the current fashion of formally reducing aggregate behavior to stylized behavior took hold'.[8] On the other hand, he did insist that the 'model of the economy used by the relevant agents (businessmen, bankers, and managers of money) in forming their expectations is of vital importance'[9] in determining the price level of assets and the future trajectory of asset markets. Accordingly, Minsky called for the emergence of an economics-psychology synthesis to explain financial system relations, an approach which is not inconsistent with BDT in rejecting the formal assumptions of modern finance theory in favour of the view that investors' decisions are not immune to certain psychological influences.[10] As a result, Minsky posits that investors, lenders and other market participants are predisposed to expectations-changing influences such as optimism, uncertainty and overconfidence,[11] concepts more 'redolent of

---

[8] Benjamin M. Friedman, David I. Laibson & Hyman P. Minsky, 'Economic Implications of Extraordinary Movements in Stock Prices' (1989) Brookings Papers on Economics 137, 177–78 (hereinafter Friedman et al, 'Extraordinary Movements').

[9] Ibid. 'Current views about financing reflect the opinions … [investors] … hold about uncertainties they must face. These current views reflect the past … A history of success will tend to diminish the margin of safety that business and bankers require and will thus tend to be associated with increased investment; a history of failure will do the opposite. Investment therefore is a financial phenomenon … asset prices, financing conditions, and income flows affect investment.' See Hyman P. Minsky, *Stabilizing an Unstable Economy* (2nd edn, McGraw-Hill, 2008) (hereinafter Minsky, *Stabilizing an Unstable Economy*) 209.

[10] 'The psychology of uncertainty and the social psychology of waves of optimism and pessimism are two points at which economists need guidance from the relevant sister social sciences. Throughout any discussion of uncertainty and of economic policy in the framework of uncertainty psychological assumptions must be made. At times the conclusions depend in a critical manner upon the psychological assumptions.' See Minsky, *Financial Instability Revisited* 24, n 21.

[11] Minsky, *Stabilizing an Unstable Economy* 114. In this context, a cursory glance at recent interpretations of Minsky's work reveals the extensive parallels between the axioms of behavioural finance and the expectations-based tenets of the FIH. For example, see Dimitri B. Papadimitriou & L. Randall Wray who note '[i]nnovation, itself, is endogenously generated by the apparent tranquillity of the

psychology rather than rational economic man'.[12] The key notion of Minsky's work, whilst of course 'based on a clear and detailed analysis of modern financial capitalism … is also rooted in human psychology and behavior'.[13] Accordingly, Minsky's work concurs with the concept of investor-bounded rationality, and recognises that there can be no guarantee that economic agents share consistent models 'such as are needed for the existence of a rational expectations equilibrium'.[14] The FIH, he stated,

> assumes that the models of system performance that help form the expectations of businessmen and bankers are affected by the recent performance of the economy and by agents' knowledge of its more remote past … As a result, businessmen, bankers, and managers of money may markedly – and unpredictably – change their behavior in response to small changes in system

---

circular flow … This confidence, however, raises entrepreneurial spirits, inducing experimentation and encouraging innovation. Innovation, in turn, generates expansion and disrupts conventional patterns of behaviour …' See Dimitri B. Papadimitriou & L. Randall Wray, 'Introduction: Minsky on Money, Banking and Finance' in Dimitri B. Papadimitriou & L. Randall Wray (eds), *The Elgar Companion to Hyman Minsky* (Elgar, 2009) 8; see also Eric Nasica, 'Rational and Innovative Behaviors at the Core of Financial Crises: Banking in Minsky's Theory', noting that in Minsky's view '[R]ationality rests upon objective bases, but also on more conventional or subjective grounds. This means that, even if actual outcomes only confirm banks' expectations, it is likely that, on account of their increased confidence in the way they are forming their expectations, banks will augment their lending and contribute to making the economy less liquid … Indeed when Keynesian uncertainty prevails, the adoption of behaviors that are based upon a particular form of rationality, where conventions and animal spirits play an important role, implies that bankers, like other economic agents, do not act as do the robot-like decision-makers of the rational expectations theory. Other behaviors and other variables are to be considered: the level reached by the agents' indebtedness, the ratios of indebtedness that are judged acceptable, changes in the 'state of confidence', the liquidity preference of banks and the related appearance of financial and endogenous instability' in ibid. 110, 114.

[12] Sheila Dow, 'The Psychology of Financial Markets: Keynes, Minsky and Emotional Finance' in ibid. 246 (hereinafter Dow, 'The Psychology of Financial Markets').

[13] James K. Galbraith & Daniel Munevar Sastre, 'The Generalized "Minsky Moment"' in ibid. 263.

[14] Hyman P. Minsky, 'Uncertainty and the Institutional Structure of Capitalist Economies: Remarks upon Receiving the Veblen-Commons Award' (1996) 30 J. ECON. ISS. 357, 360 (hereinafter Minsky, 'Uncertainty and Institutional Structure').

behavior, if the changes affect their belief in, or the structure of, the model of the economy they use to form expectations.[15]

Consistent with this, bankers, in Minsky's view, are naturally sceptical about funding investments, and their view of risk will be influenced both by the composition of their portfolios and by their views about future economic prospects. However, these views are not objectively assessed probability calculations; these views are subjectively valued, based upon (predominantly) recent experiences. In particular, as economies move from recession into expansion, Minsky notes:

> [P]rofits in the present value calculations that had reflected expected 'recessions' are replaced by those that reflect continuing expansion. Simultaneously there is less uncertainty about the future behaviour of the economy [as] the belief in the reality of a new era[16] emerges … The shift to euphoria increases the willingness of financial institutions to acquire assets by engaging in liquidity-decreasing portfolio transformations … The desire to expand and willingness to finance expansion by portfolio changes can be so great that, unless these are serious side effects of feedbacks, an inflationary explosion becomes likely.[17]

One consequence that flows from investor behaviour is that where crises are successfully contained, the potential for future crises to occur is magnified, because 'risky practices'[18] are validated. The risky practices that contribute to asset price appreciation in this context are the loosening of financing standards and an increase in the overall volume of credit; they emerge in benign economic conditions and assist in creating financial instability, driven by confidence that strong market performance

---

[15] Friedman et al, 'Extraordinary Movements' 177.

[16] Note the similarity in terms here between the Minsky argument and the arguments proffered by Shiller on 'new era thinking' discussed in the previous chapter.

[17] Minsky, 'Financial Instability Revisited' 8–11.

[18] 'Risky practices' and the circumstances of their use have been defined as follows: 'Agents [speculate] on the future of the asset prices that are presently being financed and on the future behaviour of the financial markets, as they may have to refinance their debts. Looking for larger profits, they undertake riskier decisions for as long as stability and prosperity continue.' See Yves Rannou, 'Banking Regulation, Behavioural Finance and the Financial Crisis in Europe: Looking to the Kindleberger-Minsky Paradigm' (2010) 3 J. RISK MAN. FIN. INSTITUTIONS 278, 280.

will continue, at least in the short term.[19] According to Minsky, it is the validation of previously successful investment strategies that determine that in euphoric periods riskier strategies are adopted with greater confidence. Debt-fuelled exuberance begets investment based upon the expectation that a market will continue along its recently observed trajectory – this book has noted previously that certain heuristics undermine the attempts of market participants to correctly distinguish between the potential length of the short and long run. Accordingly, as economies recover from crisis, the institutional memories of that crisis begin to dissipate and agents may convince themselves that practices deemed too risky following the crisis are no longer so (analogous to the availability heuristic, discussed in the previous chapter), sowing the seeds for future crises in the process. Asset price increases are thereby natural products of the expectations of investors that positive economic conditions experienced in the recent past will persist, and form the basis for increased borrowing and speculative investment:

> As the memory of the [previous] 'crisis' fades, risk aversion dissipates and financing terms ease. As a modest economic expansion replaces stagnation, financial institutions and balance sheets in general become more robust. Continued success sets the groundwork for failure. Financial robustness that is deemed excessive leads to the development of new instruments. Once again, power in the belief of creative finance emerges. Even as optimism reigns, financial robustness is eroded: the domain of financial fragility increases.[20]

Underlying this theme is Minsky's rejection of perfect investor foresight, an assumption of modern finance theory. Instead, Minsky emphasises the significance of uncertainty amongst bankers and businessmen in creating the conditions necessary for boom and bust dynamics.[21] On this basis, 'the market prices of firms at every date place values on intangibles, such

---

[19] Minsky, 'Financial Instability Revisited' 20–21. As noted by Kindleberger in this context: 'Some event increases confidence. Optimism sets in. Confident expectations of a steady stream of prosperity and of gross profits make portfolio plunging more appealing. Financial institutions accept liability structures that decrease liquidity that in a more sober climate they would have rejected.' See Kindleberger & Aliber, *Manias, Panics and Crashes* 27.

[20] Hyman P. Minsky, 'Longer Waves in Financial Relations: Financial Factors in the More Severe Depressions II' (1995) 29 J. ECON. ISS. 83, 93 (hereinafter Minsky, 'Longer Waves').

[21] '[C]apitalists, observing stability in the present, have a herding tendency to extrapolate the expectation of stability out into the indefinite future, putting in place ever-more risky debt structures … that cause stability to be undermined … If everybody is simultaneously becoming more risk-seeking, risk premiums

as market position or power, and reflect the auras of optimism or pessimism about the future that are assigned to firms, industries, and economies'.[22] The uncertainty of these valuations comes with the implication that '[in] a world ruled by uncertainty, with an uncertain future linked to an actual present, a final position of equilibrium, such as one deals with in static economics, does not properly exist'.[23] The uncertainty that agents must act under necessarily amplifies the psychological factors driving investment. In the absence of certainty or perfect foresight, agents will fall back on recent experiences to use as a frame of reference to guide future investment, and thereby their behaviour.[24] These investment decisions are therefore markedly influenced by the degree of confidence held about future prospects in financial markets:

> When knowledge of the future is subjective and imperfect, as it always is, the expectations of rational agents can never be fully and adequately represented solely by probability distributions because such distributions fail to incorporate the agents' own understanding of the degree of incompleteness of their

---

shrink, the value of collateral goes up, the ability to lever increases …' See McCulley, 'Shadow Banking and Hyman Minsky' 257, 261.

22 Friedman et al, 'Extraordinary Movements' 176.

23 Keynes, *The General Theory*. As has been noted by Keynesian economists on rational choice theory: '[T]here are two related problems with the convergence to rational expectations equilibria. First, since agents learn and realized outcomes depend on expectations the uncertain process being forecast cannot possibly be stationary. Learning leads to changing expectations and changes in expectations cause changes in the underlying process … [T]his kind of learning may never reach a self-sustaining state at all … Secondly, suppose a rational expectations equilibrium exists. If the system is away from [it], any agent's expectation formation process must consider the expectations of other agents, since the actual outcome will depend on others' expectations. Hence, it is possible that even an agent who knows the properties of the [equilibrium] would forecast results different from the [equilibrium].' See Steven M. Fazzari, 'Keynes, Harrod and the Rational Expectations Revolution' (1985) 8 J. POST-KEYNES. ECON. 66.

24 'In a capitalist economy, present views about future profits determine current investment and financing decisions, even as present achieved profits determine whether what was done in the past is validated. An economic theory that is relevant to a capitalist economy cannot evade the issues involved in unidirectional historical time by assuming recontracting or the existence of universal systems of future, or contingent contracts. The essence of capitalism is that units have to take positions *in an uncertain world*.' See Hyman P. Minsky, 'Capitalist Processes and the Instability of Capitalism' (1980) 14 J. ECON. ISS. 505, 515 (emphasis added) (hereinafter Minsky, 'Capitalist Processes').

> knowledge. These functions neglect the agents' 'confidence' in the meaningfulness of the forecasts – 'how highly we rate the likelihood of our best forecast turning out to be quite wrong … if we expect large changes but are very uncertain as to what precise form these changes will take, then our *confidence* [in our ability to forecast] will be quite weak'.[25]

In this context, the degree of confidence held may be regarded as the extent to which the agents believe in the 'meaningfulness' of their forecasts or 'the degree of rational belief' the agents assign to their predictions.[26] As noted in the previous chapter, agents form this degree of confidence using heuristics.[27] Psychological research has shown that success, even if achieved only in relation to moderate expectations, boosts confidence[28] and that 'an extended period of stability and growth

---

[25] Ibid.; Keynes, *The General Theory* 148 (emphasis added).

[26] James Crotty, 'Are Keynesian Uncertainty and Macrotheory Compatible? Conventional Decision-Making, Institutional Structures, and Conditional Stability in Keynesian Macromodels' in Robert Pollin & Gary Dymski (eds), *New Perspectives in Monetary Macroeconomics* (University of Michigan Press, 1994).

[27] Minsky notes: 'In addition to periods where the likelihood of various states of nature appear stable, there are troubled periods when the subjective estimates as to the likelihood of various states of nature are held with much less confidence. The risk averter reaction to a decline in confidence is to attempt to increase the weight of assets that yield flexibility in portfolio choices, in other words, to increase the value not only of money but also of all assets that have broad, deep, and resilient markets. Any increase in uncertainty shifts the liquidity preference function, and this shift can be quite marked and sudden. Obviously, the reverse – a decrease in uncertainty – can occur. If risk-averters are dominant then it is likely that an increase in uncertainty can be a rapid phenomenon, whereas a decrease will require a slow accretion of confidence. There is no need for a loss in confidence to proceed at the same pace as a gain in confidence.' Minsky, 'Financial Instability Revisited' 20–21.

[28] The psychology underpinning the FIH has received further theoretical support from distinguished scholars who highlight 'emotional finance' as a further explanation for the inflation of bubbles: 'Bubbles start with some novelty which causes excitement. Not only is the excitement of a euphoric state a response to a novel stimulus, but … we may actively crave novel stimuli. And yet the excitement itself alters judgement … Bubbles then follow an emotional sequence: patchy excitement turns into growing excitement and in turn manic/euphoric excitement. There is normally some conflict between emotion (wishful thinking) and normal asset valuation (reality-based cognition). This conflict increases as asset valuation diverges more and more from a reality-based valuation, causing anxiety. Market players avoid this anxiety by increasingly ignoring reality as the euphoria builds up. Indeed the market tends to be dominated by those who are willing to act, i.e. those who resolve the tension by privileging phantasy; those who continue to retain reality-based thinking will

by itself increases the confidence of economic units because of the tendency of the latter to discount or to forget about the past'.[29] Conversely, a sharp drop in confidence will lead inexorably to a sharp decline in the price of assets: 'the professional investor is forced to concern himself with the anticipation of impending changes … of the kind by which experience shows that the mass psychology of the market is most influenced'.[30] These psychological factors include 'spontaneous optimism … animal spirits [and] nerves and hysteria …'.[31] As Keynes notes further:

> We should not conclude from [a discussion on speculation] that everything depends on waves of irrational psychology. [But we must remind] ourselves that … our rational selves [are] choosing between alternatives as best we are able, calculating where we can, but often falling back for our motive on whim or sentiment or chance.[32]

This view is therefore also consistent with some of the tenets of each of the alternative theories surveyed in the previous chapter, in that Minsky holds that human behaviour has an irreducibly significant effect on both the structure and performance of the financial system, thereby refuting

---

drop out of the market as the euphoria is perceived to be excessive … It is only when reality breaks through in some form that phantasy is challenged and the bubble bursts, and panic ensues. But the continuing dominance of wishful thinking is evident in the prevalence of blame rather than guilt when the bubble bursts; guilt would require acknowledgement that there had been a major departure from reality-based thinking … This analysis treats emotion or sentiment as integral to market behaviour, given rein by uncertainty compounded by the tensions in attitudes to asset valuation. It therefore has the potential to flesh out a Minskian account of the psychology of the market. The notion of reality-based thought may be taken to imply some notion of objective valuation as a benchmark. For Minsky, as for Keynes, asset valuation is not an objective process, since it is conducted under uncertainty. Nevertheless, if we consider Keynes's notion of weight of argument, we can consider degrees of uncertainty, or conversely degrees of confidence, with respect to expectations, on the basis of experience, or evidence. Reality-based thinking therefore draws more on evidence than wishful thinking, which involves self-deception.' Dow, 'The Psychology of Financial Markets' 246–62, 257–58.

29 Eric Tymoigne, 'The Minskyan System, Part II: Dynamics of the Minskyan Analysis and the Financial Fragility Hypothesis' (2006) UMKC Department of Economics Working Paper.

30 Keynes, *The General Theory* 155.

31 Ibid. 162.

32 Ibid. 163.

the orthodox view that the economy is predisposed to a static equilibrium.[33] Accordingly, human behaviour is inherently pro-cyclical, leading to herding and feedback processes which may generate boom and bust cycles.[34] Similarly, Minsky focuses upon the often unpredictable actions of market participants, who might not necessarily act rationally, but instead adopt the investment strategy of 'following the crowd' or herding. Empirical research confirms that in euphoric conditions, investors often take more risks as an environment of easier lending terms becomes established, and increasing levels of financial returns from investments are achieved.[35] Models confirm that the financial system becomes more fragile based on the behaviour of investors and their reduced risk aversion in euphoric economic conditions: 'as the most recent crisis becomes a more distant memory, the relevant actors in the economy change their behaviour so as to erode the financial system's ability to withstand a major shock …'.[36] Even large-scale price collapses may not affect long-term market expectations if the shock is not enough to overcome the underlying confidence levels which agents use to form their expectations concerning future prices. In this way, his work arguably treads similar ground to that of other heterodox scholars, especially in his rejection of neoclassical economic assumptions of investor behaviour, and in providing a convincing explanation for the potential inflation of asset bubbles.

---

[33] On this basis, in the context of governing financial markets Lo proposes 'a framework for regulatory reform that begins with the observation that financial manias and panics cannot be legislated away, and may be an unavoidable aspect of modern capitalism – a consequence of the interactions between hardwired human behavior and the unfettered ability to innovate, compete, and evolve'. See Lo, 'Regulatory Reform' 5.

[34] Emilios Avgouleas, *Governance of Global Financial Markets: The Law, the Economics, the Politics* (CUP, 2012) 83. See also George A. Akerlof & Robert J. Shiller, *Animal Spirits: How Human Psychology Drives the Economy, and Why It Matters for Global Capitalism* (Princeton UP, 2008).

[35] In research into the 'dot.com bubble', investors polled claimed that 'they believed that the stock they invested in during the bubble period was over-valued but invested in it anyway in anticipation of further increases in price'. See William N. Goetzmann & Ravi Dhar, 'Bubble Investors: What Were They Thinking?' (2006) Yale ICF Working Paper No. 06-22, 3.

[36] Friedman et al, 'Extraordinary Movements' 160.

THE FINANCIAL INSTABILITY HYPOTHESIS

Minsky's work is therefore predicated upon the role uncertainty plays in investment behaviour, and the inherent instability in the financial structure of the economy that this may generate. This forms the basis of his most significant contribution to understanding the behaviour of the financial system, the FIH, which is of particular relevance to the modern financial system. The FIH is important in the context of this book, not simply for its critique of orthodox economic theory but because it explains, inter alia, (a) how the pricing of assets may be imperfect due to factors endogenous to the financial system; and (b) the importance of the banking sector in creating financial instability, and thereby transmitting distress from the financial system to the stock market and in particular the bank equity market.

THE FIH TAXONOMY AND CRISIS

The FIH postulates that financing arrangements within a given economy progress through various stages of stability. For analytical purposes, it is useful to separate these stages, and discuss the implications for asset prices and financial stability.

(i) 'Market Euphoria'

Minsky's analysis begins with the first stage of market development, which is an economy in which businesses are making steady returns, but both firms and banks remain conservative in their financing decisions, both in terms of the projects that firms are willing to undertake, and the loans that banks are willing to advance. This is normally due to the memory of a recent system-wide economic contraction and/or financial collapse. However, the combination of a growing economy and conservative financing structures lead to most business ventures succeeding, resulting in both businesses and banks coming to regard the safety margins written into loan contracts as excessively risk averse. Any assets bought during previous recessions at low prices, allied with the strong liquidity positions of surviving producers (funded by conservative cash flow commitments) lead to new opportunities for capital investment and business growth. Benign economic conditions lead to both an increase in debt-financing and an increase in the adoption of 'risky practices' (mentioned earlier) such as loosened financing conditions on behalf of banks and an increased willingness amongst investors to borrow.

Minsky's emphasis on the period of expansion is critical to the FIH and is a corollary to the behavioural analysis of markets that was undertaken in the previous chapter. The expansionary phase sets the stage for what Minsky termed 'euphoria', a period analogous to speculative fever. The FIH postulates that 'euphoria is a necessary prelude to a financial crisis and … euphoria is almost an inevitable consequence of the successful functioning of an enterprise economy'.[37] During this stage in the economic cycle, lenders and borrowers, acting under uncertainty but with the memories of financial failure replaced in their minds by more recent memories of financial success, begin to invest in greater volumes and asset prices are revalued upwards. Commercial banks' capacity to extend credit varies dependent upon certain economic variables. Thus, even if short-term interest rates are high, in order to maximise profit opportunities, banks may push for an increase in loans, as a higher short-term interest rate means a higher opportunity cost for banks which do not lend.[38] Banks will always, therefore, push the limits of lending as far as is possible under prevailing capital regulations. Moreover, if bankers hold sufficiently optimistic expectations concerning future economic prospects, loan volumes will increase; in this phase '[e]xisting debts are easily validated and units that [are] heavily involved in debt prosper: it [pays] to lever.'[39] This presages the inevitable introduction of new financial instruments for loan investment, adding layers of complexity which may increase the opacity relating to systemic credit and leverage levels.[40] The process of securitisation, for example, is

---

[37] Minsky, 'Financial Instability Revisited' 51.

[38] When Minsky was writing, no interest was paid on banks holding reserves with the Federal Reserve. Following the GFC, in order to incentivise banks to hold reserves and increase market liquidity, and as a consequence of the central bank's asset purchasing programme launched to shore up bank balance sheets, the Federal Reserve in the US began to offer interest on bank reserves. This power was granted under the Emergency Economic Stabilization Act of 2008, Division A of Pub. L. 110–343, 122 Stat. 3765 § 128. For discussion, see David Bowman, Etienne Gagnon & Mike Leahy, 'Interest on Excess Reserves as a Monetary Policy Instrument: The Experience of Foreign Central Banks' (2010) Board Of Governors of the Federal Reserve System, International Financial Discussion Paper No. 996.

[39] Hyman P. Minsky, 'Can "It" Happen Again?' in *Essays on Instability and Finance* (M.E Sharpe, 1982) 66 (hereinafter Minsky, 'Can "It" Happen Again?').

[40] 'A given amount of bank loans and demand deposits supports a higher volume of finance to the whole economy.' See Ricardo Bellofiore, 'The Financial Instability Hypothesis and the "New" Capitalism', Paper presented to the workshop 'The complexity of financial crisis in a long-period perspective: facts,

a method through which illiquid and non-tradable assets can be converted into financial products (usually with perceived lower aggregate risk than the underlying assets) to be bought and sold. Similarly, financial derivatives, the market for which stood at approximately $700 trillion in 2009, as well as allowing financial institutions to hedge risks, permits them to take huge speculative positions on market movements. The complex financial engineering employed to create this debt allowed for the 'artificial increase of the total amount of credit (leverage effect), freeing the balances of the institutions from credit given in this way in order to create new loans'.[41] Provided that the market judges them to be liquid, banks may increase their assets without a correspondingly large increase in their capital reserves.[42] Accordingly, these products facilitated banks in evading reserve and capital requirements, and moved many of the risks in the financial system off balance sheet.

We may thus elucidate how benign economic conditions contribute to the potential for future financial instability. As economic conditions become more benign and memories of previous crises recede, lending standards drop. The dynamics subsisting during periods of euphoria generate a reflexive feedback loop within the economy, which ensures that price rises beget and reinforce positive market movements. The pressure on financial institutions to generate returns and increased earnings (to be discussed in the context of the GFC in the following chapter) in these conditions encourages financial innovation on an extensive scale and, if no shocks occur in the medium term, Minsky's 'risky practices' become validated, and relative levels of financial debt will begin to increase, facilitated by the banking system. Efficient market theorists argue that behavioural forces have little or no effect on the level of prices because market forces will operate to bring them back to rational levels. However, this view relies upon the assumption that market forces are powerful enough to overcome those behavioural influences that lead agents to underestimate risk.[43] Based on recent events in financial markets, it is far from clear that this assumption may be relied upon. The aggregate effect is that financial institutions begin to accept

theory and models', University of Siena, 23–24 March 2009, http://www.storep.org/workshopsiena/Bellofiore3.pdf (hereinafter Bellofiore, 'The "New" Capitalism').

41 Christian Marazzi, *The Violence of Financial Capitalism* (MIT Press, 2011) 37.

42 This issue will be discussed in detail in the following chapter.

43 Andrew W. Lo, 'The Adaptive Markets Hypothesis' (2004) J. PORTFOLIO MAN. 30th Anniversary Issue 15, 18.

liability structures – for both themselves and their borrowers – 'that, in a more sober climate, they would have rejected'.[44] The instability in the modern financial system is thus a function of the arrangements employed to satisfy financial commitments, and the uncertainty which underpins the entire process. Based on this premise, Minsky highlights three forms of financing arrangement used by borrowers and lenders in incremental stages: hedge, speculative and Ponzi financing.[45]

Hedge financing is largely asset based; that is, hedge financing units expect the cash flow from operating capital assets to meet future contractual payments, of both principal and interest. This remains true of the unit, even in consideration of any change in the short-term interest rate. Outstanding debts tend to fall and the value of equity and cash reserves increases over time. Notwithstanding any shocks in labour or macroeconomic conditions, a hedge unit remains impervious to changes in the financial market environment. Speculative financing units, however, are not reliant on the income from capital assets; instead, they rely on refinancing their positions or increasing debt. The cash inflows to a speculative unit will exceed the interest payments it is contractually obliged to make; however, the loan principal must be constantly refinanced in the near to medium term. On this basis, a speculative finance unit will generate long-term cash surpluses, which alleviate possible short-term deficits; however, if economic conditions deteriorate, there may be a reversal from positive to negative present values. Because of this, speculative financing is not as stable as hedge financing due to the exposure to financial market risk, and the potential destabilising effects of interest rate and financing variables. Ponzi finance units, in contrast, must continually sell assets to fund future payment commitments and are, in this sense, entirely dependent upon the anticipated increase in the value of the assets they hold. Ponzi speculators are willing to incur debts which are outsized in comparison to the value of the assets they hold, as they expect to be able to sell those assets on at a profit. The cash inflows that Ponzi units receive are insufficient either to meet the interest payments on their contractual loan obligations or to reduce the principal. Accordingly, any drop in asset prices will result in Ponzi units experiencing an inability to refinance their debts. Ponzi financing therefore has an important role in pushing up market interest rates, and a commensurate role in whittling away the economy's ability to withstand a reduction in asset values.

44 Minsky, 'Can "It" Happen Again?' 120–25.
45 Minsky, 'The FIH'.

(ii) The Denudation of Credit Quality

A period of tranquil growth (stability) thereby encourages an expansion in credit to capture increased profits. The transition from the various forms of financing regime has two main consequences: (i) the financial system becomes progressively more fragile; (ii) the credit agreements that were extended in more benign economic conditions become difficult to manage.[46] The more powerful the boom, the greater the potential for an asset bubble to emerge, because financial assets, in particular, are a prime object of speculative finance.[47] In these periods speculators begin to purchase assets and securities, not simply for their use, but also to benefit in an anticipatory manoeuvre to capture future profits from increases in asset values. The purchases that investors make in these periods are not necessarily based purely on consideration of the fundamentals of particular securities; instead, these processes are driven by investor psychology as agents become progressively more optimistic.[48] At the centre of this pattern is irreversibility.[49] Agents in a booming and over-confident economy will carry forward asset positions acquired in the past which tie them to balance sheet commitments in the present. The FIH demonstrates that it is these financial commitments established across the economy during a boom which are the key to instability: 'the liability structures that geniuses of leverage exploited in the high-growth days become nooses for aggressive-growth firms when low growth

---

[46] Kindleberger & Aliber, *Manias, Panics and Crashes* 64.

[47] For example, prior to the recent GFC, a property bubble developed and its deflation was the primary driver of financial distress amongst global banks. However, *many* asset bubbles had emerged due to the availability of cheap credit; bubbles developed in such areas of the economy as stocks, consumer loans, commercial property and commodities.

[48] As noted: 'Minsky's theory of the basic cycle involves important psychological influences. The move between financing stages is in part driven by [optimism]. That optimism manifests itself in increasingly optimistic valuations of assets and assessments of revenue streams, combined with increased willingness to take on more risk in the belief that good times are here forever. This optimistic psychology afflicts both borrowers and lenders, and not just one side of the market. That is critical because it means market discipline is weakened.' See Thomas I. Palley, 'A Theory of Minsky Super-Cycles and Financial Crises' (2011) 30 CONTRIBUTIONS TO POLIT. ECON. 30, 34.

[49] Gary A. Dymski, 'A Spatialized Approach to Asset Bubbles and Minsky Crises' in Dimitri B. Papadimitriou & L. Randall Wray (eds), *The Elgar Companion to Hyman Minsky* (Edward Elgar, 2010) 235.

hits'.[50] The resulting focus on short-term profits provides incentives for management (particularly at financial institutions) to expand their trading in order to capture rents from their firms. Each of these factors acting in combination may push up *general* asset prices, including the aggregate stock market, the fortunes of which are implicitly linked to the stability of the financial system;[51] indeed, Minsky explicitly linked the instability in financial markets with dislocations in the stock market, because of the pervasive effects of bank finance on asset price increases.[52] Accordingly, distress in financial institutions due to asset price collapses will almost certainly lead to problems in the stock market. In this context, the FIH predicts that the stock market (and bank stocks in particular) will typically become inflated during periods of economic euphoria, as investors' appetite for risk and speculation is amplified and banks earn greater profits from lending activities.[53] Axiomatically, of course, this also means that financial institutions themselves will become more leveraged.[54]

---

[50] Ibid. 236.

[51] Kindleberger notes: 'If ... the anticipated profit opportunities improve in at least one important sector of the economy: the profit share of GDP increases. In the early 1980s, US corporate profits were 3 per cent of GDP; toward the end of the 1990s [during the Internet stock boom] this ratio had increased to 10 per cent. That corporate profits were increasing one-third more rapidly than US GDP in turn contributed to the significant increase in stock prices.' See Kindleberger & Aliber, *Manias, Panics and Crashes* 23.

[52] Dominico Delli Gatti & Mauro Gallegati, 'Financial Instability, Income Distribution, and the Stock Market' (1990) 12 J. POST-KEYNES. ECON. 356 (hereinafter Delli Gatti & Gallegati, 'Financial Instability').

[53] Minsky, *Stabilizing an Unstable Economy* 162.

[54] There are three widely accepted forms of leverage: balance sheet, economic and embedded. Balance sheet leverage is the most recognised form, and measures the ratio at which the value of a firm's assets exceeds its equity base. Banks typically engage in leverage by borrowing to acquire more assets, with the aim of increasing their return on equity. Economic leverage means that a bank is exposed to a change in the value of a position by an amount that exceeds what the bank paid for it. A typical example is a loan guarantee, which is a contingent commitment that may materialise in the future but does not presently appear in the balance sheet. Finally, embedded leverage refers to holding a position that is itself leveraged. A simple example is a minority investment held by a bank in an equity fund that is itself funded by loans. While critical for the stability of the financial institutions and of the financial system, embedded leverage is extremely difficult to measure. See The World Bank Group, Financial Sector & Private Sector Development Vice-Presidency, *The Leverage Ratio: A New Binding Limit*

The stability of a financial system is dependent upon the proportion of the various types of financing employed by market participants in a given economy; in other words, the spread of financial leverage within the system:

> The overall robustness or fragility of an economy's financial structure is determined by the mix of hedge, speculative and Ponzi financing units. A liability structure in which units mainly engage in equity financing will lie towards the robust end of the spectrum. A liability structure in which units are heavily in debt so that speculative and even Ponzi finance are common will be towards the fragility end of the spectrum.[55]

It is therefore through the build-up of leverage amongst economic units that crisis is instigated. Accordingly, the key characteristic of banks which makes them crucial to the inflation of asset values is their (unique) capacity to assume huge levels of leverage. This capacity is important because leverage levels exert an explicit and powerful effect on asset prices: when leverage goes up, asset prices increase, and when leverage goes down, asset prices fall.[56] This encapsulates the so-called 'leverage cycle',[57] which, in accordance with the FIH, is

> a self-reinforcing dynamic. Declining margins, or, equivalently, increasing leverage, are a consequence of the happy coincidence of universal good news and the absence of danger on the horizon. With markets stable and the horizon looking clear, lenders are happy to reduce margins and provide more cash. Good, safe news events by themselves tend to make asset prices rise, but they also encourage declining margins, which in turn causes massive borrowing that inflates asset prices still more.[58]

On Banks (2009), http://www.worldbank.org/financialcrisis/pdf/levrage-ratio-web.pdf.

55 Hyman P. Minsky, 'The Capital Development of the Economy and the Structure of Financial Institutions' (1992) Levy Institute of Bard College Working Paper No. 72, 5.

56 John Geanakoplos, 'Solving the Present Crisis and Managing the Leverage Cycle' (2010) FRB NEW YORK ECON. POL. REV. 101, 103 (hereinafter Geanakoplos, 'Managing the Leverage Cycle').

57 A leverage cycle ends with: '1) bad news that creates uncertainty and disagreement, 2) sharply increasing collateral rates, and 3) losses and bankruptcies among the leveraged optimists.' See ibid. 102.

58 Ibid. 104.

Accordingly, financial leverage is hazardous if left unchecked, particularly when the base value of collateral assets is volatile or unstable.[59] The consequences of volatility in these collateral prices may be exacerbated by the use of financial innovation to increase leverage levels. A natural limiting factor to increasing leverage is the scarcity of collateral; however, financial engineering (for example securitisation) allows banks to stretch collateral, so the same asset backs several sets of loans, or the collateral is used to pyramid loans.[60] By reason of this, Minsky contended that as economies evolve and become more complex, crises become more likely. This is especially relevant in relation to the modern financial system, as the size, complexity and interconnectedness of the institutions comprising it mean that localised financial shocks may have systemically significant consequences.[61] The FIH predicts that finance allows for a higher rate of expansion in income and capital growth but, at the same time, increases the amount of debt in an economy and the financial commitments in relation to that debt affect the levels of anticipated cash flows. As the financing of positions in assets becomes more complex and the layers of intermediaries that subsist on these financing arrangements become deeper, the number of economic agents dependent upon the stability of financial markets – based on a myriad of debt claims – increases, leading to 'an accumulation of indebtedness relative to the cash flows that enable units to fulfil their payment commitments'.[62] The breed of money management that characterises modern-day Anglo-American finance encourages this deepening; finance specialists have 'concocted increasingly esoteric and opaque financial instruments that quickly spread around the world'.[63] The increase in leverage enabled by these instruments had two specific consequences: (i) it drove a race to lever, as highly leveraged funding drives up prices for

---

[59] As Minsky notes: '[T]he payment commitments that involve the pledging of collateral are important – for they provide a direct and quick link between a decline in market value of assets and the need to make cash payments … This margin or collateral maintenance payment commitment can be a source of considerable disorganisation and can lead to a sharp decline in asset prices.' Minsky, 'Financial Instability Revisited' 55.

[60] Geanakoplos, 'Managing the Leverage Cycle' 102–103.

[61] This point finds support in network theory, discussed in the previous chapter.

[62] Minsky, 'Longer Waves' 85.

[63] L. Randall Wray, 'Financial Keynesianism and Market Instability' (2011) Levy Economics Institute of Bard College Working Paper No. 653, 2 (hereinafter Wray, 'Financial Keynesianism').

the underlying assets, providing incentives for excess risk; and (ii) it increased the probability of financial distress.

On this basis, the greater the financial sophistication of the relevant economy, and therefore the deeper and more interconnected its financial relations, the greater its tendency towards instability. More importantly, the greater the degree to which the economy becomes financialised, the greater the importance to its stability that assets underlying the various financial claims present across the economy trade at fundamental values (in other words, collateral maintains thc valuc on which the leverage levels adopted were based).[64] If they do not, wild fluctuations in the value of assets pledged as collateral may place severe strain on financial intermediaries, as increased leverage and lowered margins of safety mean that banks and other financial institutions will find it difficult to maintain profitability if assets are revealed to have been overpriced.[65] The financialisation of Anglo-American economies is reflected in the massive growth of private sector debt; both financial and non-financial debt in the US accelerated rapidly between the mid-1990s and 2008. In particular, the rapid growth of financial sector debt is striking. In 1980 US financial institution debt was 20 per cent of GDP; by 2008 it had reached 120 per cent. This, as Wray notes, 'represents a leveraging or layering of financial commitments on top of national income flows' and leaves highly financialised economies such as those of the US, EU and UK vulnerable to asset price fluctuations.[66]

In periods of economic euphoria, the margins of safety that financial institutions demand are denuded: '[t]he ratio between uncertain (income) cash inflows, subject to sharp and sudden revaluation, and certain (balance sheet) cash outflows is the key factor in assessing the liability structure of economic units'.[67] Investor opinion on the likelihood of success in speculative ventures affects the margins charged on credit to

---

64 In this context, Gorton & Metrick note that the margins ('haircuts') charged on structured credit began to rise in August 2007, from a level of virtually zero, before reaching approximately 10% in March 2008, indicating that the market (finally) began to react to the fragility of the structured credit market in late 2007/early 2008. See Gary Gorton & Andrew Metrick, 'Securitized Banking and the Run on Repo' (2009) NBER Working Paper No. 15223, Figure 4.

65 'With an increase in leverage relative to gross profits, the ratio of payment commitments (because of liabilities) to gross profits rises; the margins of safety in cash flows are eroded. As this occurs, the financial system becomes fragile.' See Minsky, 'Capitalist Processes' 515.

66 Wray, 'Financial Keynesianism' 11.

67 Bellofiore, 'The "New" Capitalism' 11.

be used for investment, including investment in the stock market. This is significant for aggregate portfolios because, as investors become less risk averse, they are more willing to hold stocks, and correspondingly less willing to hold assets which offer lower perceived risk-adjusted returns.[68] Moreover, as was noted in Chapter 2, the price of stocks is affected by factors extrinsic to the companies that they represent, and '[more] confident expectations of a steady stream of prosperity and of an increase in profits induce investors to buy riskier stocks. Banks make riskier loans in this more optimistic environment. The optimism increases and may become self-fulfilling until it evolves into a mania.'[69] Investment may therefore flow towards stock markets, not because of any change in fundamental prospects of the corporations, but because investors are operating under greater confidence levels and looser financing regimes than previously was the case. These factors alone place significant limits on the capacity of stock prices to capture long-run value during euphoric episodes.

Through their role as credit originators, banks may provide the impetus for asset price increases, with no change in economic fundamentals, and driven by bankers' desire to increase earnings, summarised by Minsky as follows:

> [a]ggregate retained earnings can lead bankers to aim at a rate of growth of bank assets and liabilities that may be incompatible for overall, real economic expansion. For instance, an assumption underlying many of the standard policy arguments about monetary growth is that the real growth potential of the economy is at most 4 per cent per year. To many standard economists this implies that a steady 4 per cent increase in the money supply will lead to noninflationary growth if velocity is constant. In our example, the bank that earns 15 per cent on equity will endeavor to grow at 10 per cent per year, whereas the bank that earns 9 per cent will endeavor to increase at 4 per cent per year. If the world is populated by banks that earn 15 per cent and distribute one-third of earnings as dividends, then a need for bank assets to rise at 10 per cent per year to sustain the assets equity ratio and bank profitability will introduce a tension into the economy: banks will try to grow at 10 per cent per year while the authorities try to constrain the growth of bank liabilities to 4 per cent per year.[70]

---

[68] Friedman et al, 'Extraordinary Movements' 162.
[69] Kindleberger & Aliber, *Manias, Panics and Crashes* 37.
[70] Minsky, *Stabilizing an Unstable Economy* 263.

(iii) The Crash

As Minsky notes, not all financial failures, even of large institutions, cause a mass panic. The key determinant of the likelihood and impact of a financial crisis is the spread of liability structures that were instigated in the euphoric boom of the cycle: '[the] building into the financial structure of asset prices that reflect boom or euphoric expectations'.[71] Depending upon the alignment between expectations and reality of growth, economic units may be forced to unexpectedly refinance existing debts, often causing unforeseen risk to the lender. Refinancing debt remains risky as any new borrowing may be on less favourable terms than the original loan. Selling assets to meet liabilities is inherently risky because the market for sale may be illiquid, or a secondary market may not exist.

Where significant portfolio transformations have occurred due to the boom, the consequent misalignment between short-term and long-term interest rates invariably ensures that a speculative bubble will deflate. A higher debt–equity ratio is associated with a greater degree of short-term financing of fixed capital and long-term financial assets.[72] Speculative-unit status is sustainable only when interest rates are constant and there is market liquidity; when the supply of finance is constrained through central bank intervention or more prudent bank attitudes (often a combination of both), however, the 'outcome … is a *sudden*, *severe* and *unexpected* increase in the cost of financing'.[73] The required refinancing due to the upward change in interest rates is driven by the escalation of cash outflows relative to cash inflows, in the form of debt servicing.[74] In these conditions, some firms which were found in the 'hedge' finance group are shunted into the 'speculative' finance group whilst those in the 'speculative' finance group are shunted into the 'Ponzi' finance group. Where refinancing is unavailable to firms whose structure is fragile, these firms will fail. In these situations, in all likelihood, a crash will ensue; a flight to quality (i.e. cash and 'safe' capital such as Treasuries) means

---

71 Minsky, 'Financial Instability Revisited' 60.

72 Bellofiore, 'The "New" Capitalism' 12.

73 Ibid. 13.

74 As Minsky notes: '[T]he payment commitments that involve the pledging of collateral are important – for they provide a direct and quick link between a decline in market value of assets and the need to make cash payments … This margin or collateral maintenance payment commitment can be a source of considerable disorganisation and can lead to a sharp decline in asset prices.' Minsky, 'Financial Instability Revisited' 55.

that financiers no longer extend loanable capital to industry and consumers who require credit to settle bills and to bridge the gaps in the business cycle. As credit is withdrawn, industry can no longer fund production and the chain of payments is broken, provoking bankruptcy in many quarters and a contraction in economic output in others, and a general fall in aggregate stock market values will follow. The circulation of capital is restricted greatly and faith in future financial performance is shaken: 'When net worth destruction and illiquidity have spread to a significant number of units, investments completely stop and gross profits plummet. Even hedge-financing units become speculative or Ponzi.'[75]

Indeed, eventually, the spread of speculative and/or Ponzi liability structures will reach a critical mass, and 'units with cash flow shortfalls will be forced to try to make position by selling out position. *This is likely to lead to a collapse of asset values*.'[76] This failure is often associated with deterioration in the confidence of the strength of credit products and the underlying values which they represent. Banks are themselves essentially speculative units because they engage in the long-term financing of business through short-term debt.[77] On this basis, the financial system may be left vulnerable because expectations of continued growth and a significant increase in asset prices lead to an overextension of credit and the adoption of fragile financial structures, leading to mass writedowns of loans and credit previously extended for investment.[78] In conditions of crisis, bank-originated structured finance products amplify the effects of negative price movements and can lead to financial contagion.[79] These innovations, whilst augmenting risk allocation in 'good times', contribute to illiquidity in financial markets during crises. As noted, '[w]hen the "good times" end, this progressive illiquidity turns into a systemic crisis of unpayable debts – and it can happen in

---

[75] Bellofiore, 'The "New" Capitalism' 13.

[76] Minsky, 'The FIH' 8 (emphasis added).

[77] Ricardo Bellofiore & Joseph Halevi, 'A Minsky Moment? The Subprime Crisis and the "New" Capitalism', The Fourth Forum of the World Association for Political Economy (WAPE), Nation, State, and Democratic Governance of the Global Economy and Politics, May 2009, Paris, 151, http://www.wrpe.org/WAPE/WAPE%20papers%202009/BELLOFIORE&HALEVI.pdf.

[78] Minsky, 'Financial Instability Revisited' 50. See also, Steve Keen, 'A Monetary Minsky Model of the Great Moderation and the Great Recession' (2013) 86 J. ECON. BEHAVIOR & ORGAN. 221.

[79] Markus K. Brunnermeier, 'Deciphering the Liquidity & Credit Crunch 2007–08' (2009) 23 J. ECON. PERSPECTIVES 77.

a flash'.[80] Accordingly, 'a key element in the escalation of financial distress to system-wide instability and crisis is the appearance of financial distress amongst financial institutions [and a] necessary condition for a deep depression is a prior financial crisis'.[81]

In the event of a financial crisis, a spiral of deleveraging and bankruptcies may ensue, as in a Ponzi-based financial environment 'a shortfall of cash flows from the income stream, which in a low indebted environment is readily contained, can, in a highly indebted environment, reach and break through the barriers so that a cumulative interactive debt deflation takes place'.[82] Thus, the link between financial crisis and significant dislocations in all areas of the economy is satisfied. The FIH dictates that crises in the financial sector are inevitable, and that disruption to asset values in other sectors of the economy will always follow a financial crisis. The following section thus discusses the link between financial instability and general asset prices, before the analysis proceeds to consider the specific effects on banks and the equity values of financial institutions.

THE FIH AND ASSET BUBBLES: IMPLICATIONS FOR COMPENSATION INCENTIVES AT FINANCIAL INSTITUTIONS

Previous sections have described the processes which may lead to asset bubbles in securities and financial markets. This chapter will now conclude with a section discussing the consequences for stock prices and executive compensation which flow from the operation of these forces. As previously noted, both heterodox theories (surveyed in the previous chapter) and the FIH explain why prices in securities markets may be driven away from fundamental value by these factors. Each has serious implications for the design of executive compensation systems, particularly those at financial institutions. Behavioural finance demonstrates why bubbles may inflate due to investor behaviour; the FIH explains how that behaviour is allowed to take hold, and how it manifests in the

---

[80] Anastasia Nesvetailova, 'Ponzi Finance and Global Liquidity Meltdown: Lessons from Minsky' (2009) City University Working Paper on Transnational Politics Working Paper CUTP/002, 9–10.

[81] Minsky, 'Financial Instability Revisited' 61–62.

[82] For the original formulation, see Irving Fisher, 'The Debt-Deflation Theory of Great Depressions' (1933) 1 ECONOMETRICA 337. For a restatement incorporating bank finance, see Minsky, 'The FIH'.

liability structures of economic units. More importantly, it explains the importance of financial institutions in directing this process.

Of course, the banking system is central to this phenomenon. The financial sector is a crucial driver of instability because it is the financial sector that provides credit to the real economy, and it is the unstable positions that credit permits units to adopt which have the potential to destabilise financial systems. Naturally, many of these risks arise from the increased volumes of loans and finance available to borrowers during euphoric periods, which are validated by the higher profits realised during economic booms. The FIH predicts that finance allows for a higher rate of expansion in income and capital growth but, at the same time, increases the amount of debt in an economy relative to output and the financial commitments in relation to that debt affect the levels of anticipated cash flows.[83] The liability structures of firms, and the value of the products that they trade, thereby operate in a symbiotic dynamic with the stability of the financial system, especially as it is the financial system that facilitates increased leverage levels.

The importance of the Minsky model to this view is that the various stages of economic performance within the cycle may be exemplified in the price of assets and/or stocks. The price of stocks is affected by factors extrinsic to the companies that they represent (notwithstanding the effects that general economic conditions have on the prospects of businesses). If there are mechanisms which prevent the efficient pricing of assets, including behavioural influences and inherent uncertainty in financial investment, then the accuracy of market prices may be undermined. The effects on stock prices in particular may be significant, due to the prevailing function of uncertainty in investment decisions. One of the main obstacles to the efficient incorporation of information into prices is the pro-cyclicality of human nature, which may lead to groupthink, feedback effects and other reflexive social processes, which lead the price of financial assets to levels justified on nothing other than confident expectations of future profitability. Accordingly '[i]nvestors as a whole may under- or overestimate the value of a particular stock if they lack information or succumb to sweeping market tides of bullishness or bearishness'.[84]

On this basis, large aggregate levels of speculative investment mean that 'from time to time, capitalist economies exhibit inflations and debt

---

[83] Delli Gatti & Gallegati, 'Financial Instability'.

[84] Lynn A. Stout, 'Are Takeover Premiums Really Premiums? Market Price, Fair Value, and Corporate Law' (1990) 99 YALE LAW J. 1235, 1249.

deflations which seem to have the potential to spin out of control. In such processes, the economic system's reactions to a movement of the economy amplify the movement – inflation feeds upon inflation and debt deflation feeds upon debt deflation.'[85] In relation to financial markets, as noted in the previous chapter, these environments may result in investor herding and investment according to momentum, rather than considerations of fundamental value (and panic when losses begin to mount). Significantly, this often has ramifications not only for shareholders of the corporations concerned, but society as a whole, especially when the lending practices of financial institutions feed asset bubbles and create financial instability. These lending practices often do not incorporate an adequate risk premium, because of optimistic expectations concerning future financial performance.[86] On this basis, it has been noted by researchers who confirm Minsky's predictions:

> Expectations over the cycle are the main driving force behind over-leveraging and investing in riskier projects … after a period of good realization of returns, riskier projects become more appealing to financial institutions, which increase their borrowing to expand their balance sheet. Creditors are willing to provide credit at lower interest rates, since the prospects of the economy have improved from their perspective as well. This results in much higher defaults and financial instability once a bad state realizes.[87]

We have already examined how modern compensation contracts remain flawed in light of their reliance on an imperfect market pricing mechanism. To be sure, many of these pricing imperfections do not last for a protracted period, and are quickly corrected. However, certain market phenomena – bubbles in particular – demonstrate that prices may be pushed away from underlying value for protracted periods, driven by behavioural dynamics, including the debt-fuelled exuberance characteristic of periods of euphoria. Periods of euphoria invariably preface a collapse in prices in some area of the economy because of the overconfidence that this euphoria breeds in investors about future economic

---

85 Minsky, 'The FIH' 1.

86 'A sequence of periods characterised by low borrowing constraints induces optimistic expectations about the continuation of such regimes and leads to an underpricing of risk, high leverage, over inflated collateral values and a sharp collapse after realization of a tighter constraint.' See Sudipto Bhattacharya, Charles A.E. Goodhart, Dimitrios P. Tsmoscos & Alexandros P. Vardoulakis, 'Minsky's Financial Instability Hypothesis and the Leverage Cycle' (2011) LSE Financial Markets Group Paper Series Special Paper 202, 4.

87 Ibid.

prospects. Thus, prices, at the peak of a bubble, may lack validity as they are driven not simply by consideration of fundamental factors, but by market sentiment (optimism).[88] Notwithstanding this, the compensation that may be awarded to executives in euphoric markets fails to recognise the FIH's prediction that crisis in expansionist financial markets is preordained and that, during certain given periods, asset prices (including equities) will collapse in value.[89]

Financial institution stock price imperfections are amplified by the debt structure utilised by those institutions in periods of economic prosperity. As demonstrated by the FIH, periods of economic expansion are normally accompanied by an upsurge in leverage, as financial institutions migrate from stable financial structures, and increase their lending levels. This has a distorting effect on the stock prices of those firms; leverage allows financial institutions to boost their value, often without a concerted change in firm fundamentals. Where extending credit produces short-term earnings, financial institutions may find themselves in the paradoxical situation where their stock price appreciates due to the increased profits they garner, yet their financial position becomes more perilous because of the complexity and leverage employed in pursuit of those returns. In theory, credit and stock analysts ought to adjust their securities ratings to recognise the increased fragility in the structure of financial institutions but as this book noted in the previous chapter, there

---

[88] See Nicholas Mangee, 'The Long Swings Puzzle in Equity Markets: Evidence from *Bloomberg News's* Market Wraps' (2011) University of New Hampshire Working Paper. Mangee uses data from *Bloomberg News* daily market-wrap (end of day) stories in his experiment on the factors driving market participants' trading decisions. This data was collected from every trading day between 4 January 1993 and 31 December 2009. The data tracks the proportion of days over the sample in each month that a particular category or piece of news was reported to have moved stock prices. Fundamental factors (factors relating to actual information regarding a company or sector) were, as to be expected, cited in 99% of the trading days in the sample period. However, psychological considerations were cited in 55% of the trading days during the sample. This, as even behavioural finance sceptics acknowledge, indicates that psychological factors 'play an important role in underpinning price fluctuations in equity markets'. See Roman Frydman & Michael D. Goldberg, *Beyond Mechanical Markets: Asset Price Swings, Risk and the Role of the State* (Princeton UP, 2011) 134.

[89] Of course, recent regulatory interventions now require that bonuses and other equity-based compensation are paid out in stages (typically three to five years). However, as will be discussed in Chapter 7, the length of these deferments is not nearly long enough to rectify the issues highlighted by the FIH.

are serious obstacles preventing this sort of analysis and/or arbitrage to correct prices.

Naturally, those price distortions reveal an acute flaw in the design of compensation contracts – increased avenues for profit from linking remuneration to asset prices will encourage compensation systems linked to those assets. Executives who are rewarded with remuneration linked to stock price benefit from increases in leverage because of the effects that leverage increases have on equity prices (to be discussed in the context of the GFC in the following chapter). However, it is the very pursuit of profit that may condemn the economy to experience crisis in future episodes: the debt-centred account of instability results in 'a sudden realization that assets were overvalued and that peoples' collateral constraints were too lax'.[90] Accordingly, the role of leverage to this process is crucial, and leverage and capital regulations may be used to prevent damaging accumulations of debt which lead to financial fragility. Moreover, this surely ought to have some bearing on the design of compensation plans linked to stock performance; if – as according to Minsky – financial markets are inherently unstable and crisis prone, corporate governance systems ought to reflect the potential for sharp asset price revaluations in any remuneration structures linked to market prices (including stock-related pay), especially where this has been achieved through increasing debt.

Perhaps most significantly, analysis of executive investment behaviour reveals that one of the consequences of modern compensation contracts is that bubbles may themselves be driven by perverse incentives. As a boom develops, 'competition between [corporations] … push[es] toward more risk-taking. Part of the reason for this is that their compensation systems … remain inherently pro-cyclical and, as times get better, they will load up on risk.'[91] In other words, the huge returns on offer from particular strategies demand that senior executives at financial institutions herd into profitable markets, whether or not earnings from these markets are likely to be long term. Part of the reason for this is shareholder pressure to

---

[90] Gauti B. Eggertsson & Paul Krugman, 'Debt, Deleveraging, and the Liquidity Trap: A Fisher-Minsky-Koo Approach' (2010) FRBNY Working Paper, 6.

[91] Peter Boone & Simon Johnson, 'Will the Politics of Global Moral Hazard Sink Us Again?' in Adair Turner, Andrew Haldane, Paul Woolley, Sushil Wadhwani, Charles Goodhart, Andrew Smithers, Andrew Large, John Kay, Martin Wolf, Peter Boone, Simon Johnson & Richard Layard (eds), *The Future of Finance: The LSE Report* (LSE, 2010) 274 (hereinafter Turner et al, *The Future of Finance*).

assume risk; there is strong evidence that persistent focus on short-term return on equity is a direct cause of financial dislocation in financial markets, as managers pursue investments for short-term profits on behalf of firm owners.[92] Accordingly, as financial markets recover from crisis, and shareholders' risk appetites return, compensation systems will provide a convenient incentive for management to extend further excessive lending. Of course, this view is also cognisant of the arguments put forward by both behavioural finance scholars and Minsky, concerning the effects that flawed investor memories and imperfect risk valuations exert on investment behaviour. This has significant consequences for the use of stock options and stock-related awards as the basis for executive compensation, as they implicitly encourage excessive focus on short-term returns.

CONCLUSION

Despite these observations, few executive pay arrangements explicitly recognise that financial markets may experience bubbles or price swings which are not merited after consideration of fundamentals. Further, despite recent reforms, they also do not incorporate into their design the potential for significant implosions of asset prices. Executives may capture rents which are not based on the underlying fundamentals of a particular sector, but through inflated asset and stock prices driven by overconfident expectations of prosperity and the hardwiring of leverage into the financial system. If prices are not wholly indicative of – and deviate for considerable periods from – intrinsic value, then compensation awards based upon stock prices must recognise this. Moreover, even when asset prices collapse, executives who captured personal advantages in rising markets normally retain their financial rewards. Based upon the financing relations prevalent in Anglo-American economies, and as predicted by the FIH, asset prices will always collapse; whether the collapse is small or large is immaterial for present purposes. Prevailing compensation arrangements are thus flawed.

It is the contention of this book that this factor ought to be recognised in compensation awards. The following chapter will discuss these themes, together with those of the previous chapter on executive compensation, in the context of the GFC, to demonstrate how the observations

[92] Emilios Avgouleas & Jay Cullen, 'Market Discipline and EU Corporate Governance Reform in the Banking Sector: Merits, Fallacies, and Cognitive Boundaries' (2014) 41 J. LAW & SOCIETY 28.

that financial markets are prone to mispricing, investor herding and bubbles discredit the current use of equity-related compensation plans. The consequences of these system attributes, on banks and the stock market, will be also be analysed, which will lay the foundations for an analysis of contemporary reform to executive compensation systems at financial institutions.

5. The Global Financial Crisis and the complex relationship between asset prices, leverage and financial instability

INTRODUCTORY REMARKS

In the previous chapter, I attempted to explain why asset prices may become inflated and, arguably, divorced from fundamental value, often for protracted periods. This is, of course, concurrent with the predictions of the FIH, which holds that the lending policies of banks (the main sources of finance), shaped by memories of recent financial market performance, will create unsustainable levels of debt within an economy, and generate the potential for asset bubbles. Whilst this notion remains contentious amongst some neoclassical economists, it is clear that virtually every serious financial crisis in the modern era has been preceded by a bubble in one or more asset markets.[1] Accordingly, these bubbles may be confined to particular sectors, or be diffused across the economy, as was the case in the lead-up to the most serious financial crisis since the Great Depression, the GFC. Whilst the focus of this book is on the propensity of stock market bubbles to affect executive compensation, it is clear that stock bubbles may themselves be propelled by asset price bubbles in other areas of the economy, which are transmitted to the stock market from other sectors.[2]

---

[1] For discussion, see Kindleberger & Aliber, *Manias, Panics and Crashes.*

[2] Peter C.B. Phillips & Jun Yu, 'Dating the Timeline of Financial Bubbles During the Subprime Crisis' (2011) 2 QUANT. ECON. 455; Didier Sornette & Ryan Woodard, 'Financial Bubbles, Real Estate Bubbles, Derivative Bubbles, and the Financial and Economic Crisis' in Misako Takayasu, Tsutomu Watanabe & Hideki Takayasu (eds), *Econophysics Approaches to Large-Scale Business Data and Financial Crisis* ((Springer, 2010); Ricardo J. Caballero, Emmanuel Farhi & Pierre-Olivier Gourinchas, 'Financial Crash, Commodity Prices and Global Imbalances', NBER Working Paper No. 14521 (2008).

In keeping with the subject matter of this book, this chapter will consider the experience of Anglo-American financial markets which have, since only the turn of the twenty-first century, experienced several severe episodes of crisis. Virtually all of these financial crises have exhibited similar characteristics; namely, huge growths in private sector debt, a consequent and unsustainable inflation of asset prices, followed by mass asset price deflation.[3] In the case of financial institutions, large short-term gains were created, only for prices to return to levels approximating long-term value, often causing severe long-term losses of stockholder wealth. Notwithstanding the destruction to shareholder wealth resulting from these price corrections, it is the effects on the wider economy that have caused these episodes to become embedded in the public consciousness. In these instances, public and political ire has often been directed toward corporate executives, who captured large compensatory windfalls through the exercise of stock options, or bonuses related to corporate performance, as gains made in the relevant sectors fed into compensation packages. These gains were often realised despite the fact that it was arguably behavioural dynamics which drove the market price increases in question; these increases, by their nature, did not reflect fundamentals and, without exception, were subject to correction. This, of course, accords with the predictions of the FIH, which suggests that financialised economies are, fundamentally, subject to endogenously generated boom and bust cycles.

This cycle of asset price appreciation feeding into greater assumption of debt, and from debt into asset price inflation, was witnessed across the private sector in the run-up to the GFC, which became increasingly heavily indebted as credit terms for loans were loosened and financial innovation exploded.[4] Accordingly, this chapter will undertake an analysis of the GFC with a particular focus on the 2000–07 real estate bubble, the effects of which were transmitted to asset prices in virtually every market, and fed private levels of consumption previously unseen in the US and Europe. Whilst the underlying causes of the GFC were legion,[5] it is clear that the price inflation of several asset classes (and

[3] Kindleberger & Aliber, *Manias, Panics and Crashes.*

[4] For example, by 2007, the US ratio of debt to GDP reached an all-time peak of 500% (in other words, 5 dollars of debt to service out of each dollar of income). See Yeva Nersisyan & L. Randall Wray, 'The Global Financial Crisis and the Shift to Shadow Banking' (2010) Levy Economics Institute of Bard College Working Paper No. 587.

[5] In the US, the Financial Crisis Inquiry Commission concluded that the GFC was both manmade and avoidable. According to the Commission the causes

subsequent price crashes) was, at least, partially responsible.[6] A key tenet of my argument is that euphoric views concerning the future trajectory of asset prices may prevent accurate pricing of risk, and thereby distort market pricing. Moreover, this implicitly encourages the adoption of incentives in executive compensation contracts which are linked to asset values. The effects of this dynamic are attenuated by the structure of equity-based executive compensation systems, which remain inherently pro-cyclical, rewarding strategies which encourage stock price growth, but largely failing to provide incentives to consider long-term sustainability. Whilst proponents of linking compensation packages to equity prices contend, of course, that doing so provides a strong interconnection between pay and performance, the utility of these systems is called into question by the inflation of asset bubbles; as noted following the GFC, '[i]t would be hard to argue that pay for performance increases incentives

---

were 'Widespread failures in financial regulation, including the Federal Reserve's failure to stem the tide of toxic mortgages; Dramatic breakdowns in corporate governance including too many financial firms acting recklessly and taking on too much risk; An explosive mix of excessive borrowing and risk by households and Wall Street that put the financial system on a collision course with crisis; Key policy makers ill prepared for the crisis, lacking a full understanding of the financial system they oversaw; and systemic breaches in accountability and ethics at all levels.' See The National Commission on the Causes of the Financial and Economic Crisis in the United States, *The Financial Crisis Inquiry Report*, Pursuant to Public Law 111–21 (hereinafter FCIC, *Inquiry Report*) *Conclusions xv* (2011). In the UK, the FSA identified the causes as: (i) The growth of the financial sector; (ii) Increasing leverage – in several forms; (iii) Changing forms of maturity transformation: the growth of shadow banking; (iv) Misplaced reliance on sophisticated maths; (v) Hard-wired pro-cyclicality: ratings, triggers, margins and haircuts. The specific problems that this led to within the financial system were attributable to: (i) failures in underwriting standards for sub-prime mortgages; (ii) market discipline for securitisation; (iii) rating agency assessments of securitised mortgage products; (iv) risk management in US and European banking institutions; and (v) regulatory policies to mitigate failures in risk management systems. See FSA, *The Turner Review* 16. See also G-20, *The Declaration of the Washington Summit on Financial Markets and the World Economy*, November 2008, Washington DC, USA.

[6] In the context of the GFC, for example, the availability of cheap credit fuelled the real-estate bubble which inflated prior to 2007, which itself powered several other bubbles across Anglo-American markets, most notably the stock market. For discussion, see L. Randall Wray, 'The Commodities Market Bubble: Money Manager Capitalism and the Financialization of Commodities' (2008) Levy Economics Institute of Bard College Public Policy Brief No. 96.

for risk when times are good and then argue that such incentives did not lead to too much risk taking given the crisis'.[7]

Of course, substantial increases in executive compensation levels characterised the pre-GFC environment.[8] However, absolute pay levels are not the crucial factor in this debate. Instead, I will attempt to show in this chapter that the two phenomena – the bubble in the real estate market, and executive compensation at financial institutions – were implicitly linked. In particular, I will explain how a reinforcing dynamic existed between house prices, the stock prices of banks, and compensation levels at financial institutions. Specifically, I will demonstrate that it was arguably due to the incentives of senior executives themselves – motivated as they were by perverse compensation structures and the capacity to leverage their banks' balance sheets – that the bubbles in question were inflated. This will go some way to demonstrating that the share pricing mechanism may not only be a poor proxy for corporate executive performance, but that reliance upon it to determine compensation awards creates incentives for corporate executives at financial institutions to assume excess risk, through credit creation and overleveraging, with potentially disastrous consequences for the real economy. This ought to help explain why incentive systems – in particular, at financial institutions – should not over-rely on measures of performance such as market prices, as this may actually reduce the effectiveness of those systems in delivering long-term and sustainable growth.

The next section will briefly draw out the development of the GFC. This will set the scene for a discussion of the fundamental drivers of the housing bubble, the links between this bubble and compensation incentives, and the consequences for executive compensation.

---

[7] Recommendation 1a, 'Governance, Executive Compensation, and Excessive Risk in the Financial Services Industry: A Research Symposium', Columbia Business School (27–28 March 2010) http://www4.gsb.columbia.edu/rt.

[8] Executive compensation in the US, in real terms, increased by 5% per year from 1980 to 1996. See Xavier Gabaix & Augustin Landier, 'Why Has CEO Pay Increased So Much?' (2008) 123 Q. J. ECON. 49. The US has the highest CEO-pay to worker-pay ratio in the world – in 2005 the ratio was 39:1. In the same year the UK had the second highest ratio at 31.8:1. See Heather Landy, 'Behind the Big Paydays', *The Washington Post* (Washington, 15 November 2008).

THE GLOBAL FINANCIAL CRISIS

The story of the GFC has been recounted many times, although attributing relative weight to its fundamental causes remains a contentious issue.[9] One may claim with some certitude, however, that one of the chief underlying factors was the inflation of a huge global real estate bubble,[10] fed through the recycling of savings excesses from China and other emerging economies and through the ultra-loose monetary policies of the US Federal Reserve; these excesses were ploughed back into financial assets in the US and elsewhere, including the mortgage market.[11] On this basis, Wray notes that the GFC was 'a natural outcome of these processes – an unsustainable explosion of real estate prices, mortgage debt, and leveraged positions in collateralized securities and derivatives in conjunction with a similarly unsustainable explosion of commodities prices and equities. The crash was inevitable.'[12]

The vast majority of mortgages issued during this period were pooled and securitised (to create so-called 'mortgage-backed securities' or 'MBS') and sold on in secondary markets, normally to other financial institutions (often combined with other forms of loan in asset-backed

---

[9] For discussion see Emilios Avgouleas, *Governance of Global Financial Markets: The Law, The Economics, The Politics* (CUP, 2012) (hereinafter Avgouleas, *Governance of Global Financial Markets*).

[10] Property price increases outpaced inflation in all developed jurisdictions during this period. Between 1997 and 2007, for example, in Spain and Ireland house prices increased by 190% and 240% respectively. See Brent W. Ambrose, Piet Eichholtz & Thies Lindenthal, 'House Prices and Fundamentals: 355 Years of Evidence' (2013) 45 J. MONEY, CREDIT & BANKING 477.

[11] Michael Pettis, *The Great Rebalancing: Trade, Conflict, and the Perilous Road Ahead for the World Economy* (Princeton UP, 2013). For example, the US mortgage giants, Fannie Mae and Freddie Mac (officially, the Federal National Mortgage Association and the Federal Home Loan Mortgage Corporation, respectively), alone owned nearly $5 trillion in mortgage assets at the end of 2007. These two bodies are 'publicly traded financial institutions that were created by Acts of Congress in order to fulfill a public mission. These charter Acts imbue the two GSEs with important competitive advantages (most notably, implied public-sector support for their obligations) and define the scope of their permissible activities. Over time, Fannie Mae and Freddie Mac became exceptionally large, profitable, and politically powerful.' See W. Scott Frame, 'The 2008 Federal Intervention to Stabilize Fannie Mae and Freddie Mac' (2009) FRB Atlanta Working Paper No. 2009-13, 1–2 (notes omitted).

[12] L. Randall Wray, 'Minsky's Money Manager Capitalism and the Global Financial Crisis' (2011) Levy Economics Institute of Bard College Working Paper No. 661, 15.

securities known as 'collateralised debt obligations' or 'CDOs').[13] These securities were often granted triple-A status credit ratings; however many contained lower-quality mortgages, with various tranches securitised to provide contractual payment streams of differing creditworthiness. Through the increasing interconnectedness of the financial system,[14] virtually all banks and other financial institutions became exposed to the MBS market. When the US housing market began to slow in 2006, resulting mortgage defaults destroyed the value of many of the securitised products that had been created from underlying payment sources. On this basis, the value of MBS began to drop, and financial markets experienced severe dislocation, resulting in a 'credit crunch' during which market liquidity dried up. In July 2007 one of the five major US investment banks,[15] Bear Stearns, closed two of its specialised mortgage funds, which had $18 billion in assets.[16] Bear Stearns later had to be rescued by JP Morgan Chase, causing substantial losses to Bear's shareholders.[17] At around the same time in the UK, Northern Rock, a medium-sized UK bank heavily reliant on wholesale funding, was forced to ask for emergency financial support from the Bank of England and,

[13] The securitisation process converts lower-grade individual financial products into higher-grade securities. For example, structured finance products may convert a portfolio of BBB-rated products into a security with AAA-rated senior tranches. Securitisation of assets allows banks to cater to a wide pool of investors with heterogeneous preferences and risk tolerance. Furthermore, it allows institutional investors to hold indirectly assets which capital regulations would ordinarily deem too risky and would therefore prevent them from holding, if they had not been securitised. See Jeremy C. Stein, 'Securitization, Shadow Banking & Financial Fragility' (2010) 139 DAEDALUS 41.

[14] 'Rethinking the Financial Network', Speech given by Andrew G. Haldane, Executive Director, Financial Stability, Bank of England, at the Financial Student Association, Amsterdam, 28 April 2009, http://www.bankofengland.co.uk/archive/Documents/historicpubs/speeches/2009/speech386.pdf.

[15] The others, prior to the GFC (following which some ceased to be distinct entities, or collapsed) were Goldman Sachs, Merrill Lynch, Morgan Stanley and Lehman Brothers.

[16] Jonathan Davis, 'How a Fat Tail Comes Home to Roost', *Financial Times* (London, 30 July 2007), http://www.ft.com.

[17] JP Morgan Chase eventually paid $10 per share for the entire share capital of Bear Stearns, valuing the company at $1.2 billion. As late as January 2007, Bear Stearns had been valued at $172 per share (giving a market capitalisation of $20.64 billion).

despite attempts to find a private buyer, was eventually taken into public ownership.[18]

The collapses at Northern Rock and Bear Stearns of 2007 were simply portents of a global systemic collapse. The GFC reached its peak with the collapse of Lehman Brothers, the fourth-largest global investment bank, in September 2008.[19] The failure of Lehman caused mass panic in financial markets, driving the prices of financial assets into a calamitous descent. Governments in the US and Europe were forced to undertake massive rescue packages to shore up the banking system and recapitalise financial institutions. In the US, the Troubled Asset Relief Program authorised the use of more than $700 billion to purchase assets and equity from financial institutions,[20] whilst the US government was forced to rescue the world's largest insurer, AIG, and the mortgage giants Fannie Mae and Freddie Mac with direct infusions of equity capital.[21] Shortly thereafter, the UK government was forced to rescue the world's largest bank, RBS, in October 2008, followed by a rescue of Lloyds Banking Group in 2009.[22] The global cost of the GFC in bank rescues alone has been estimated at £7 trillion (c. $11 trillion).[23]

THE REAL ESTATE BUBBLE

The inflation of the real estate bubble was propelled by a marked increase in bank lending.[24] There were two main drivers of the increased bank lending into the property market. Firstly, there was a flawed

---

18 Jane Croft, 'London to Nationalise Troubled Mortgage Lender', *Financial Times* (London, 8 February 2008), http://ft.com.

19 For a detailed discussion of the GFC, see FCIC, *Inquiry Report*; FSA, *The Turner Review*.

20 This amount was later reduced to $475 billion.

21 Ashley Seager & Philip Inman, 'US Steps in to Rescue Failing Home Loan Giants', *The Guardian*, 8 September 2008.

22 Andrew Porter, James Kirkup & Gordon Rayner, 'Financial Crisis: HBOS and RBS "to be nationalised" in £50 Billion State Intervention', *The Daily Telegraph* (London, 12 October 2008).

23 Edmund Conway, 'IMF Puts Total Cost of Crisis at £7.1 Trillion', *The Daily Telegraph* (London, 8 August 2009). The cost in lost output to the US economy alone was estimated at $22 trillion.

24 The balance sheets of global banks doubled between 2004 and 2007. See Emilios Avgouleas & Jay Cullen, 'Excessive Leverage and Bankers' Pay: Governance and Financial Stability Costs of a Symbiotic Relationship' (2014), http://papers.ssrn.com/sol3/papers.cfm?abstract_id=2412869 (hereinafter Avgouleas & Cullen, 'Excessive Leverage and Bankers' Pay').

expectation that real estate prices would continue to appreciate in line with recent price level changes: investors were (over)confident that future price increases would follow, and were therefore comfortable in extending further mortgage finance, and willing to trade in increasing volumes of securitised mortgage products.[25] This also, of course, affected the expectations of mortgage borrowers who, in most cases, were convinced that the real estate market would continue to increase in value. Poor lending and underwriting practices at many mortgage originators compounded these problems.[26] The originate-to-distribute model generated fees for loan officers trading in mortgages, and for traders in securitised products with no immediate default risk to the financial institution or employees concerned. Secondly, as was touched upon in the previous chapter and will be expanded upon below, compensation incentives at financial institutions were poorly structured and encouraged the assumption of leverage. Senior bank executives were incentivised by equity-based remuneration to increase short-term returns on the basis of credit extension, which was most easily achieved through maximising the leverage of their firms, and which was facilitated through lax capital regulation. The chapter will now examine these central claims in depth.

(i) Overconfidence in the Real Estate Market

It is now accepted by virtually all academics and policymakers that real estate prices in several developed economies prior to 2007 exhibited increases which were not consistent with prevailing supply and demand considerations.[27] In the US, property prices experienced approximately a 60 per cent increase between 2000 and 2007: the average cost of a new

---

[25] Atif Mian & Amir Sufi, 'The Consequences of Mortgage Credit Expansion: Evidence from the U.S. Mortgage Default Crisis' (2009) 124 Q. J. ECON. 1449.

[26] John C. Duggan, Comptroller of Currency, Speech Given at the Annual Convention of The American Bankers Association, 8 October 2007, http://www.occ.treas.gov/ftp/release/2007-109a.pdf). Duggan observed that with the increasing use of the originate-to-distribute model of lending, lending standards shifted from evaluating the likelihood of repayment to evaluating the likelihood that the loan could be sold.

[27] An authoritative study notes: 'analysts generally understood that falling prices would have disastrous consequences but assigned that outcome a low probability … Our bottom line is that the problem largely had to do with expectations about home prices.' See Kristopher Gerardi, Andreas Lehnert, Shane M. Sherlund & Paul Willen, 'Making Sense of the Subprime Crisis' (2008) Brookings Papers On Economic Activity 69, 69–70.

home in the US at the beginning of 2000 was $195,600; by 2007, this had reached $313,900,[28] a rise of 33 per cent in real terms.[29] This house price appreciation was tacitly encouraged by and supported the granting of mortgage loans to less-creditworthy Americans, underwritten by Fannie Mae and Freddie Mac. Figure 5.1 demonstrates the increase in house prices for both new and existing houses. This chart contains data from three separate measures of house price growth: the national average, the 10-city composite and the 20-city composite.[30] Whilst each measure provides slightly differing aggregate percentage change figures, the market trend is obvious.

Further evidence for an overvaluation in US real estate may be derived from an analysis of the ratio of house prices to rents, which can be thought of as equivalent to a dividend–price ratio for the stock market.[31] Accordingly, if this ratio rises significantly above its fundamental (or long-run) value, the possibility of a bubble in real estate values is raised. In the US, between 2002 and 2006, this ratio accelerated to 90 per cent above its long-run value, far outstripping any previously recorded level.[32]

A similar (yet more pronounced) trend regarding real estate prices was evident in the UK: the average house price at the beginning of 2000 was £111,714; by mid-2007 the figure had reached £222,013.[33] In Figure 5.2 the average real price (adjusted for inflation) of UK house prices is

---

[28] This figure is adjusted for inflation. See http://www.census.gov/const/uspriceann.pdf.

[29] James A. Kahn, 'What Drives Housing Prices?' (2008) FRB New York Report No. 345.

[30] The 10-city composite includes: Greater Boston; Chicago Metropolitan Area; Denver-Aurora Metropolitan Area; Las Vegas Metropolitan Area; Greater Los Angeles; South Florida Metropolitan Area; New York Metropolitan Area; San Diego County; San Francisco; and Washington Metropolitan Area. The 20-city composite adds to the foregoing areas the following areas: Phoenix Metropolitan Area; Tampa Bay Area; Atlanta Metropolitan Area; Detroit Metropolitan Area; Minneapolis-Saint Paul Area; Charlotte Metropolitan Area; Greater Cleveland; Portland Metropolitan Area; Dallas/Fort Worth Metroplex; and Seattle Metropolitan Area.

[31] Joshua Gallin, 'The Long-Run Relationship between House Prices and Rents' (2008) 36 REAL ESTATE ECON. 635.

[32] Janet Yellen, President & CEO, Federal Reserve Bank of San Francisco, 'A Minsky Meltdown: Lessons for Central Bankers', Presentation to the 18th Annual Hyman P. Minsky Conference on the State of the US & World Economies: Meeting the Challenges of the Financial Crisis, Levy Economics Institute of Bard College New York City, 16 April 2009.

[33] This figure is adjusted for inflation. See http://www.nationwide.co.uk/hpi/downloads/UK_house_price_since_1952.xls.

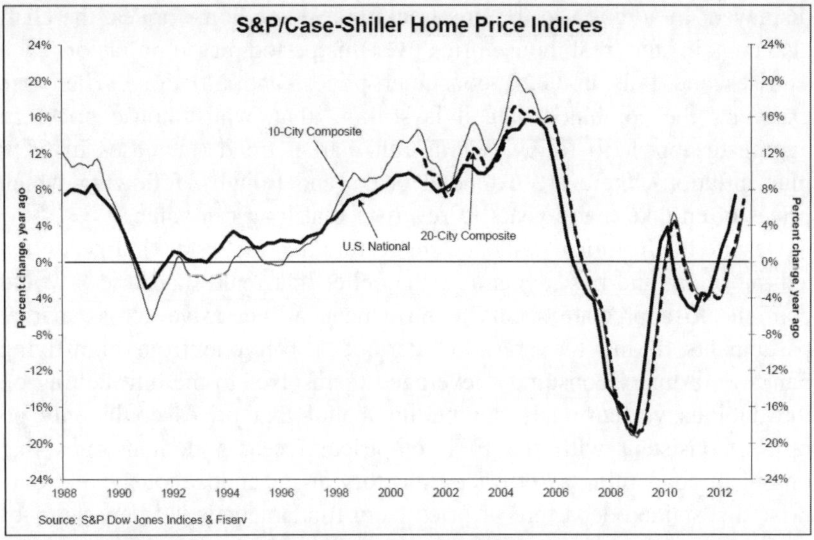

Source: S&P Dow Jones Index & Fiserv.

Figure 5.1 US Case-Shiller House Price Index 1990–2013

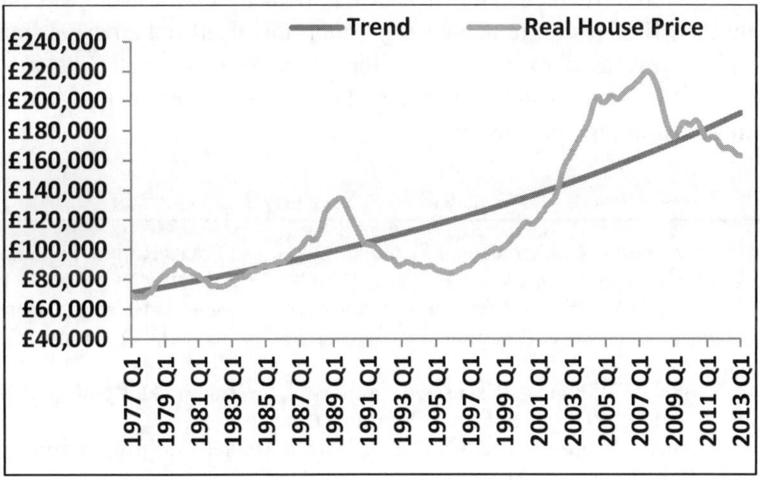

Source: Nationwide Building Society.

Figure 5.2 UK House Real Price Growth 1977–2013

displayed. In addition to the line tracking average home prices, the chart also contains the 'real' house price over this period, based on factors such as rises and falls in GDP, consumer prices, and inflation. When one examines the combined data it is striking that, whilst house prices in aggregate appear to follow a long-run market trend (increases in GDP plus inflation), there are extended peaks and troughs, following which prices often take many years to revert to real long-run value.[34]

Despite the historical evidence suggesting that real estate markets often exhibit boom and bust dynamics, the belief that real estate prices would continue to appreciate seems to have been all-pervasive across market participants during the pre-2007 period: '[e]veryone from high-flying banks to ordinary consumers leveraged themselves to the hilt, betting on the dubious yet curiously compelling belief that prices could only go up'.[35] Consistent with the FIH, empirical research demonstrates that optimism concerning asset price trajectory arises endogenously, and may drive a sustained departure of price from fundamentals.[36] Many years of substantial returns in the MBS market and year-on-year increases in the value of property therefore led bank management to consistently underestimate the probability that the value of mortgages and related MBS products might become impaired, especially in conditions of market panic.[37] Naturally, memories of previous housing crises faded as returns from the MBS market remained consistent; this itself fed an expansion in bank lending, as bankers underestimated the risks of a decline in real estate values, and which had the additional consequence that bankers' compensation also increased:[38]

---

[34] Vyacheslav Mikhed & Petr Zemčík, 'Do House Prices Reflect Fundamentals? Aggregate and Panel Data Evidence' (2009) 18 J. HOUSING ECON. 140.

[35] Nouriel Roubini & Stephen Mihm, *Crisis Economics: A Crash Course in the Future of Finance* (Penguin, 2010) (hereinafter Roubini & Mihm, *Crisis Economics*) 13.

[36] John C. Williams, 'Excessive Optimism, Leverage and Boom and Bust Cycles' (2013) FRB San Francisco Working Paper.

[37] Frank J. Fabozzi, 'The Structured Finance Market: An Investor's Perspective' (2005) 61 FIN. ANALYSTS J. 27.

[38] Luc Laeven & Ross Levine, 'Bank Governance, Regulation and Risk Taking' (2009) 93 J. FIN. ECON. 259; Carl R. Chen, Thomas L. Steiner & Ann Marie Whyte, 'Does Stock-Option-Based Compensation Induce Risk-Taking? An Analysis of the Banking Industry' (2006) 30 J. BANKING & FIN. 915; Anthony Saunders, Elizabeth Strock & Nickolaos G. Travlos, 'Ownership Structure, Deregulation, and Bank Risk Taking' (1990) 45 J. FIN. 643.

> [I]n benign markets with no recent history of negative events managers will potentially take high risks, as they essentially underestimate low-probability, high-risk events … The reward structures currently observed in the banking and investment industry can play their part in cyclical risk taking because they exacerbate the short-term focus and provide incentives for disaster myopia.[39]

These observations are, of course, highly reflective of the FIH analysis of financial markets outlined in the previous chapter. In the case of the real estate market, memories of recent large gains in the housing market were fresh, and some investors (wishing not to be excluded from profits in this market) began to herd in the view that property prices would continue rising.[40] As evidence for this, several mortgage companies raised record amounts for mortgage loans prior to the collapse in the housing market.[41] Many of these loan originators were aware that mortgage loan quality had deteriorated; in fact, many mortgage companies and banks in both the US and UK were complicit in facilitating fraudulent mortgage applications.[42] However, in most cases, lenders believed that house prices

---

39 Financial Services Authority, *Reforming Remuneration Practices in Financial Services: Feedback on CP09/10 and Final Rules PS 09/15* (2009) 4.24–4.27 (hereinafter FSA, *Reforming Remuneration Practices*).

40 This interpretation of events is supported by a great deal of anecdotal evidence from the period preceding the crash. See Andrew Redleaf & Richard Vigilante, *Panic: The Betrayal of Capitalism by Wall Street and Washington* (Richard Vigilante Books, 2010) 145–60; see also Michael Lewis, *The Big Short: Inside The Doomsday Machine* (Allen Lane, 2010).

41 For example, New Century Financial (NCF), which collapsed in early 2007, was one such firm. In 1997, its first year of trading, it raised $2 billion for loan originations; in 2005 it raised $56.1 billion. However, this extra lending at NCF occurred against a backdrop of declining equity capital. In 2004 NCF had equity of $987 million, yet by 2006 its equity had dropped to $457 million, despite 'the appearance of the warning flags [regarding the housing market which] … did not influence management'. See Allen B. Frankel, 'The Risk of Relying on Reputational Capital: A Case Study of the 2007 Failure of New Century Financial' (2009) BIS Working Paper No. 294, 12; Michael Missal, Final Report of Michael Missal, Bankruptcy Court Examiner, in *re: New Century Holdings, Inc. Chapter 11*, case no. 07-10416 (KJC), US Bankruptcy Court of the District of Delaware, February.

42 Many mortgages in the period up to 2007 were granted on the basis of self-certification. However, 90% of self-certified mortgage loan applications contained some element of fraud. This led to self-certification mortgages being granted the uncharitable moniker, 'liars' loans'. By 2006, 40% of mortgage originations in the US were self-certified; in the UK, the proportion was 45%. Thus, over two million loans made in the year 2006 across the US and UK were obtained through the use of inaccurate or fraudulent submissions to brokers. For

would continue to appreciate and borrowers would be able to refinance their loans in the future (or, indeed, that the mortgage loan would be sold on to other investors and the risk of delinquency would therefore be transferred), a classic form of FIH Ponzi financing.[43] In fact, for significant numbers of mortgage defaults to occur, home prices did not have to fall; they simply had to stop rising. In the event, after rising consistently from 1997 to 2005, house prices in the US stopped rising in 2006, and fell in 2007, yet credit default swap (CDS) spreads on financial institutions which traded heavily in the MBS markets were not affected until mid-2007 and did not widen substantially until later that year.[44] This suggests that investor sentiment regarding the real estate market – and those institutions trading in the MBS market in the US – remained irrationally positive despite the clear danger that a drop in real estate values would pose to the financial system. In this context, empirical modelling confirms that the predictions of the FIH hold true in relation to the real estate market prior to the US sub-prime meltdown of 2008. The authors of this study found in particular that financial innovation, interacting with credit constraints, led to underpricing of the risk in relation to securitised mortgages, which in turn produced a surge in credit and asset prices (in this case, real estate). Of course, when optimism concerning the real estate market evaporated, and risk premiums increased, prices collapsed.[45]

Similar investor sentiments concerning the real estate market were also prevalent in the UK; such sentiments, as elucidated in the following observation from a leading UK economist, were overly optimistic (and perhaps, irrational):

> Many British people seem to believe that it is somehow inevitable that house prices rise by 10pc, 15pc or 20pc every year … GDP rises, on average, at 2pc to 3pc per year, as do real average earnings. Add 2pc to 3pc inflation to that and you have a good starting point for what you should expect for the progress of most money values over time – 4pc to 6pc per annum. So why should house prices rise by 10pc plus, year after year? … As with other bubbles, prices went up much further than was justifiable on the economic

---

further discussion see William K. Black, 'When Liars' Loans Flourish' *Wall Street Journal* (New York, 30 January 2011).

[43] Yuliya Demyanyk & Otto Van Hemert, 'Understanding the Subprime Mortgage Crisis' (2011) 24 REV. FIN. STUD. 1848.

[44] FSA, *Turner Review* 46–47.

[45] Emine Boz & Enrique G. Mendoza, 'Financial Innovation, the Discovery of Risk, and the U.S. Credit Crisis' (2010) IMF Working Paper No. 10/164 (hereinafter Boz & Mendoza, 'Financial Innovation').

> fundamentals, as the experience of past price rises caused the expectation of further price rises, and as mortgage money became more freely available on extremely attractive terms … It has been normal for house prices to fall back a long way after excessive rises. It is just that, in the past, high rates of inflation made it possible for this to happen in real terms without a fall in nominal prices, thereby sustaining the popular myth that house prices never go down.[46]

Research conducted just prior to the time that the housing bubble burst in the UK confirms that house prices were overvalued by as much as 25 per cent, with a large portion of that figure driven by momentum trading, or herding.[47] Arbitraging the housing market to correct overvaluation is notoriously difficult, as it is virtually impossible to efficiently short a real asset.[48] Moreover, as noted in a previous chapter, herding is not a rational trading pattern – it is driven by price changes alone, whereby agents buy after price increases, and sell after price decreases. Price changes are therefore expectations based, and not due to analysis of long-run fundamentals.[49] As in the US, loose financing terms were prevalent in the UK, as increasing volumes of credit were extended to borrowers, often only on the basis of confidence in future real estate price rises. No-collateral ('zero-deposit') mortgages were commonplace, again reflecting the speculative and Ponzi stages of the FIH.[50] Zero-deposit mortgages are only worth issuing if the lender is confident that property prices will continue to rise yet, in the absence of severe supply shortages, there is no reason why house prices should outpace inflation for a protracted period

---

46 Roger Bootle, 'House Prices Could Fall Back A Long Way After their Excessive Rises' *The Daily Telegraph* (London, 14 July 2008).

47 Angela Black, Patricia Fraser & Martin Hoesli, 'House Prices, Fundamentals and Bubbles' (2006) 33 J. BUS. FIN. & ACC. 1535.

48 Richard Herring & Susan Wachter, 'Bubbles in Real Estate Markets' (2002) Zell/Lurie Real Estate Center Working Paper No. 402. Of course, the mortgage market was shorted by a few market participants using derivatives, but these were exceptions as there were few markets available for short-sellers to take advantage of. See Gregory Zuckerman, *The Greatest Trade Ever: How One Man Bet Against The Markets And Made $20 Billion* (Penguin, 2010).

49 J. Bradford De Long, Andrei Shleifer, Lawrence H. Summers & Robert J. Waldmann, 'Noise Trader Risk in Financial Markets' (1990) 98 J. POLIT. ECON. 703.

50 Thus, in the UK in September 2007, there were 238 mortgage products available for borrowers with no deposit. By September 2012, there were five. See Jonathan Eley, Elaine Moore & Tanya Powley, 'Rock Collapse Left Many in a Hard Place' *Financial Times* (London, 14 September 2012).

of time.[51] Much of the price rise in the UK real estate market in the lead-up to the GFC may therefore simply be attributable to over-confidence.

(ii) Bank Leverage

The real estate boom was fed by a rapid and sustained expansion in debt levels in the banking sector,[52] particularly through the expanded use of novel techniques in structured finance. As noted in the previous chapter, the FIH holds that increasing fragility in the financial structure of the economy is indicated by increasing leverage levels, and the figures – both in relation to leverage within the financial system and reduced margins in relation to house purchases – evidence this trend. Accordingly, between 2000 and 2006, ABS (asset-backed security) issuance increased by a factor of almost four, from $337 billion to over $1,250 billion. Over the same period, 'non-agency-sponsored' (non-GSE) MBS rose from roughly $100 billion to $773 billion.[53] Of course, one of the effects of asset bubbles is to swell bank balance sheets, and the expansion of MBS markets contributed to a pronounced build-up in systemic leverage, as the explosion in asset prices allowed the aggregate stock of debt within the global economy to expand.[54] These increases were used to justify greater levels of credit extension through 'complicated additional structures whose assumed values became, in turn, articles of faith and the basis for further leverage'.[55] There is considerable research to suggest, contrary to the predictions of 'orthodox' economic theory, that increases in both house prices and stock markets are products of higher bank leverage.[56] Data from the Bank of International Settlements supports this position.[57]

---

[51] Stijn Van Nieuwerburgh & Pierre-Olivier Weill, 'Why Has House Price Dispersion Gone Up?' (2010) 77 REV. ECON. STUD. 1567.

[52] Almost all of the reports commissioned following the GFC cite financial leverage as a significant cause of the crisis. For a flavour of these critiques, see FCIC, *Inquiry Report*.

[53] The De Larosiere Group, *The High Level Group on Financial Supervision in the EU* (2009) 8 (hereinafter *De Larosiere Group*).

[54] Roubini & Mihm, *Crisis Economics* 127. Debt within the US financial sector alone increased from 22% of GDP in 1987 to 117% of GDP in 2008.

[55] Andrew Smithers, *Wall Street Revalued: Imperfect Markets and Inept Central Bakers* (John Wiley & Sons, 2009) 2.

[56] '[H]ouse price (and share price) bubbles are always and everywhere a phenomenon of rising bank leverage, and anywhere that has high and rising levels of household debt (relative to GDP) is a candidate for being a bubble economy. This is a non-mainstream argument in economics, because for decades

The capacity to increase leverage affected business lines in several divisions within financial institutions, most notably retail lending at the individual consumer level, and aggregate MBS trading by investment and trading desks.[58] This was true particularly of conglomerates that focused on investment banking and complex finance, which grew their balance sheets rapidly via derivatives and MBS trading. This is, of itself, dangerous, because thinly capitalised banks are more exposed to changes in collateral values and they are therefore more fragile.[59] Accordingly, asset write-downs during the GFC were more strongly related to asset volatility in highly leveraged financial institutions: there was 'a positive and significant interaction between [firm risk] and leverage'.[60] Moreover, as Minsky outlines (noted in the previous chapter), there is a strongly evidenced link between increases in risk taking by banks (particularly increased leverage) and the various stages of the leverage cycle, a process governed largely by investor expectations.[61]

Of course, imperfections in banking regulation and regulatory arbitrage contributed to the crisis. Whilst the capital adequacy rules under Basel II were meant to restrict leverage to some degree through requiring the maintenance of a prescribed ratio of risk-weighted assets to capital,[62] it is

---

the so-called "efficient markets hypothesis" and "capital assets pricing model" have dominated academic economics, and they both argue that leverage has no effect on the price of assets.' Steve Keen, 'How to Spot a Housing Bubble Before It Bursts', *Business Spectator*, 15 June 2013, http://www.businessspectator.com.au/article/2013/10/15/economy/how-spot-housing-bubble-it-bursts.

57 Data from the BIS relating to 15 separate countries between 1985 and 2012 suggests that there is a significant relationship between the levels of household debt (including mortgages) and house price inflation. See ibid.

58 For example, according to its consolidated balance sheets, UK bank Barclays had derivatives (speculative) positions of approximately £248 billion in 2007; £984.8 billion in 2008; and £324.5 billion in 2013.

59 Hyman P. Minsky, 'Financial Instability Revisited: The Economics of Disaster', Policy Paper prepared for the Steering Committee for the Fundamental Reappraisal of the Discount Mechanism Appointed by the Board of Governors of the Federal Reserve System (January 1970).

60 See Marc Chesney, Jacob Stromberg & Alexander F. Wagner, 'Managerial Incentives to Take Asset Risk' (2012) Swiss Financial Institute Research Paper No. 10-18, 26 (hereinafter Chesney et al, 'Managerial Incentives').

61 See Sudipto Bhattacharya, Charles A. E. Goodhart, Dimitrios P. Tsmoscos & Alexandros P. Vardoulakis, 'Minsky's Financial Instability Hypothesis and the Leverage Cycle' (2011) LSE Financial Markets Group Paper Series Special Paper 202; Boz & Mendoza, *Financial Innovation.*

62 So, some observers have pointed to the fact that whilst asset price levels increased markedly in the years leading up to the GFC, reported leverage levels

clear that reported leverage levels at both commercial and investment banks were inaccurate.[63] This was due largely to two factors. Firstly, prevalent rules on bank capital were exploited, mainly by the establishment of large off-balance sheet vehicles, which were undercapitalized, thanks to flawed accounting rules and reliance on short-term repurchase agreements.[64] The vast majority of ABS and MBS issues in this period were warehoused in off-balance sheet conduits, which benefitted from higher capital relief than on-balance sheet assets. However, these conduits exposed sponsor banks to extremely similar risks as those related to on-balance sheet financing. For example, banks used asset-backed commercial paper (ABCP) to fund the assets held in conduits; however, banks were forced to guarantee the credit of the conduit for investors to purchase their ABCP issues. If the cash flows generated by the conduit were not sufficient to refinance its ABCP, and conduits could not roll over their funding, sponsor banks would have to assume the losses arising from this refinancing failure. The reputational risks which would have arisen if banks had failed to support these conduits were severe.[65] On this basis, whilst conduits were not on banks' consolidated balance sheets, the credit risk attached to conduits remained with the bank. Any lines of credit extended to these conduits were subject to less than 20 per cent of the capital requirement for on-balance sheet assets, as long as

---

at large commercial banks remained constant. For example, reported commercial bank leverage was largely unchanged between 2000 and 2009, which would tend to suggest that, whilst banks expanded asset levels aggressively, they maintained capital levels, which preserved stable leverage ratios. See Sebnem Kalemli-Ozcan, Bent Sorensen & Sevcan Yesiltas, 'Leverage Across Firms, Banks and Countries' (2012) 88 J. INT. ECON. 284. It is clear, however, that official figures do not present the full picture.

[63] *De Larosiere Group* 6. Leverage levels at European banks in 2008 included: ING, 49:1; Deutsche Bank, 53:1; and Barclays, 61:1.

[64] As noted by the Turner Review, accounting rules relating to these vehicles did not reflect underlying fundamentals: 'At the individual bank level, the classification of these as off-balance sheet proved inaccurate as a reflection of the true economic risk, with liquidity provision commitments and reputational concerns requiring many banks to take the assets back on balance sheet as the crisis grew, driving a significant one-off increase in measured leverage. But even if this had not been the case, the contribution of SIVs and conduits to total system leverage … would still have increased total system vulnerability.' See FSA, *Turner Review* 20. By 2007, commercial banks' off-balance sheet vehicles had total assets of $2.2 trillion, more than the assets of hedge funds ($1.8 trillion) and more than half of the total of the five largest investment banks ($4 trillion).

[65] Charles A.E. Goodhart, 'The Regulatory Response to the Financial Crisis' (2008) CESIFO Working Paper No. 2257, 9.

such lines had a term of less than a year.[66] On this basis, banks extended credit lines to conduits with durations of less than 365 days and, crucially, did not retain capital buffers to withstand any losses from those conduits.[67] Moreover, on the basis of these guarantees and the accounting treatment of the assets held in conduits, sponsor banks could assume much higher degrees of leverage (up to 10 times more for a given pool of loans) than if loans had been included on their balance sheets.[68] The consequences in terms of financial distress during the GFC were that banks with the largest securitisation operations suffered the greatest losses and lost most in equity valuation.[69]

Banks used other techniques to game the risk-weights under Basel, a process known as 'risk-weight optimisation' ('RWO'). Firstly, following securitisation of loans, and the consequential movement of those loans into an off-balance sheet vehicle, banks would often reinvest in the AAA-tranches of the securitised products they had created. As these securities were rated so highly, they attracted much higher capital relief than traditional loan assets. For example, AAA-rated securities were rated at less than half of the risk of commercial and mortgage loans, and were therefore granted only a 20 per cent risk weight, compared to 50 per cent for mortgages, and 100 per cent for corporate bonds.[70] Secondly, banks purchased credit protection against losses arising from these securities in the form of CDS. Where a CDS was purchased on AAA-securities from a AAA-rated issuer (for example, AIG), the securities would attract a zero per cent capital weight.[71] This consequentially further reduced the capital available to withstand losses from securitised

---

66 Viral A. Acharya & Philipp Schnabl, 'How Banks Played the Leverage "Game"' in Viral V. Acharya & Matthew Richardson (eds), *Restoring Financial Stability: How To Repair A Failed System* (John Wiley & Sons, 2009) (hereinafter Acharya & Schnabl, 'The Leverage "Game"') 83, 85.

67 IMF, *Global Financial Stability Report: Containing Systemic Risks and Restoring Financial Soundness* (April 2008) Box 2.5.

68 Viral V. Acharya, Nirupama Kulkarni & Matthew Richardson, 'Capital, Contingent Capital, and Liquidity Requirements' in Viral V. Acharya, Thomas F. Cooley, Matthew P. Richardson & Ingo Walter (eds), *Regulating Wall Street: The Dodd-Frank Act and the New Architecture of Global Finance* (John Wiley & Sons, 2011) 148 (hereinafter Acharya et al, 'Capital, Contingent Capital, and Liquidity Requirements').

69 Acharya & Schnabl, 'The Leverage "Game"' 83–84.

70 Hyun Shin, 'Securitisation and Financial Stability' (2009) 119 ECON. J. 309.

71 Acharya et al., 'Capital, Contingent Capital, and Liquidity Requirements' 148.

assets. These trends are demonstrated in Figure 5.3 on US bank leverage ratios, which shows the dramatic effect on leverage levels exerted by this forced incorporation of conduit finance on bank balance sheets from 2007.

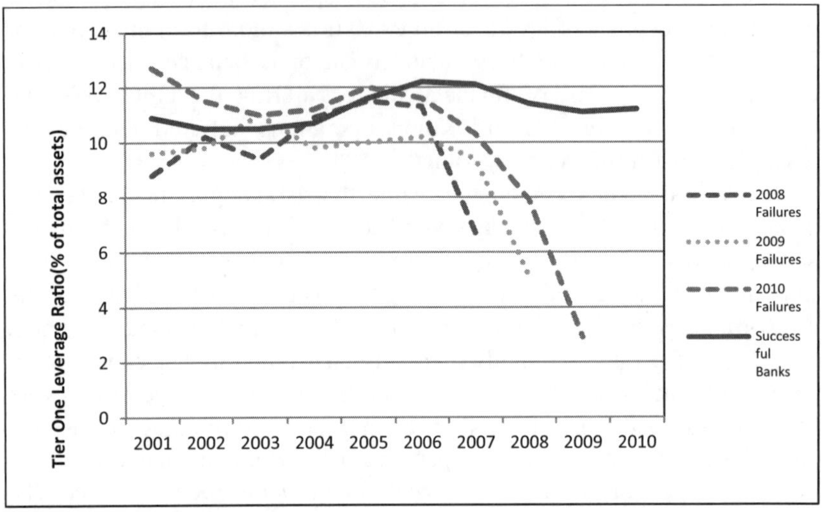

Source: Federal Deposit Insurance Corp.

Figure 5.3 US Bank Leverage Ratios 2001–2009

Leverage levels at large European conglomerate banks exhibited similar trends, particularly as these banks operated with both commercial and investment banking divisions (in the US, investment banks were often separate from commercial banks, although there were exceptions). Figure 5.4 traces the burgeoning leverage levels amongst certain large European banks in the run-up to the GFC (note that leverage levels at all exhibited banks spiked following the introduction of the Basel II Accord).

Secondly, strides made in financial innovation masked a poor understanding of the levels of interconnectedness and complexity at the heart of the financial system.[72] Due in part to this, systemic leverage levels

[72] Research suggests that the complexity and opacity of many MBS products led to investors mispricing those products, which, in combination with an excess supply of mortgage finance, contributed to an (unseen) build-up of risk within the financial system. See Adam J. Levitin & Susan M. Wachter, 'Explaining The Housing Bubble' (2012) 100 GEORGETOWN LAW J. 1177.

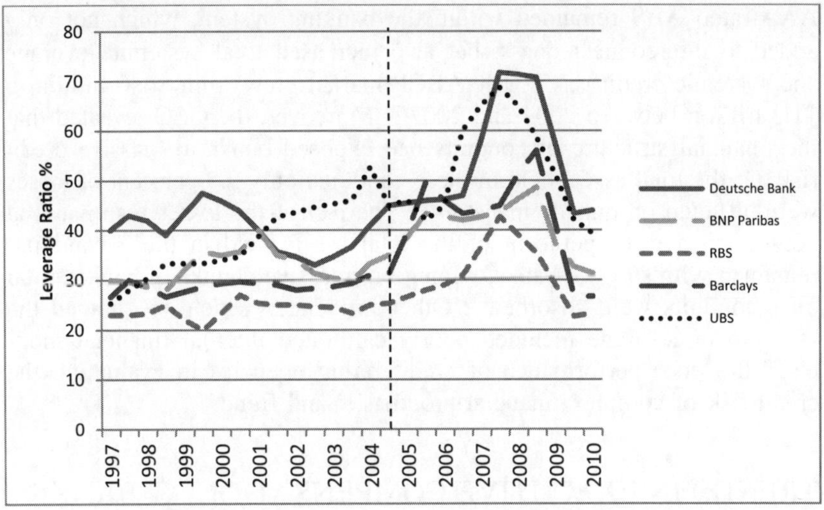

Source: Adapted from Blundell-Atkinson 2011. Alexander Blundell-Wignall & Paul E. Atkinson, 'Global SIFIs, Derivatives and Financial Stability' (2011) 1 OECD J: FIN. MARKET TRENDS, Figure 14.

Figure 5.4 Selected European Bank Leverage Ratios Total Assets/Tier One Capital

were underestimated. Of course, once again, there are parallels between the events of the GFC and the predictions of Minsky's FIH. In particular, money managers operating under light-touch, unobtrusive regulations concocted increasingly complex and esoteric financial instruments with which to trade, increasing leverage levels in the process. Prior to the GFC, it was assumed that by diversifying and spreading risk throughout the financial system through securitisation, the financial system would be more stable and more resilient to shocks. Instead, these risk management techniques increased homogeneity, thereby resulting in the entire financial system being exposed to fluctuations in the market for complex MBS, as '[a] positive feedback loop was created [by the housing boom] as the rapid appreciation of the underlying assets seemed to justify a large triple-A tranche for derivative collateralised debt obligations … and related products'.[73] Some of the most active purchasers of structured financial products were banks themselves: approximately 50 per cent of

[73] Richard J. Caballero, 'The "Other" Imbalance and the Financial Crisis' (2009) MIT Working Paper 09-32, 4.

AAA-rated ABS remained within the banking system, which not only added to interconnectedness, but also increased total systemic leverage and systemic credit risk.[74] The ABCP market grew from $650 billion to $1.3 trillion between 2004 and 2007.[75] Moreover, the GFC revealed that the financial structure of conduits had exposed banks to massive credit risk. Of the total assets held in these conduits, only 2.5 per cent of losses were inflicted on outside investors.[76] The rest of the losses (estimated at between 5 and 15 per cent of the total assets held in those conduits) remained with sponsor banks, wiping out massive chunks of bank capital once conduits were absorbed.[77] Other influences which encouraged the build-up of leverage included poorly calibrated internal financial models,[78] the poor performance of credit rating agencies in evaluating the credit risk of complex financial products,[79] and fraud.[80]

TRENDS IN EXECUTIVE COMPENSATION AT BANKS PRIOR TO THE GFC

The analysis conducted above provides some insights into the incentives created by executive compensation to assume excessive risk. However, any analysis of this issue would not be complete without considering the structure of compensation in the financial sector prior to 2008, and the potential contribution of that composition to the assumption of those

---

[74] Viral V. Acharya, Philipp Schnabl & Gustavo Suarez, 'Securitization Without Risk Transfer' (2011) NBER Working Paper 15730.

[75] Ibid. 2.

[76] Ibid. 26.

[77] Acharya et al. calculate a consequential loss of between $68 billion and $204 billion on this basis. See ibid.

[78] Michael Simkovic, 'Secret Liens and the Financial Crisis of 2008' (2009) 83 AM. BANKRUPTCY LAW J. 253.

[79] Andrew Johnston, 'Corporate Governance Is the Problem Not the Solution: A Critical Appraisal of the European Regulation on Credit Rating Agencies' (2011) 11 J. CORP. LAW STUD. 395.

[80] For example, it was documented by the lead counsel in the Lehman Brothers bankruptcy case that Lehman systematically attempted to conceal its true leverage ratio by using accounting techniques to remove liabilities from the core bank to its SIVs. This allowed Lehman to build up unreported leverage and remove debt from its balance sheet 'to create a materially misleading picture of the firm's financial condition in late 2007 and 2008 …'. See Final Report of Anton R. Valukas, Bankruptcy Court Examiner, *In Re: Lehman Brothers Holdings Inc. Et Al*, Chapter 11 Case No. 08-13555 (JMP) US Bankruptcy Court of the District of New York, 11 March 2010, Volume I, 732–33.

risks. This section will therefore briefly discuss the composition of executive compensation prior to the GFC. The link between compensation and excessive risk may thereby be established.

Through analysing the composition of pay of senior management at US banks, there are trends which suggest that bankers' compensation, in general, was structured in a way that would create increased risk in the lead-up to GFC. As noted in Chapter 2, senior managerial compensation at firms comprises several forms, most commonly salary, bonuses, stock options and restricted stock (equity) and other perquisites. Moreover, it also noted that studies have found that equity incentives (in relation to non-equity incentives) are likely to induce risk taking, due to the convexity added explicitly by stock options to managers' pay, and implicitly through performance conditions when restricted stock is used. Figure 5.5 demonstrates the marked increase in the use of equity-based pay to reward senior executives at US financial institutions between 1995 and 2008.

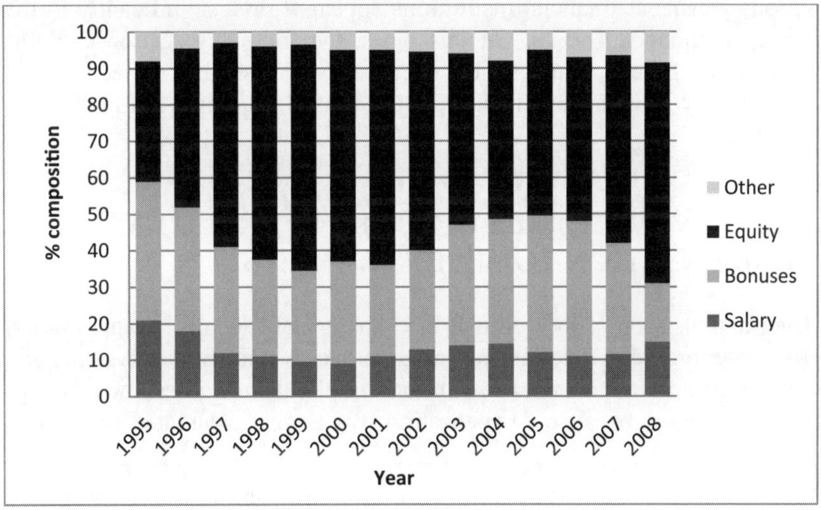

Source: Adapted from Balachandran, Kogut & Harnal. Sudhakar Balachandran, Bruce Kogut & Hitesh Harnal, 'The Probability of Default, Excessive Risk, and Executive Compensation: A Study of Financial Services Firms from 1995 to 2008' (2010) Columbia Business School Research Paper, Figure 4, Panel B (hereinafter Balachandran et al, 'Probability of Default').

Figure 5.5 Senior (Named) Executive Compensation Proportions at US Financial Firms

One can discern from the data that equity grants steadily increased as a proportion of pay until the height of the dot.com boom in 1999. When the market for technology stocks collapsed, stock-based pay reduced. However, in the years leading up to the GFC – particularly between 2005 and 2008 – the proportion of equity-based compensation awards at US banks appreciated considerably, resulting in stock and bonus awards making up approximately 80 per cent of total compensation by the time of the GFC.[81] There also appears to be a pro-cyclical rise in the proportion of equity-based compensation used prior to the downturns of 2001 and 2008. As noted by the authors of the research upon which this data is based: 'The … results indicate quite strongly that strong incentives through equity-based pay were not a deterrent to excessive risk-taking; to the contrary the financial institutions led by executives whose remuneration was heavily weighted in equity (stock and options) were more likely to be marked by excessive risk-taking.'[82] Whilst this correlation does not necessarily provide a concrete link between the phenomena, it is clear that the proportion of equity-based pay employed in compensation systems at financial institutions appears to rise significantly in the run-up to financial crises. On this basis, the following section explains why equity-based compensation encourages excess risk, especially via the capacity of financial institutions to expand lending quickly through leverage.

THE CONSEQUENCES OF LINKING EXECUTIVE COMPENSATION TO ASSET MARKETS

The previous section showed that the structure of executive compensation may have provided incentives to assume excess risk. Bonus systems and options awards at financial institutions implicitly rewarded the assumption of leverage because compensation was largely calculated on metrics

---

[81] Lucian A. Bebchuk, Alma Cohen & Holger Spamann, 'The Wages of Failure: Executive Compensation at Bear Stearns and Lehman 2000–2008' (2010) Harvard Law School Discussion Paper No. 657. This study examined the pay, bonuses and stock option awards of the CEOs and top executives at Bear Stearns and Lehman Brothers prior to the GFC to determine the levels of compensation awarded to the executive teams at these investment banks prior to the collapse in the market values of each. The top executives (defined as the top two to five executives) at Bear Stearns cashed out $1.1 billion in stock between 2000 and 2007 and those at Lehman cashed out $850 million during the same period.

[82] Ibid. at 32.

such as 'return on equity' ('RoE'), which encourages asset-building and a reduction in capital levels.[83] Leverage increases RoE when achieved returns on assets are above the borrowing rate of interest, by magnifying the impact that rises in asset values have on earnings:

> For a given return on assets (RoA), higher leverage mechanically boosts a banks' ROE. The decision by many banks to increase leverage appears to have been driven, at least in part, by a desire to maintain ROE relative to competitors … virtually all of the increase in the ROE of the major UK banks during this century appears to have been the result of higher leverage. Banks' return on assets – a more precise measure of their productivity – was flat or even falling over this period.[84]

High RoE thereby tends to increase the stock price of the relevant corporation, but it is clear that the leverage component underlying increases in RoE is generally underpriced by investors, because of the implicit and explicit guarantees provided to financial institutions by governments and state-backed insurance systems;[85] arguably, therefore, the selective focus on RoE represented by prevailing compensation

---

[83] For example, at one of the major casualties of the GFC, Bear Stearns, the board determined top executives' compensation with reference only to RoE. At the fiscal year end of 2007, Bear Stearns had net equity of $11.1 billion supporting $395 billion in assets, giving it a leverage ratio of 35.5 to 1. See Roddy Boyd, 'The Last Days of Bear Stearns', *Fortune* (31 March 2008), http://www.money.cnn.com/2008/03/28/magazines/fortune/boyd_bear.fortune/. The US Options Clearing Corporation (OCC), for example, commented on CitiGroup's corporate culture in 2005 that: 'Earnings and profitability growth have taken precedence over risk management and internal control.' See Comptroller of the Currency, *Memo: Examination of Citigroup Risk Management (CRM)*, 13 January 2005, 3. However, '[t]he use of unadjusted [earnings] or net [earnings] is a particularly poor metric for measuring performance since it can provide an incentive for employees to pay insufficient regard to the quality of the business undertaken or the services provided.' See FSA, *Reforming Remuneration Practices* 3.13.

[84] See Andrew G. Haldane, Simon Brennan & Vasileios Madouros, 'The Contribution of the Financial Sector: Miracle or Mirage?' in Turner et al, *The Future of Finance* 99 (hereinafter Haldane et al, 'Contribution of the Financial Sector').

[85] Anat R. Admati, Peter M. DeMarzo, Martin F. Hellwig & Paul Pfleiderer, 'Fallacies, Irrelevant Facts, and Myths in the Discussion of Capital Regulation: Why Bank Equity is Not Expensive' (2013) Rock Center for Corporate Governance at Stanford University Working Paper No. 161.

systems was part of a process of 'risk illusion'.[86] However, focusing on RoE was common practice across financial institutions in determining bonuses, which as Figure 5.5 shows, comprised a significant proportion of compensation at financial institutions:

> Many … banks take net revenue (typically, revenues after deduction of expenses) and then determine bonus pools by reference to a revenue to compensation ratio, frequently in the range of 45–50%. Profit is a better measure, but only a few firms were making satisfactory measures to adjust profit data for future risks. Few firms were accruing bonuses after accrual of profits at a rate which was sufficient to award shareholders a minimum risk adjusted return on the capital employed in the firm.[87]

Under incentive systems dominated by equity compensation, bank management will be focused on increasing stock prices through managing the rate of profitability which accrues, through leveraging the balance sheets of their banks to increase net earnings per unit of asset. It is, of course, significant in the context of executive compensation that more highly levered institutions are able to expand more quickly, and therefore capture higher RoE.[88] Moreover, in the financial sector – which is a highly competitive environment where shareholders pressure managers to assume risk and there are significant career concerns at play[89] – short-termism will be introduced into business models because the more quickly banks are able to expand, in general, the more competitive they will become, through undercutting rival institutions, or acquiring them. On this basis, it has been noted that '[banks] operate aggressively because they have to – the global financial marketplace is now extremely competitive, and mandates are won or lost based less on the ideas

---

[86] Haldane et al, 'Contribution of the Financial Sector' 99. On this theme, the (then) FSA made the following observation on the incentive structures prevalent at RBS employed prior to the GFC: '[The board] [s]et incentives for the RBS CEO which made it rational for him to focus on increasing revenue, profit, assets and leverage, rather than on capital, liquidity and asset quality. The CEO's annual remuneration was heavily influenced by operating profit, EPS growth and return on equity, as distinct from return on assets. There was less regard to non-financial performance measures. *This type of incentive package was, however, not dissimilar to those at other large banks*.' (Emphasis added.) It was also noted that RBS had one of the lowest equity/asset ratios of any major European bank. See FSA Board Report, *The Failure of the Royal Bank of Scotland* (2011) (hereinafter FSA Board Report, *Failure of RBS*) 225.

[87] FSA, *Reforming Remuneration Practices* 2.8.

[88] Minsky, *Stabilizing An Unstable Economy* 263.

[89] Avgouleas & Cullen, 'Excessive Leverage and Bankers' Pay'.

proposed than on the tightness of the pricing and the willingness to bear risk.'[90] In the lead-up to the GFC, money managers and bankers adopted excess risk because '[c]ontrary to economic theory, markets generate perverse incentives for excess risk, punishing the timid with low returns. Those playing along are rewarded with high returns because highly leveraged funding drives up prices for the underlying assets ...'[91] This naturally introduces short-termism into bank business models because the more quickly banks are able to expand their balance sheets, in general, the more market share they will attract, and the more investment they will have recourse to. Shareholders will therefore tend to favour managers who are able to expand their financial institutions and provide the highest returns which, in so-called benign financial conditions, are most easily achieved by increasing leverage. On this basis, it is highly plausible that short-termism will become embedded in the incentive structure at financial institutions. However, this pursuit of market share also renders banks more vulnerable to asset write-downs and confidence shocks because of the extreme leverage used in order to expand, and therefore undermines the use of equity prices as measurements of value. Further, the prevailing accounting rules which mark asset prices to market create incentives for firm management to concentrate on enlarging banks' trading books through additional asset expansion. There is a serious problem with certain asset price booms, because they demonstrate a high interdependence with price explosions in other sectors. For example, research indicates that the price movements of stocks and real estate (together with oil) are highly correlated in both tranquil and crisis periods.[92]

Consistent with the FIH, there is a considerable body of research which demonstrates clear links between asset prices and the supply of

---

90 Matthew Richardson, Roy C. Smith & Ingo Walter, 'Large Banks and the Volcker Rule' in Viral V. Acharya, Thomas F. Cooley, Matthew P. Richardson & Ingo Walter (eds), *Regulating Wall Street: The Dodd-Frank Act and the New Architecture of Global Finance* (John Wiley & Sons, 2011) 191.

91 L. Randall Wray, 'Minsky Crisis' (2011) Levy Economics Institute of Bard College Working Paper No. 659, 7.

92 Kam Fong Chan, Sirimon Treepongkaruna, Robert Brooks & Stephen Gray, 'Asset Market Linkages: Evidence from Financial Commodity and Real Estate Assets' (2011) 35 J. BANKING & FIN. 1415 (finding that under tranquil regimes, returns from stocks, oil and real estate are positive, whereas gold and bond prices tend to fall; in crisis regimes, returns from stocks, oil and real estate fall, whilst returns from gold and bonds increase).

credit.[93] It has been shown that significant credit expansion may lead to an increase in the value of stock markets by up to 40 per cent. Further, these effects may be transmitted to the real estate sector.[94] On this basis, there is a strong suggestion of a reciprocal relationship between bank lending policies and house price appreciation.[95] This dynamic link runs both ways and is, itself, mutually reinforcing: credit influences house prices, and house prices influence credit.[96] Further research demonstrates a strong correlation between the acceleration of mortgage debt and changes in US house prices (which purports to explain approximately four-fifths of the change in house prices over the last 25 years).[97] It may be posited that this pattern was evident in the build-up to the collapse in the sub-prime market in the US in 2007, as increased credit and bank leverage fuelled the real-estate bubble.[98]

---

93 Claudio Borio & Philip Lowe, 'Asset Prices, Financial and Monetary Stability: Exploring the Nexus' (2002) BIS Working Paper No. 114; Minsky, 'Can "It" Happen Again?'; Carsten Detken & Frank Smets, 'Asset Price Booms and Monetary Policy' (2004) ECB Working Paper No. 364.

94 Franklin Allen & Douglas Gale, 'Bubbles and Crises' (2000) 110 ECON. J. 236, 238.

95 Claudio Borio & Philip Lowe, 'Securing Sustainable Price Stability: Should Credit Come Back from the Wilderness?' (2004) BIS Working Paper No. 157; Charles A.E. Goodhart & Boris Hofmann, 'Deflation, Credit and Asset Prices' in Richard C.K. Burdekin & Pierre L. Siklos (eds), *Deflation: Current and Historical Perspectives* (CUP, 2004); Miguel A. Segoviano Basurto, Charles A.E. Goodhart & Boris Hofmann, 'Default, Credit Growth and Asset Prices' (2006) IMF Working Paper 06/223.

96 Charles A.E. Goodhart & Boris Hofmann, 'House Prices, Money, Credit, and the Macroeconomy' (2008) 24 OXF. REV. ECON. POL. 180, 202; Boris Hofmann, 'The Determinants of Private Sector Credit in Industrialised Countries: Do Property Prices Matter?' (2004) 7 INT. FIN. 203.

97 Steve Keen, 'The Debtwatch Manifesto' (2012) 15, http://keenomics.s3.amazonaws.com/debtdeflation_media/2012/01/TheDebtwatchManifesto.pdf.

98 Paul McCulley, 'The Shadow Banking System and Hyman Minsky's Economic Journey' in Larry Siegel (ed), *Insights into the Global Financial Crisis* (The Research Foundation of CFA Institute, 2009). On this theme, it has been noted: 'In the ten years up to the start of the financial crisis, house prices tripled. Many people think this is because there were not enough houses around, but that is only part of the picture. A major cause of the rise was that banks have the ability to create money every time they make a loan. During the period in question the amount of money banks created through mortgage lending more than quadrupled! This lending was a major driver of the massive increase in house prices.' See 'Why Are House Prices So High?' (Positive Money, 15 March 2014), http://www.positivemoney.org/issues/house-prices/.

Not only does real estate lending increase the prices of houses themselves, but it also has a pervasive effect on the value of stock markets. Changes in property prices, driven by lending, often exert upward pressure on corporate profitability and, on this basis, the stock prices of those corporations. This is due to the changes on the asset side of corporate balance sheets brought about by increases or decreases in real estate asset prices, which will affect the value of their fixed assets. Naturally, this also allows corporations to leverage those assets as collateral to obtain higher levels of bank finance for investment and expansion.[99] Again, this pattern is redolent of the earliest (euphoric) stages of the FIH: corporations borrow more for investment on the basis of higher collateral values of their assets, driven by optimistic views concerning future economic prospects and as a result, margins are reduced and financial fragility increases.

Moreover, as a large degree of bank lending is concentrated in property markets, the effect on bank stocks of collapses in property prices is magnified relative to the effects on stocks more generally.[100] This is depicted in Figure 5.6, which contains data on the UK housing market, UK equity market and a narrower sub-sample of UK bank stocks, and which forcefully demonstrates the disproportionate effect that falls in the real estate market exert on the stocks of financial institutions.

One can discern from Figure 5.6 that there appears to be a strong correlation between bank stock prices and real estate prices, and reveals the extent to which bank stock prices are dependent upon the volume and

---

[99] Daniel C. Chan & Sheridan Titman, 'Do Real Estate Prices and Stock Prices Move Together? An International Analysis' (1999) 27 REAL ESTATE ECON. 183; Colin Lizieri & Stephen Satchell, 'Interactions Between Property and Equity Markets: An Investigation of Linkages in the United Kingdom 1972–1992' (1997) 15 J. REAL ESTATE FIN. & ECON. 11; Nicholas Apergis & Lambros Lambrinidis, 'More Evidence on the Relationship between the Stock and the Real Estate Market' (2011) 85 BRIEFING NOTES IN ECON. 1, 3. These links have arguably become more prominent following the introduction of real estate investment trusts (REITs) to the stock market. There are two general forms of REIT: equity REITs, which invest directly into properties, and mortgage REITs, which invest in mortgage securities. Investors purchase stock in these REITs which are then listed on exchanges. As they invest exclusively in real estate, REIT prices are contingent entirely on property market performance and, as such, act as channels through which both the real estate market and securitised mortgage markets affect stock prices.

[100] Graciela L. Kaminsky & Carmen M. Reinhart, 'The Twin Crises: The Causes of Banking and Balance-of-Payments Problems' (1999) 89 AM. ECON. REV. 473.

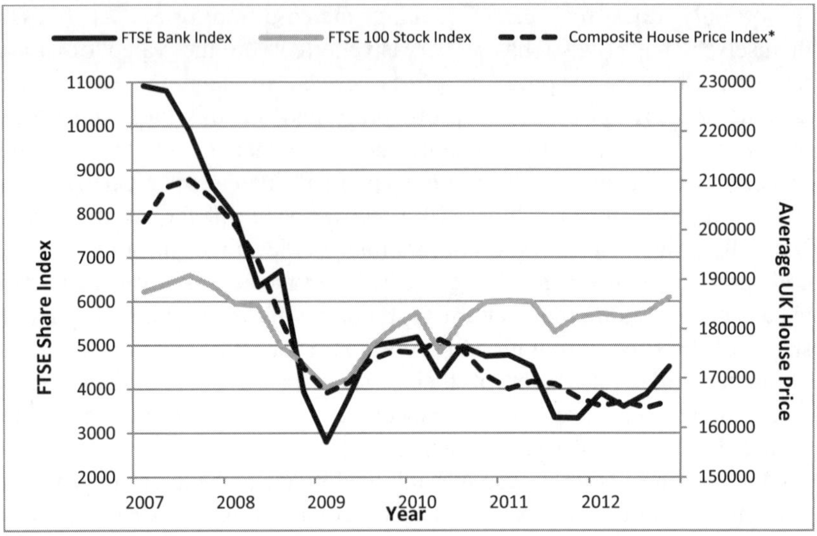

Source: Author's calculations based on share index data.
*Composed of the HBOS and Nationwide average house price data (adjusted for inflation).

Figure 5.6 Correlations between Bank Stock Prices and House Prices

quality of real estate lending. The aggregate FTSE 100 Stock Index suffered large losses in value during the GFC and subsequent fall in demand across the economy, but it recovered to something approaching its pre-crisis levels by late 2010. In contrast, the collapse in bank stock prices virtually mirrored the collapse in real estate values, and continued to track those values until 2013, when both started to recover. This is suggestive of a relationship between real estate values and bank stocks. In some ways, of course, one would expect such a relationship to exist; a high proportion of bank lending is advanced for real estate and commercial property, and so falls in real estate values hit banks and other financial institutions harder than other corporations.[101] Bank balance sheets contain both mortgage books and securitised trading books, and banks are affected by economic slowdowns and falls in asset values because of the leverage they employ. Accordingly, banks and other

[101] In 2010, 45% of UK bank lending was to individuals for property purchases, with a further 15% to commercial real estate. See Andrew Jackson & Ben Dyson, *Modernising Money: Why Our Monetary System Is Broken and How It Can Be Fixed* (Positive Money, 2013) 113.

financial institutions whose investments were concentrated most in real estate and mortgage securitisation suffered the greatest relative losses.[102] Moreover, not only banks, but also purchasers of real estate were becoming more highly leveraged in the run-up to the GFC. Until 2006 many house purchasers were borrowing with very low margins, often with no deposits. This led to the overleveraging – or 'double leveraging' – of both financial institutions and borrowers, leading to an extremely fragile financial structure: '[The pre-GFC] cycle is really a double leverage cycle: not only are the mortgage securities subject to the leverage cycle, but their "fundamental" cash flows (namely homeowner mortgage payments) are also subject to the leverage cycle. These two cycles feed off each other.'[103]

INCENTIVES AND THE REAL ESTATE LOAN MARKET

What has not been explored sufficiently is the link between the lending policies of financial institutions and the incentives systems prevalent in financial institutions, outlined above, which were rewarding of strategies which increased short-term returns. As outlined in the introduction to this chapter, there is a strong logical argument, consistent with the FIH, that incentives at financial institutions – especially compensation systems – to some degree acted as amplification mechanisms in relation to real estate values, which were a key driver of the stock prices of large financial institutions. Expectations of future real estate price increases and commensurate expectations of stability in the MBS market provided the basis for compensation systems which encouraged focus on increasing leverage. We have noted in preceding discussions that these returns were themselves largely contingent on increasing credit levels. Therefore, not only did the incentive systems at financial institutions reflect the overall increases in bank lending which occurred prior to the GFC, but they actually a priori drove the inflation of the real estate bubble, because managers had financial incentives to increase lending and reduce the capital base of their institutions. Real estate (mortgage) investment, together with associated MBS trading, was particularly conducive to leveraged finance. In the case of banks, because senior executives at

[102] Adrian Blundell-Wignall, Gert Wehinger & Patrick Slovik, 'The Elephant in the Room: The Need to Deal with What Banks Do' (2009) 2 OECD J: FIN. MARKET TRENDS 10.

[103] John Geanakoplos, 'Solving the Present Crisis and Managing the Leverage Cycle' (2010) FRB NEW YORK ECON. POL. REV. 101.

financial institutions usually hold significant equity positions in their firms, or are rewarded with stock options, their compensation awards are determined to a great extent by the banks' stock prices, which are themselves often contingent on the asset prices in markets in which the banks trade (in the case of commercial and investment banks, mostly real estate and real-estate-based securities) even where these price movements were short-term.[104] Bank managers will therefore be focused on increasing stock prices through managing the rate of profitability which accrues to their institutions, and increased RoE. This is most easily achieved through expanding bank leverage, and greater investment in rising asset markets, each of which indirectly amplifies their pay through the equity market:

> As holders of stock options, bank management is interested in the share price, on the exchanges, of their bank's shares. The price of any stock is related to the earnings per share, the capitalization rate on earnings of the bank's perceived risk class, and the expected rate of growth of such earnings. If bank management can accelerate the growth of rate of earnings by increasing leverage without a decrease in the perceived security of the bank's earnings, then the price of shares will rise ...[105]

There is a further extension to this argument which suggests that, as bank stock market values are contingent to some degree on real estate values, the entire market pricing mechanisms for both bank stocks and real estate values are interdependent, and mutually reinforcing. This naturally creates severe and perverse incentives to structure compensation systems to reward expansions in bank lending for real estate investment. If so, this would suggest that linking executive compensation to equity prices in the financial sector which, based on the factors discussed, are subject to potential distortion, is counter-productive, and may itself lead to asset price booms and collapses, if checks on factors such as credit extension, leverage and mortgage financing are not mandated. Naturally, in the absence of focused reform to bank financing capacity, this would require increased monitoring of bank financing and business models by the market. In this vein, many regulatory proposals (to be analysed in the following chapter) have placed increased shareholder power at the centre of regulatory reform.[106] However, the GFC demonstrated the impotence

---

[104] Lucian A. Bebchuk & Holger Spamann, 'Regulating Bankers' Pay' (2010) 98 GEORGETOWN LAW J. 247.

[105] Minsky, *Stabilizing An Unstable Economy* 266.

[106] Costas Stephanou, 'Rethinking Market Discipline: Lessons from the Financial Crisis' (2010) World Bank Policy Research Working Paper Series 5227.

of market discipline as a regulatory tool, amongst other things for the design and regulation of compensation contracts.

THE PROBLEM OF BANK GOVERNANCE THEORY

There are a number of possible reasons for this. Perhaps the most serious is that agency theory has proven extremely limited in explaining how governance ought to be structured at financial institutions. As was noted in Chapter 2, agency theory suggests, inter alia, that firm ownership structure and the relative power of shareholders determine the capacity of firm owners to influence risk taking. This framework, however, is incomplete in explaining how corporate governance works within financial institutions. Agency theory – like all theories wedded to notions of market efficiency – assumes that financial firms operate in competitive markets which are structured by market forces to operate in the same managerial way as all other types of firm.[107] There are, however, several limitations to this view, which may be drawn out by a brief overview of some of agency theory's core assumptions:

(i) for the capital structure of the firm to be optimal, limited leverage is required (the so-called Modigliani-Miller theorem[108]);
(ii) the locus of information asymmetry exists between managers and owners of the firm (the principal–agent problem); and
(iii) the firm operates in normal and competitive markets.

In the case of banks, however, these assumptions simply do not apply. Firstly, as we have noted in this chapter, the business models of financial institutions require the use of significant leverage. The nature of financial institutions is to operate with a maturity mismatch between assets (usually long-term loans) and liabilities (usually short-term demand deposits), with a reserve requirement constraint. A bank's profits increase directly in proportion to the number of (good) loans it makes. Axiomatically this requires a high degree of financial leverage, which renders banks vulnerable to confidence and liquidity shocks. More importantly from a corporate governance perspective, this provides shareholders with strong incentives for banks to operate with low capital levels, as higher leverage and riskier business strategies will generally increase the stock price of

---

[107] Penny Ciancanelli & Jose Antonio Reyes Gonzalez, 'Corporate Governance in Banking: A Conceptual Framework' (2000), http://ssrn.com/abstract=253714.

[108] Francis Modigliani & Merton Miller, 'The Cost of Capital, Corporation Finance and the Theory of Investment' (1958) 48 AM. ECON. REV. 261.

the firm, and thereby shareholder wealth. More specifically, managers have an incentive to increase the bank's leverage, particularly if the ownership structure of the bank is dispersed.

Secondly, the agency problem in relation to financial institutions is much more complex than agency relationships in non-financial corporations. Due to the high default risks associated with bank business models, and the attendant vulnerability to systemic contagion, banks are provided with regulatory safety nets, including deposit guarantee schemes and lender-of-last-resort facilities. These guarantees add layers of complexity to the traditional agency dynamic. Bank executives – agency theory's agents – must have regard to a much more diverse group of principals than merely their shareholders, particularly bank regulators. These regulators may constrain certain corporate activities, and may even insist upon the implementation of prescribed governance mechanisms.[109] Moreover, the balance sheets of banks are much more opaque than those of non-financial firms, and therefore monitoring their activities is much more difficult. The complexity of certain financial assets and their often hidden exposures to one another makes the task of valuing banks much more demanding.[110] For example, in the context of the GFC, Avgouleas notes:

> There is clear evidence that, in the time leading to the GFC, market discipline … failed. The two most important market-based indices of a bank's financial health, the CDS premium and the share price showed (with the exception of Northern Rock) no sign of the trouble that lay ahead. Moreover, investors and analysts, instead of exercising any kind of discipline over bank management by asking for the building up of higher capital buffers, were just pushing for higher returns at the height of the boom. Such pressure from the markets provided even bigger incentives to bank management to take ever higher amounts of debt to leverage the bank's balance sheet to expand its profits.[111]

These factors place severe limits on the capacity of incentive contracts to be effective in aligning the long-term interests of managers and shareholders, and simultaneously safeguarding financial stability, either at the institutional or systemic level.

---

[109] For discussion, see Peter O. Mulbert, 'Corporate Governance of Banks after the Financial Crisis – Theory, Evidence, Reforms' (2010) ECGI Law Working Paper No. 130/2009.

[110] For example, studies demonstrate that analysts disagree more in valuing bank bonds than in valuing other non-financial company debt. See Donald P. Morgan, 'Rating Banks: Risk and Uncertainty in an Opaque Industry' (2002) 92 AM. ECON. REV. 874.

[111] Avgouleas, *Governance of Global Financial Markets* 120.

Thirdly, and related to the second point, the markets that banks operate in are heavily regulated and controlled. Banks have traditionally operated under the implicit guarantee of rescue in the event of insolvency.[112] Deposit insurance has the effect of lowering incentives for outsider control, weakening market discipline. This creates several competing issues, and means that a large degree of moral hazard is generated by the fragility of banks' capital structure. In relation to executive compensation in particular, government guarantees to bail out financial institutions may provide incentives for extreme risk taking by bank managers. Research reveals that the value of this 'too-big-to-fail' (TBTF) subsidy in terms of reducing funding costs is significant; for example, estimates for its value to UK banks range from £30 billion to £120 billion per year.[113] Any upside benefits accrue to top executives and shareholders by virtue of the positive effect on stock prices that high risk taking has on bank value, whereas downside costs are borne by taxpayers and governments. The incentives generated to assume excess risks place bank executives and shareholders in conflict with those who bear the costs of deposit insurance and the TBTF subsidy. This, in itself, may affect the sensitivity of pay and performance at banks, especially in periods leading up to financial crises.[114]

LEVERAGE, GOVERNANCE AND RISK TAKING

On the basis of these discussions, it is clear that compensation systems are pro-cyclical and, particularly during euphoric periods, there are profound incentives for firm management to link compensation to equity prices, especially in the financial sector, which has the advantage of a debt structure under which gains are amplified by leverage.[115] This is

---

[112] Renée Adams & Hamid Mehran, 'Is Corporate Governance Different for Bank Holding Companies?' (2003) FRB NEW YORK, http://papers.ssrn.com/sol3/papers.cfm?abstract_id=387561.

[113] For a discussion on this literature, see Joseph Noss & Rhiannon Sowerbutts, 'The Implicit Subsidy of Banks' (2012) Bank of England Financial Stability Paper No. 15, 10; see also Stefan Jacewitz & Jonathan Pogach, 'Deposit Rate Advantages at the Largest Banks' (2013) FDIC Working Paper, https://papers.ssrn.com/sol3/papers.cfm?abstract_id=2018474.

[114] Sudhakar Balachandran, Bruce Kogut & Hitesh Harnal, 'The Probability of Default, Excessive Risk, and Executive Compensation: A Study of Financial Services Firms from 1995 to 2008' (2010) Columbia Business School Research Paper, http://ssrn.com/abstract=1914542.

[115] Haldane et al, 'Contribution of the Financial Sector' 99.

apparent in the choice of compensation systems at banks prior to the GFC: 'leverage was an endogenous managerial choice variable during the crisis, affected by managerial compensation'.[116] If an executive cashes in his shares prior to any revaluation, there is no downside risk to leveraging, because the costs of failure are not internalised. In this vein, there have been a large number of studies which show, inter alia, a positive association between risk taking and the sensitivity of the CEO's wealth to return volatility[117] and the sensitivity of the CEO's compensation to short-term earnings per share;[118] a greater need for government assistance for firms with compensation incentives that promoted higher risk taking;[119] and higher volumes of share sales and low volumes of

---

[116] Sjoerd Van Bekkum, 'Inside Debt & Bank Risk', 19 December 2013, https://www.aeaweb.org/aea/2014conference/program/retrieve.php.

[117] Chesney et al, 'Managerial Incentives', finding that 'stock holdings can induce substantial risk-taking incentives, qualifying common beliefs regarding the central role of stock options. Finally, only asset incentives explain asset risk-taking of U.S. financial institutions before the 2007/08 crisis'; Robert DeYoung, Emma Y. Peng & Meng Yan, 'Executive Compensation and Business Policy Choices at U.S. Commercial Banks' (2010) http://ssrn.com/abstract=1544490, finding 'strong evidence that bank CEOs responded to contractual risktaking incentives by taking more risk; systematic evidence that bank boards altered CEO compensation to encourage executives to exploit new growth opportunities; and more limited evidence that bank boards set CEO incentives in a manner designed to moderate excessive risk-taking. These relationships are strongest … after deregulation and technological change had expanded banks' capacities for risk-taking, and for the largest banking companies, which are better strategically positioned to exploit these opportunities'; Felix Suntheim, 'Managerial Compensation in the Financial Service Industry' (2010) http://ssrn.com/abstract=1592163, finding that '[b]anks which endowed their CEO with high risk taking incentives performed worse in the period after the Lehman collapse in terms of accounting performance … [and] … over time bank risk has been positively correlated with CEOs' risk taking incentives.'

[118] See Sugato Bhattacharyya & Amiyatosh K. Purnanandam, 'Risk-Taking by Banks: What Did We Know and When Did We Know It?' (2011) AFA 2012 Chicago Meetings Paper, finding that '[t]he composition of risks assumed by U.S. commercial banks underwent a dramatic transformation over the years leading up to the financial crisis: between 2000 and 2006 idiosyncratic risk dropped by almost half while systematic risk doubled. These patterns, more pronounced in banks with heavy involvement in residential mortgage lending and securitization, were accompanied by higher earnings per share performance. Their managers … earned significant amounts through compensation plans heavily geared to short-term earnings.'

[119] Amar Gande & Swaminathan L. Kalpathy, 'CEO Compensation and Risk-taking at Financial Firms: Evidence from U.S. Federal Loan Assistance'

share purchases by bank CEOs than would be expected if banks were being managed with long-term performance in mind.[120] Consistent with these findings however, the increase in leverage encouraged by these incentive systems may be paradoxical; high leverage also magnifies losses when returns on assets are low and a small negative return on an asset relative to the borrowing rate can wipe out much, or even all, of a bank's equity. Leverage therefore, whilst boosting short-term returns, also increases financial fragility, and exposes the institution concerned to huge financing risks, which may result in severe losses in stock value over the medium or long term.

There are studies since the GFC which have purported to show that banks with 'good' corporate governance and remuneration systems, i.e. those in which shareholder and manager interests were most aligned, performed worse than other banks during the GFC, and suffered the most losses. Many commentators, most notably Fahlenbrach and Stulz,[121] for example, highlight the significant equity positions that senior management at financial institutions controlled and the paper losses that they incurred once stock prices began to fall sharply. Bankers at institutions which failed also did not take massive risks; most of the MBS products purchased by banks were low-yield, low-risk.[122] However, in a key caveat

(2013) http://ssrn.com/abstract=1865870, finding that 'those firms where CEOs had the highest risk-taking incentives, as measured by high levels of vega, received federal financing for a longer period of time'.

[120] In a sample of 14 large US financial institutions between 2000 and 2008, the CEOs of these banks, as a group, bought shares in their respective banks 73 times, yet sold their shares 2,048 times. The value of the shares bought was $36 million, yet the shares sold totalled $3.46 billion. Even after accounting for the precipitous collapse in share prices in 2008, the net gain to the CEO sample was $649 million. It is also noteworthy that the 'losses' that top executives at these firms incurred were *unrealised* – or paper – losses. The *realised* gains were immense. Over the 14 firms in the sample, officers and directors received almost $127 billion in bonuses and stock awards *alone* between them. See Sanjai Bhagat & Brian J. Bolton, 'Investment Bankers' Culture of Ownership?' (2010), http://ssrn.com/abstract=1664520.

[121] Rudiger Fahlenbrach & Rene M. Stulz, 'Bank CEO Incentives and the Credit Crisis' (2011) 99 J. FIN. ECON. 11 (hereinafter Fahlenbrach & Stulz, 'Bank CEO Incentives'). The value of stock and options in the 'average' bank CEO's portfolio was more than 10 times the value of the CEO's salary in 2006 and CEOs on average owned 1.6% of the outstanding stock of their bank. See also Jeffrey Friedman, 'Bank Pay and the Financial Crisis', *Wall Street Journal* (New York, 28 September 2009).

[122] Viral V. Acharya & Matthew Richardson, 'Causes of the Financial Crisis' (2009) 21 CRITICAL REV. 195.

to the findings expressed in the paper, Fahlenbrach and Stulz acknowledge that their thesis holds only if the market for stocks is efficient. If the market is not efficient, the market 'might put more weight on short-run results and mis-valuation could create pressure on management to take actions it would not take in an efficient market'.[123] On the basis of foregoing discussions, it is clear that assumptions of market efficiency, in relation to the financial sector especially, are almost certainly flawed. Consistent with this, in relation to the GFC, evidence shows that 'insiders' at banks heavily exposed to sub-prime markets increased their equity selling from mid-2006 onwards, suggesting that executives at banks at least partly perceived the significant risks their banks were assuming.[124] Moreover, there is strong evidence of a positive link between the level of residual executive pay and a firm's risk measures.[125] Further, optimal compensation might place more weight on short-term results to take advantage of speculative behaviour in the stock market and CEOs might favour cash bonuses rather than increasing their equity wealth if their options are not realisable until a later period.[126]

There are therefore competing views as to the role of equity-based pay in contributing to the causes of the GFC. However, the ramifications of either side of the debate on this issue mean that the continued use of stock-based compensation is an exercise in futility. If, as contended by this book, this compensation provided incentives for short-termism, which was facilitated by the complexity, opacity and regulatory arbitrage engaged in by bankers, stock options and other forms of equity compensation are an inefficient method of incentivising managers and, further, contribute to financial instability. Moreover, if financial markets are not efficient at pricing risk, there are opportunities to exploit these inefficiencies in the short term by making compensation awards contingent on asset price increases, without causing alarm to regulators and investors, simply through the imitation of competitor strategies and increased leverage. On the other hand, if these options did not a priori provide

---

[123] Fahlenbrach & Stulz, 'Bank CEO incentives' 12.

[124] Peter Cziraki, 'Trading by Bank Insiders Before and During the 2007–2008 Financial Crisis' (2014) http://ssrn.com/abstract=1962719.

[125] Ing-Haw Cheng, Harrison G. Hong & Jose A. Scheinkman, 'Yesterday's Heroes: Compensation and Creative Risk-Taking' (2011) ECGI Finance Working Paper No. 285/2010; see also Marco Becht, Patrick Bolton & Ailsa Roell, 'Why Bank Governance Is Different' (2011) 27 OX. REV. ECON. POL. 437.

[126] Patrick Bolton, Jose Scheinkman & Wei Xiong, 'Executive Compensation and Short-Termist Behaviour in Speculative Markets' (2006) 73 REV. ECON. STUD. 577.

inappropriate risk-taking incentives, current corporate governance arrangements remain fundamentally flawed; the use of stock options and other forms of incentive pay did *not* guard against the build-up of excessive risk. This poses serious questions regarding the assumptions underpinning their use – that good governance requires the use of stock options and other performance-related pay to align the interests of managers with shareholders. On this basis, the actual state of knowledge of market participants is irrelevant. Even where it can be shown that there is no overt assumption of risk linked to stock-based compensation awards, the net result will not differ, due to market short-termism, and because market participants are boundedly rational, have limited computational abilities and may be pressured into pursuing risk by professional career concerns.[127] As posited by Minsky, the transition to fragility is driven by competition between banks for market share. Herding may thereby be tacitly encouraged by investments which appear to provide commensurate risk-adjusted returns and regulation which requires banks to hold 'safe' capital.[128] The risk premia attached to these investments might appear valid but mask latent dangers which require greater analysis of the economic or financial environment; however, the cognitive limitations of market participants may prevent executives from recognising the dangers in these products, or price distortions in the market. This line of argument does not contradict the findings of the studies on stock option wealth at banks cited previously; instead, it reveals the futility of relying on stock-based governance to a significant extent, because (if one accepts the findings of those studies) stock-based governance provided no protection for shareholders. Of course, this may mean that future attempts to reform compensation incentives are doomed to fail, because

---

[127] See discussions of behavioural finance in the previous chapter. Further, '… it is worth asking what would have happened if Mr. Fuld had somehow realized in 2005 that the mortgage business was a time bomb and had gotten Lehman out of it. Within a year, its profits would have sagged and its share price collapsed. Mr. Fuld would have been labeled a dunce, and might have lost his job. The same can be said of Jimmy Cayne of Bear Stearns and Stan O'Neal of Merrill Lynch, the two runners-up in the richest bank C.E.O. sweepstakes of 2006.' See Floyd Norris, 'It May be Outrageous, but Wall Street Pay Didn't Cause the Crisis', *New York Times* (New York, 30 July 2009), http://www.nytimes.com/2009/07/31/business/31norris.html?_r=0.

[128] Jeffrey Friedman & Wladimir Kraus, *Engineering The Financial Crisis: Systemic Risk and the Failure of Regulation* (University of Pennsylvania Press, 2011).

they are predicated on a fallacy – that equity-based pay remains the best way to incentivise management to protect shareholder equity, and thereby the bank.

CONCLUSION

The ramifications of the foregoing analysis are far reaching, and have serious consequences for the design of executive compensation systems. Whilst the concept of pay for performance is certainly a laudable mechanism when used correctly, it is limited when compensation is not adjusted for long-term risk. On the basis of the foregoing analysis of the GFC, it is reasonable to postulate that there is a self-reinforcing dynamic between compensation systems and asset bubbles. In the case of the pre-GFC real estate bubble, it is likely that the massive rewards at stake, when coupled with the view that the housing market would consistently exhibit above-inflation price rises, convinced bank executives to increase leverage in the pursuit of greater returns.[129] This itself fed the boom in real estate prices, as credit was extended to fund both increased lending in the mortgage markets and greater volumes of securitisation and derivative trading.

There is no doubt that the postulated relationship is highly complex, and there is a complicated pattern of causation running from executive compensation packages to stock prices, and to real estate values. However, there is strong evidence that this dynamic exists and, if so, it is important to consider asset price increases beyond the stock market and their potential effects on executive compensation, because large price changes in certain asset markets, especially real estate, will generally affect equity prices.[130] It is precisely because bubbles in one market will indirectly boost prices in other asset markets, including stock markets, that the use of stock prices as proxies for long-run value is entirely undermined, if expectations of future price rises are carried by unwarranted optimism.

---

[129] For example, one of the key findings of the FSA in its investigation into the failure of RBS was based on a management philosophy, which, amongst other things, emphasised the importance of 'an overt focus on capital "efficiency", i.e. on high leverage'. See FSA Board Report, *Failure of RBS* 233.

[130] For example, see David G. McMillan, 'Long-Run Stock Price-House Relation: Evidence from an ESTR Model' (2012) 32 ECON. BULL. 1737; Nicholas Apergis & Lambros Lambrinidis, 'More Evidence on the Relationship between the Stock and the Real Estate Market' (2011) 85 J. ECON. LIT. 1.

Whether one views the GFC as a product of compensation awards, or due to a deficiency in market discipline, or views these factors as two sides of the same coin, it is clear that focus must be diverted from using options linked to equity prices as a singular metric with which to assess executive performance, through the introduction of safeguards into executive compensation contracts to mitigate the effects of short-term strategies, alternative measures of performance evaluation, and even structural reform of the banking sector. Any compensation packages for executives which contain these elements ought to rccognise the potential for a collapse in asset prices. Where asset prices fall, (generally) stock prices fall also.[131] Moreover, banking crises often lead to a prolonged slump in asset values, particularly in housing and equity markets.[132] The build-up of leverage within the system through the increased availability of credit is the most significant sign that a potential asset collapse is imminent. On this basis, measures ought to be adopted to limit the incentives to inculcate financial conditions under which asset prices are likely to collapse. The potential for a sharp reduction in asset values would suggest that utilizing stock-based pay awards with short-term time horizons prior to vesting, or bonuses based upon the performance of share prices over a short-term period ought to be limited. Reducing incentives to leverage will therefore reduce the probability of financial crashes.

The following chapter comprehensively reviews the reforms made to executive compensation systems at financial institutions following the GFC across the US, UK and EU, before making proposals for further reforms in a later chapter.

---

[131] Francis A. Longstaff, 'The Subprime Credit Crisis and Contagion in Financial Markets' (2010) 97 J. FIN. ECON. 436.

[132] Typically following a banking crisis, housing prices drop 35% and equity prices drop 55% over a period of between three-and-a-half and six years. See Carmen M. Reinhart & Kenneth S. Rogoff, 'The Aftermath of Financial Crises' (2009) NBER Working Paper No. 14656.

6. Post-Crisis reform to executive compensation at financial institutions

INTRODUCTORY REMARKS

The previous chapter observed that the GFC was caused to some extent by a flawed understanding of the operation of financial markets and poor incentives in executive compensation contracts. Compensation systems at banks remained largely unfettered until the banking collapses of 2008. Of course, on the basis of those collapses, severe doubt was cast on the capacity of market discipline to act as an effective tool in constraining harmful risk taking,[1] and on the provisions of existing legislation to regulate risks generated by executive compensation structures at financial firms. The view that poor incentives and insider rent seeking were partly to blame for the eruption of the crisis is supported by analysis of the events. Euphoric financial conditions combined with behavioural biases to drive an increase in credit expansion and leverage. The risk management systems and compensation structures at financial institutions were skewed heavily in favour of increased lending volumes and weak due diligence. Executives were rewarded for achieving short-term earnings targets even where earnings from these trades evaporated and it became clear that risk had been underestimated. On this basis, executive compensation reform has been placed at the heart of the regulatory response to the GFC.[2]

---

[1] Costas Stephanou, 'Rethinking Market Discipline: Lessons from the Financial Crisis' (2010) World Bank Policy Research Working Paper Series 5227; Kern Alexander, Rahul Dhumale & John Eatwell, *Global Governance of Financial Systems: The International Regulation of Systemic Risk* (OUP, 2005); Joseph E. Stiglitz, 'Capital Market Liberalization, Economic Growth, and Instability' (2000) 28 WORLD DEVELOPMENT 1075.

[2] See especially, Financial Stability Board, *FSF Principles for Sound Compensation Practices: Implementation Standards* (2009) (hereinafter FSB, *Sound Compensation Practices*). As noted by one renowned economist: 'Whoever dreamed up this crazy compensation system? That's a good question, and the answer leads straight to the doors of the top executives of the companies. So

Accordingly, the regulatory response to these factors will be analysed in this chapter, which will conduct an examination of the reforms to executive compensation post-GFC produced by national and global regulators.[3] For the sake of practicality, description of the reforms will be

---

let's consider the incentives facing the CEO and other top executives of a large bank or investment bank… For them, it's often: Heads, you become richer than Croesus ever imagined; tails, you receive a golden parachute that still leaves you richer than Croesus. So they want to flip those big coins, too.' Alan Blinder, 'Crazy Compensation and the Crisis', *Wall Street Journal* (New York, 28 May 2009).

[3] Of course, there had been some far-reaching reforms to corporate governance in the US following the accounting scandals of the early 21st century. The Public Company Accounting Reform and Investor Protection Act of 2002, Pub. L. No. 107-204, 116 Stat. 745 (July 30, 2002) (Sarbanes-Oxley Act, or 'SOX') in particular instigated some far-reaching reforms in relation to executive conduct. For example, the following measures were included:

(a) SOX prohibits outright any publicly held corporation from making loans to its directors or officers (§ 402);
(b) SOX forces the executive and financial officers of every public company to certify each periodic report filed or submitted to the SEC, and makes it a federal crime to certify such statements knowing they are false (§ 302);
(c) SOX forces the CEO and CFO of any publicly held corporation that is required to file a financial restatement as a result of misconduct to reimburse the corporation for any bonuses received or profits from stock sales realised in the 12-month period following the restatement (§ 304);
(d) SOX prohibits directors and executive officers from selling company stock during benefit plan 'black-out periods' (§ 306); and
(e) SOX makes it unlawful for any officer or director to pursue conduct 'to fraudulently influence, coerce, manipulate, or mislead' the corporation's auditor (§ 303).

The reforms under SOX were envisaged to bring greater protection to investors in public companies by improving disclosure channels and punishing officer and director complicity or negligence in the preparation of corporate accounts. One of the key measures of SOX was that it required claw-back of incentive-based compensation in the event of a financial restatement. This was designed of course to promote the accuracy of corporate accounts. However, as the GFC demonstrated, the legislative response did not address the basic weaknesses in corporate governance in Anglo-American markets, as it focused entirely on improving corporate disclosure by penalising conduct which might give rise to accounting misstatements. This focus was too narrow: there are many ways of producing short-term profits which do not involve accounting tricks or fraudulent financial reporting. Thus, SOX – and other contemporaneous corporate governance reforms – missed the salient weakness in executive compensation contracts which manifested prior to the GFC; these contracts provided incentives for conducted geographically, with discussion of the key regulatory measures adopted in each region (specifically, the US, UK and European Union (EU)), and the recommendations of highly respected supranational regulatory bodies. Each of these geographical levels will have effects on the model of banking and remuneration that subsists in Anglo-American markets; an overwhelming proportion of large financial institutions maintain stock exchange listings in these territories. This will set the stage for a thematic discussion of proposals for future reform in the following chapter.

US REFORM

The Wall Street Reform and Consumer Protection Act of 2010[4] ('Dodd-Frank') was the major piece of US legislation to emerge from the GFC. Its provisions in relation to corporate governance at banks and financial firms are far reaching. Section 956 of Dodd-Frank contains provisions authorising the Federal Reserve and/or the SEC to adopt rules in relation to executive officers, employees or directors of 'covered financial institutions' to limit 'excessive compensation, fees, or benefits' or compensation that 'could lead to material financial loss' at certain systemically significant financial companies.[5] This led to the proposal in 2011 for a rule requiring the deferral of certain forms of variable compensation at covered institutions, although the exact details of this provision have still

---

executives to pursue strategies which would allow them to benefit from short-term positive changes in firm value whilst generating latent issues which might cripple their firms in later years. SOX ought to have focused on reforming the methods through which executives were paid; instead it provided severe penalties for individuals engaging in accounting manipulation. This also had the perverse effect of decreasing pay for performance; in lieu of forfeitable bonus compensation, executives were granted larger base salaries. For discussion, see Roberta Romano & Sanjai Bhagat, 'Reforming Executive Compensation: Focusing and Committing to the Long-term' (2009) 26 YALE J. REG. 359, 363 (hereinafter Romano & Bhagat, 'Reforming Executive Compensation'); see also Daniel A. Cohen, Aiyesha Dey & Thomas Z. Lys, 'The Sarbanes-Oxley Act of 2002: Implications for Compensation Structure and Managerial Risk-Taking' (2007), http://ssrn.com/sol3/papers.cfm?abstract_id=568483.

4 Dodd-Frank Wall Street Reform and Consumer Protection Act, Pub., L. No. 111/203 (July 21, 2010) Pub. L. No. 124 Stat. 1376.

5 The term 'covered financial' includes most financial institutions (banks, investment banks, credit unions, broker-dealers, etc.) that have assets in excess of $1 billion. Dodd-Frank Act § 956 (codified at 12 U.S.C. § 5641).

not been agreed upon by the relevant agencies.[6] Dodd-Frank § 953 requires that companies' annual proxy statements provide an exposition of the relationship between executive compensation and the firms' financial performance, as measured by share price appreciation, dividends and distributions. The explanation must be transparent and give shareholders a clear opportunity to compare executive compensation to firm performance over the relevant period. The proxy statement must also declare whether or not individual employees are permitted to hedge the value of stock they own. Companies must also report the median value of the total executive compensation at their firm (excluding the CEO), and the ratio of pay between the CEO and the median pay of all other employees.[7]

Dodd-Frank also mandates a periodic shareholder vote on named executive officer compensation (so-called 'say-on-pay'), in which shareholders must ratify the pay of named executive officers. Shareholders must also approve payments on severance of employment (so-called 'golden parachutes').[8] However, whilst there is a legal requirement that

---

[6] See Fed. Register Vol. 76, No. 72 / Thursday, April 14, 2011 / Proposed Rule: Incentive-Based Compensation Arrangements, 21170. In relation to incentive compensation, the FDIC notes: 'short-run revenue or profit can often diverge sharply from actual long-run profit because risk outcomes may become clear only over time. Activities that carry higher risk typically yield higher short-term revenue, and an employee who is given incentives to increase short-term revenue or profit, without regard to risk, will naturally be attracted to opportunities to expose the organization to more risk.' See FDIC: Statements of Policy, Guidance on Sound Incentive Compensation Policies, September 16, 2013, http://www.fdic.gov/regulations/laws/rules/5000-5350.html.

[7] This has the potential to be burdensome to companies: '[It] means that for every employee, the company would have to calculate his or her salary, bonus, stock awards, option awards, nonequity incentive plan compensation, change in pension value and nonqualified deferred compensation earnings, and all other compensation (e.g. perquisites). This information would undoubtedly be extremely time-consuming to collect and analyze, making it virtually impossible for a company with thousands of employees to comply with this section of the Act.' See Warren J. Casey & Richard Leu, 'United States: New Executive Compensation Disclosures Under Dodd-Frank', 3 August 2010, http://www.mondaq.com/unitedstates/article.asp?articleid=106962. Despite this, the SEC (as of March 2014) is consulting on a proposed final rule to implement § 953. See SEC, Proposed Rule: Pay Ratio Disclosure, 17 Cfr Parts 229 And 249 Release Nos. 33-9452; 34-70443; File No. S7-07-13.

[8] Dodd-Frank § 951, which amends § 14A of the Securities Exchange Act 1934 to require companies to conduct a shareholder advisory vote on specific executive compensation not less frequently than every three years.

the votes themselves be carried out, these votes do not bind the board of directors, and are not to be construed as capable of overruling the board. Accordingly, these shareholder votes are not to be construed as creating any additional fiduciary duties for directors to follow. The 'say-on-pay' votes may also not limit the power of shareholders to include executive compensation proposals for inclusion in proxy materials.[9]

Under Dodd-Frank § 954 (amending Sarbanes-Oxley Act (SOX) § 304), compensation paid to certain executives at firms is also now subject to potential clawback. SOX § 304 allowed for the clawback of any compensation received by the CEO or the CFO arising in the 12 months following the misreporting of financial information, along with any profit from stock sales during this period. SOX § 304 also required that the CEO or CFO or firm be guilty of misconduct in order for clawback to operate[10] and may only be invoked by the SEC.[11] Dodd-Frank expands both the range of employees this clawback may be invoked against and the timespan over which the power may be invoked. On this basis, § 954 requires that issuer firms devise and disclose clawback policies to reclaim any excess compensation paid to *any* current or former executive officers on the basis of a financial misstatement, and expands the period that clawback may operate in from one year to three years following the date of the original misstatement.[12] 'Excess' compensation in this context refers to the difference in the level of compensation between what the executive was paid and what he/she would have been paid absent the misstatement.[13] These provisions have been criticised in some quarters as unnecessary and unduly prescriptive.[14]

---

[9] On this basis, shareholders may include proposals for compensation packages for senior executives and board members in the proxy statement although, of course, these proposals are not binding.

[10] This was confirmed by the courts in *SEC v Jenkins*, 718 F. Supp. 2d 1070, 1074–77 (D, Ariz. 2010).

[11] *Neer v Pelino*, 389 F. Supp. 2d 648, 657 (E.D. Pa. 2005). This has in practice occurred very rarely. See Jerry W. Markham, 'Regulating Excessive Executive Compensation – Why Bother?' (2007) 2 J. BUS. & TECH. 277, 299.

[12] See Kevin J. Murphy, 'Executive Compensation: Where We Are, and How We Got There' in George Constantinides, Milton Harris & René Stulz (eds), *Handbook of the Economics of Finance: vol. 2A* (North Holland, 2013) 211.

[13] Senate Report No. 111-176, *The Restoring American Financial Stability Act 2010*, 135.

[14] For example, see Stephen M. Bainbridge, 'Dodd-Frank: Quack Federal Corporate Governance Round II' (2011) 95 MINN. LAW REV. 1779 (criticising the Dodd-Frank clawback for unfairly penalising executives and describing the clawback as poorly thought out); see also, Larry E. Ribstein, 'Financial Reform

Under Dodd-Frank § 954, therefore, clawback will only operate in the event of material non-compliance with federal securities law financial reporting requirements. The fact that this does not extend to cases where apparent strong financial performance is later revealed to have been based upon an imprudent assumption of risk or persistent market inefficiencies may be a potential weakness with the legislation. This is especially the case because the recommendations on deferral of variable compensation in the US are rather vague, with a simple requirement that any deferral period be adjusted 'to reflect actual losses or other measures or aspects of performance that are realized or become better known during the deferral period'.[15] In spite of this, many US financial institutions follow guidelines issued by the Basel Committee on Banking Supervision (BCBS) and the Financial Stability Board (FSB), which recommend deferral of significant variable compensation:[16] this is discussed below, and in the following chapter.

Further miscellaneous rules in relation to compensation at financial firms mandated under Dodd-Frank and recently enforced by the SEC include the following:

(i) stock exchanges must adopt listing standards providing that the members of the compensation committee meet enhanced independence standards comparable (but not identical) to what is required for audit committee members under SOX;
(ii) compensation committees may only select compensation consultants, legal counsel or other advisers in compliance with independence standards established by the SEC;
(iii) enhanced disclosure is required regarding the use of compensation consultants and any conflicts of interest;[17] and

---

That Isn't', *FORBES*, 8 July 2010, http://www.forbes.com/2010/07/08/financial-reform-bill-hedge-funds-opinions-columnists-larry-e-ribstein.html (criticising Dodd-Frank clawback provisions as too prescriptive and arguing that the market and individual states ought to be entrusted to formulate clawback policies if they are desirable).

[15] Incentive-Based Compensation Arrangements: Proposed Rule, 76 Fed. Reg. 21,170, 21,180 (April 14, 2011).

[16] BCBS, *Range Of Methodologies For Risk And Performance Alignment Of Remuneration* (2011) (hereinafter BCBS, *Range of Methodologies*).

[17] Securities and Exchange Commission (Release No. 34-68639; File No. SR-NYSE-2012-49) January 11, 2013, Self-Regulatory Organizations; New York Stock Exchange LLC; Notice of Filing of Amendment No. 3, and Order Granting Accelerated Approval for Proposed Rule Change, as Modified by Amendment Nos. 1 and 3, to Amend the Listing Rules for Compensation Committees to

(iv) in the event of bank failure, the Federal Deposit Insurance Corporation (FDIC) is empowered to retrieve all payments made to senior executives two years prior to the start of the resolution process, if the senior executive concerned is 'substantially responsible' for the firm's failure.[18]

UK REFORM

Until the GFC, the main regulatory rules which governed corporate governance and compensation in public companies, including financial institutions, were derived from non-binding governance codes ('The Code') operated by the UK Listing Authority (now the 2012 UK Corporate Governance Code;[19] formerly, the Combined Code on Corporate Governance). The Code's provisions in relation to remuneration relate only to corporate directors; executive officers are excluded from its ambit. The Code recommends that a significant proportion of executive director remuneration should be linked to corporate and individual performance;[20] a proportion of remuneration awarded to directors ought to be deferred;[21] and clawback of remuneration implemented in some circumstances.[22] Despite these recommendations, the Code demands no

---

Comply with Securities Exchange Act Rule 10C-1 and Make Other Related Changes.

[18] Dodd-Frank Act § 210(s)(1), 124 Stat. at 1514; Orderly Liquidation Authority, 76 Fed. Reg. 16,324, 16,338 (proposed March 23, 2011).

[19] Financial Reporting Council, *UK Corporate Governance Code* (2012) (hereinafter FRC, *The Code*).

[20] Ibid. D.1.

[21] 'In normal circumstances, shares granted or other forms of deferred remuneration should not vest, and options should not be exercisable, in less than three years. Directors should be encouraged to hold their shares for a further period after vesting or exercise, subject to the need to finance any costs of acquisition and associated tax liabilities.' Ibid. Schedule A.

[22] 'Consideration should be given to the use of provisions that permit the company to reclaim variable components in exceptional circumstances of misstatement or misconduct.' See ibid. In recent developments, the Association of British Insurers (ABI) claimed that: 'The inclusion of clawback and malus provisions in scheme designs and executive contracts is a recognised way to prevent executives receiving rewards that are undeserved. Shareholders expect to see such provisions included in relevant arrangements and for them to be enforced when appropriate.' See ABI, *Principles of Remuneration* (2011).

explicit standards for director remuneration.[23] Moreover, as it is not legally binding, the Code lacks the requisite clout to ensure the wholesale adoption of risk-adjusted compensation systems across UK-listed financial institutions.

Following the GFC, the Walker Review on Corporate Governance[24] ('the Walker Review') was commissioned to examine specifically the corporate governance arrangements in UK banks. The Review entrusted the enforcement of corporate governance norms to the boards of banks and financial institutions, arguing that:

> [b]oth the UK unitary board structure and the [UK Corporate Governance Code] of the FRC remain fit for purpose. Combined with tougher capital and liquidity requirements and a tougher regulatory stance on the part of the FSA [now FCA], the 'comply or explain' approach to guidance and provisions under the [UK Corporate Governance Code] provides the surest route to better corporate governance practice ...[25]

Notwithstanding these observations, in relation to executive compensation reforms, the Walker Review made proposals for the following:

(i) Rules regarding executive remuneration policies ought to extend not only to senior management and the board of directors, but also to senior traders within the organisations concerned. As these traders were often at the centre of unsustainable build-up in leverage and balance sheet exposures, the Review proposed to extend to the remuneration committees responsibility for setting remuneration for highly paid executives below board level.[26]

---

[23] Other than to suggest that: 'Levels of remuneration should be sufficient to attract, retain and motivate directors of the quality required to run the company successfully but a company should avoid paying more than is necessary for this purpose.' FRC, *The Code* D.1.

[24] David Walker, *A Review of Corporate Governance In UK Banks and Other Financial Industry Entities: Final Recommendations* (2009) (hereinafter 'the Walker Review').

[25] Ibid. Recommendation 10.

[26] Ibid. Recommendation 29. Under Recommendation 31: 'For FTSE 100-listed banks and comparable unlisted entities such as the largest building societies, the remuneration committee report for the 2010 year of account and thereafter should disclose in bands the number of "high end" employees, including executive board members, whose total expected remuneration in respect of the reported year is in a range of £1 million to £2.5 million, in a range of £2.5 million to £5 million and in £5 million bands thereafter and, within each

(ii) Executive officers and 'high-end' employees ought to be required to maintain significant equity stakes in their firms, of an amount in line with their total historic compensation. The vesting of equity awards should not be accelerated following the cessation of employment (the 'golden parachute') unless requested on compassionate grounds.[27]

(iii) Executive remuneration in Large Complex Financial Institutions (LCFIs) ought to be calibrated to focus on long-term and sustainable investments rather than on short-term earnings. Scales of deferment ought to be used to ensure attention is given to longer-term objectives.[28] There should be a significant deferral of incentive payments for all 'high-end executives' based on specific risk adjustment mechanisms. To this end, up to two-thirds of cash bonuses ought to be deferred, with at least half of pay or bonuses to be in the form of a long-term incentive scheme with half vesting after three years and the rest after five years.[29]

The Walker Review thus endorsed the view that executive compensation rules in financial institutions ought to be both risk sensitive to changes in the financial environment and staggered in award. This, in some ways, reflects the view adopted under Dodd-Frank; the significant divergence between the two jurisdictions is that compensation clawback policies are not required of financial institutions in the UK; although the UK Corporate Governance Code recommends that firms consider such a policy, no legal requirement is in place.[30]

On the basis of the recommendations by the Walker Review, the FSA included requisite provisions in its revised Remuneration Code of August 2009,[31] updated following the abolition of the FSA in 2013 and its replacement with the Financial Conduct Authority (FCA). The FCA

---

band, the main elements of salary, cash bonus, deferred shares, performance-related long-term awards and pension contribution. Such disclosures should be accompanied by an indication to the extent possible of the areas of business activity to which these higher bands of remuneration relate.'

[27] Ibid. Recommendation 34.

[28] Ibid. Recommendation 33.

[29] Ibid.

[30] In fact, as of September 2011, only 20% of FTSE 100 companies used clawback policies. See Department for Business, Innovation & Skills, *Executive Remuneration: Discussion Paper* (2011) 117.

[31] Financial Services Authority, *Policy Statement: Reforming Remuneration Practices in Financial Services PS 09/15* (2009).

finalised its own Remuneration Code in 2014 ('Rem-Code').[32] The provisions of the Rem-Code apply to large banks although the FCA has reserved the right to apply it to other, smaller entities. The principles are subsumed under the overarching rule that: 'A firm must establish, implement and maintain remuneration policies, procedures and practices that are consistent with and promote effective risk management.'[33] There are also 12 prescriptive principles which operate under the Rem-Code, as well as detailed guidance on the structure of remuneration systems at LCFIs.[34] These principles underscore the recognition that remuneration awards in the financial sector tend to recognise short-term revenue generation and profit targets, giving staff in financial institutions incentives to pursue practices with the aim of undertaking higher risk investments or activities which provided higher income in the short run despite exposing the institution to higher potential losses in the longer run.[35] To this end, the Rem-Code requires that:

> A *firm* must ensure that the assessment of performance is set in a multi-year framework in order to ensure that the assessment process is based on longer-term performance and that the actual payment of performance-based components of *remuneration* is spread over a period which takes account of the underlying business cycle of the *firm* and its business risks.[36]

Finally, the Rem-Code recommends that non-financial indicators of performance ought to be included in the assessment of employee performance and used as the basis for a significant portion of compensation awards. In particular, the Rem-Code recommends that compensation ought to be adjusted where it can be demonstrated that effective risk management and behavioural norms are not adhered to. Specifically, the Rem-Code states that: 'Poor performance as assessed by non-financial metrics such as poor risk management or other behaviours

---

32 Financial Conduct Authority, *Remuneration Code* (2014) (hereinafter FCA, *Rem-Code*).

33 Ibid. Sysc 19A.2.1.

34 Ibid. Sysc 19A.3.7–19A.3.30. These Principles set down rules for such issues as the best practice for corporate governance, compliance and risk management, the calculation of bonus remuneration, deferral of bonus payments and risk adjustment of long-term incentive plans.

35 Financial Services Authority, *Reforming Remuneration Practices in Financial Services: Feedback on CP 09/10 and Final Rules PS 09/15* (2009) 1.5.

36 FCA, *Rem-Code* Sysc 19A.3.38 (italics in original).

contrary to firm values can pose significant risks for a firm and should, as appropriate, override metrics of financial performance.'[37]

Finally, there are also, of course, the much-talked-about limits to bankers' bonuses recommended by the European Parliament, which were implemented recently by the EU Commission. The UK government was hugely resistant to these proposals (even launching legal action to attempt to prevent their implementation[38]), although they now have legal effect in all EU countries; they are therefore dealt with in the following section, which discusses EU-level reform.

EU RECOMMENDATIONS

The EU responded to the GFC – characteristically – with piecemeal reform,[39] devolving much of the implementation of reformed financial standards to Member States.[40] The Commission has issued several Recommendations[41] in relation to executive remuneration, which amplify previous Commission pronouncements on executive pay.[42] The Commission Recommendation on Remuneration Policies in the Financial Sector[43] ('EC Recommendation') argued for the establishment of a pan-European supervision regime of executive pay arrangements at financial institutions.[44] Whilst mirroring the UK Walker Review Recommendations,

---

[37] Ibid. Sysc 19A.3.37.

[38] Alex Barker, Daniel Schäfer & George Parker, 'George Osborne takes EU to Court over Bank Bonus Cap' *Financial Times* (London, 25 September 2013) http://ft.com.

[39] Luca Enriques & Matteo Gatti, 'The Uneasy Case for Top-Down Corporate Law Harmonization in the European Union' (2006) 27 UNIV. OF PENN. J. INT. ECON. LAW 939.

[40] Guido Ferrarini, Niamh Moloney & Maria-Cristina Ungureanu, 'Executive Remuneration in Crisis: A Critical Assessment of Reforms in Europe' (2010) 10 J. CORP. LAW STUD. 73.

[41] EC Commission, Recommendation Complementing Recommendations 2004/913/EC and 2005/162 (C(2009) 3177); EC Commission, Recommendation on Remuneration Policies in the Financial Sector (C(2009) 3159) (hereinafter EC Commission, Remuneration Recommendation); see also EC Commission, Green Paper on Corporate Governance in Financial Institutions and Remuneration Policies (C(2010) 284).

[42] In particular, see Commission Recommendations 2004/913/EC and 2005/162 (C(2009).

[43] EC Commission, Remuneration Recommendation.

[44] Especially to avoid the effects of cross-border competitive pressures. See ibid. para. 6.

this stands in marked contrast to the approach adopted under Dodd-Frank, which requires oversight of the pay of bank executive officers only. The EC also recommended that more qualitative measures of bank officer performance could be utilised in place of standard quantitative metrics such as stock price or earnings.[45]

The EC Recommendation invited Member States to adopt measures in four major areas: (1) structure of the remuneration policy; (2) governance; (3) disclosure; and (4) supervision by competent authorities. Its provisions were designed to apply to staff whose 'professional activities have a material impact on the risk profile of the financial undertaking'.[46] Accordingly, remuneration awards ought to be calibrated to align the 'personal objectives of staff members with the long-term interests of the financial undertaking concerned'[47] and the assessment of performance on which this remuneration is based ought to be a longer-term horizon than currently employed at many financial institutions.[48] Clawback also ought to be considered as a risk-reducing mechanism.[49] Deferment of bonus payments should be mandated across executive compensation systems to reduce the impact of any tail-risk in a financial institution's investments.[50] Significantly, the EC Recommendation also proposed that the 'actual payment of performance-based components of remuneration is spread over the business cycle of the company',[51] which is also enshrined in the UK Rem-Code. This significant and potentially rewarding principle is also complemented by the proposals of several other regulatory bodies. It captures a much-needed principle of requisite compensation reform; namely, that payments for performance ought to be staggered across a significantly drawn-out timescale, in order to allow any latent risks attendant to the institutions concerned – and thereby any inefficiencies in

---

45 Ibid. section II, 5.4, which states: 'When determining individual performance, non-financial criteria, such as compliance with internal rules and procedures, as well as compliance with the standards governing the relationship with clients and investors should be taken into account.'

46 Ibid. para. 13.

47 Ibid. para. 14.

48 Ibid. The Recommendation notes: '… The assessment of the performance-based components of remuneration should be based on longer-term performance and take into account the outstanding risks associated with the performance. The assessment of performance should be set in a multi-year framework, for example of three to five years, in order to ensure that the assessment process is based on longer term performance …'

49 Ibid. 5.1.

50 Ibid. 4.4.

51 Ibid. 5.2.

the market-pricing mechanism – to be smoothed out. The application of this proposal will therefore be discussed further in the following chapter.

Perhaps the most contentious regulatory proposal in relation to bankers' pay to arise from the GFC has been the pan-European introduction of a cap on bankers' bonuses, which was included in the revised Capital Requirements Directive (CRD IV).[52] The cap applies to all staff at EU banks and staff at non-EU banks operating in the EU, and shall apply to any bonus payments which are made in relation to any financial year following 2013–14.[53] The basic principles are as follows:

(i) There is a default position that variable compensation must be capped to the same level as fixed compensation (1:1), although with shareholder approval, a ratio of 1:2 will be permitted. Obtaining shareholder approval in this context requires a super-majority – a 66 per cent majority from shareholders representing a quorum of at least 50 per cent of the voting shares or, if that quorum is not achieved, then a 75 per cent majority is needed.
(ii) Up to 25 per cent of the bonus may be paid in long-term instruments valued on a discounted basis (which will result in a ratio of greater than 1:2). These instruments must be deferred for at least five years to be eligible for the discount. If a bank chooses to pay more than 25 per cent of a bonus in these instruments, any excess will not benefit from the discount. The European Banking Authority (EBA) published guidelines on the applicable discount rate in March 2014.[54]
(iii) At least 50 per cent of the variable remuneration must consist of shares or equivalent instruments which reflect the credit quality of

---

[52] Directive 2013/36/EU of the European Parliament and of the Council of 26 June 2013 on access to the activity of credit institutions and the prudential supervision of credit institutions and investment firms, amending Directive 2002/87/EC and repealing Directives 2006/48/EC and 2006/49/EC [2013] OJ L176/338.

[53] The cap was not included in the AIFM Directive, and there are no plans to apply its provisions to alternative fund managers. See Directive 2011/61/EU of the European Parliament and of the Council of 8 June 2011 on Alternative Investment Fund Managers and amending Directives 2003/41/EC and 2009/65/EC and Regulations (EC) No 1060/2009 and (EU) No 1095/2010 (OJ L174/1).

[54] European Banking Authority, Guidelines on the Applicable Notional Discount Rate for Variable Remuneration', EBA/GL/2014/01, 27 March 2014, https://www.eba.europa.eu/documents/10180/643987/EBA-GL-2014-01+%28Final+Guidelines+on+the+discount+rate+for+remuneration%29.pdf.

the institution as a going concern or which can be converted to equity in adverse circumstances (for example, contingent convertible bonds). Moreover, at least 40 per cent of the variable remuneration must be deferred over a period of not less than three to five years. Where the variable remuneration component is of a particularly high amount (in the UK this is currently set at £500,000), at least 60 per cent must be deferred.

(iv) All bonus payments remain subject to malus and/or clawback, in certain circumstances.[55]

The bonus cap under CRD IV is designed to be wide ranging, and to catch all categories of staff that hold senior management positions or whose activities designate them a 'material risk taker'.[56] Moreover, recent amendments by the EBA to the scope of the cap may result in an even greater number of staff being caught by it. To this end, the following regulatory technical guidance was issued in December 2013 by the EBA to determine how to apply the term 'material risk taker' to bank staff:

(i) if the individual's total remuneration exceeds €500,000 per year. However, an individual earning up to €750,000 may be excluded from the cap if it is determined by the employer that the individual is not, in fact, taking or managing risks. Further, an individual earning between €750,000 and €1 million may be excluded from the cap if the exclusion is approved by the national regulator, and an individual earning €1 million or more may be excluded from the cap if the exclusion is approved by the EBA itself; and/or
(ii) if the individual is part of the 0.3 per cent of staff with the highest remuneration in the institution or firm; and/or
(iii) if the individual's remuneration bracket is equal to or greater than the lowest total remuneration of senior management and other risk takers.[57]

---

55 For a summary, see Freshfields Bruckhaus Deringer, 'New EU Rules on Bankers' Pay (Including the Bonus Cap)', Briefing, May 2013, http://www.freshfields.com.

56 CRD IV defines 'Identified Staff' as: 'senior management, risk takers, staff engaged in control functions and any employee receiving total remuneration that takes them into the same remuneration bracket as senior management and risk takers, whose professional activities have a material impact on their risk profile'. See Directive 2013/36/EU.

57 European Banking Authority, Final draft regulatory technical standards on criteria to identify categories of staff whose professional activities have a

INTERNATIONAL REFORM: THE FINANCIAL STABILITY BOARD, THE BASEL COMMITTEE ON BANKING SUPERVISION AND THE INSTITUTE OF INTERNATIONAL FINANCE

Global standards setting is highly challenging, particularly due to the lack of legal control that may be exerted by supranational 'soft' law.[58] However, two global authorities on the financial system working in conjunction with one another (the FSB and the BCBS), and a third working independently (the Institute of International Finance (IIF), the world's only global association of financial institutions) have produced detailed guidance on executive compensation reform.

In April 2009 the FSB published nine principles for the achievement of sound compensation practices for financial institutions[59] ('FSB Principles'). Following this, the FSB's 2010 Peer Review of its implementation standards delegated responsibility for devising methodologies for

---

material impact on an institution's risk profile under Article 94(2) of Directive 2013/36/EU, 16 December 2013, http://www.eba.europa.eu.

[58] Chris Brummer, 'How International Financial Law Works (and How It Doesn't)' (2011) 99 GEORGETOWN LAW J. 247.

[59] These comprised:

(i) The firm's board of directors must actively oversee the compensation system's design and operation.
(ii) The firm's board of directors must monitor and review the compensation system to ensure the system operates as intended.
(iii) Staff engaged in financial and risk control must be independent, have appropriate authority, and be compensated in a manner that is independent of the business areas they oversee and commensurate with their key role in the firm.
(iv) Compensation must be adjusted for all types of risk.
(v) Compensation outcomes must be symmetric with risk outcomes.
(vi) Compensation payout schedules must be sensitive to the time horizon of risks.
(vii) The mix of cash, equity and other forms of compensation must be consistent with risk alignment.
(viii) Supervisory review of compensation practices must be rigorous and sustained, and deficiencies must be addressed promptly with supervisory action.
(ix) Firms must disclose clear, comprehensive and timely information about their compensation practices to facilitate constructive engagement by all stakeholders. FSB, *Sound Compensation Practices* 2–3.

risk and performance alignment to the BCBS,[60] resulting in the publication of the BCBS Range of Methodologies ('BCBS Range').[61] One of the key principles noted in the report is that 'the adjustment of remuneration to risk and performance is a key element to reduce incentives for excessive risk-taking in banks'.[62] The BCBS Range acknowledges that the compensation systems in most international banks feature deferral and vesting periods for variable remuneration and that some have instituted clawbacks applying to senior executive officers; however, these periods vary greatly across institutions and generally apply only to very senior staff.[63] The BCBS Range also recognises that several obstacles limit the effectiveness of remuneration based upon financial performance, particularly those associated with the manner in which 'future outcomes are captured, [of] the integration and proper allocation of costs or losses, and the use of income versus revenues'.[64]

The IIF released similar principles during the most severe period of the GFC ('IIF compensation principles').[65] This was, in part, a consequence of the view that 'much of the recent criticism of industry compensation practices has focused on the use of revenues or profits to calculate bonus payouts, without adequately accounting for the risk taken to generate profits'.[66] The seven compensation principles consist of the following:

---

60 Financial Stability Board, *Thematic Review On Compensation – Peer Review Report* (2010), Recommendation 7.

61 BCBS, *Range of Methodologies.*

62 Ibid. B.4.

63 Ibid. 20–21; see also Sam Fleming, 'Bank of England Is Urged to Clamp Down on Bank Bonuses', *Financial Times* (London, 4 March 2014), http://ft.com.

64 Ibid. 33.

65 The first publication was in July 2008, prior to the apogee of the GFC and was entitled International Institute of Finance, *Final Report of the IIF Committee on Market Best Practices: Principles of Conduct and Best Practice Recommendations, Financial Services Industry Response to the Market Turmoil of 2007-2008* (2008) (hereinafter IIF, *Principles of Conduct*). The second publication was a follow-up review using surveys from its membership on the progress made since the release of its compensation recommendations. See International Institute of Finance, *Compensation in Financial Services: Industry Progress And The Agenda For Change* (2009) 1 (hereinafter IIF, *Compensation in Financial Services*).

66 Ibid. IIF, *Compensation in Financial Services* 3.2.1.1.

(i) Compensation incentives should be based on performance and should be aligned with shareholder interests and long-term, firm-wide profitability, taking into account overall risk and cost of capital.
(ii) Compensation incentives should not induce risk taking in excess of the firm's risk appetite.
(iii) Payout of compensation incentives should be based on risk-adjusted and cost of capital-adjusted profit and phased, where possible, to coincide with the risk time horizon of such profit.
(iv) Incentive compensation should have a component reflecting the impact of business units' returns on the overall value of related business groups and the organisation as a whole.
(v) Incentive compensation should have a component reflecting the firm's overall results and achievement of risk management and other general goals.
(vi) Severance pay should take into account realised performance for shareholders over time.
(vii) The approach principles, and objectives of compensation incentives should be transparent to shareholders.[67]

The IIF compensation principles were perhaps the most prescriptive voiced and the IIF was clear that remuneration ought to be reflective of the risks that sharp market swings may occur, which themselves may reveal that earnings realised in earlier years were produced as a result of asset or credit bubbles. In particular, the IIF called for compensation structures which do not reward apparent superior short-term performance which at a later date emerges to have been illusory when adjusted for risk; institutions must align compensation systems to the risk time horizon of the firm concerned. To achieve this, firms should:

> Incorporate adjustments for risk/capital usage based on the risk measures most appropriate to the business in question … Measure performance over a multi-year period where appropriate … Defer compensation delivery in businesses that have a multi-year risk time horizon … Pay compensation in units with value that is linked to the individual's future performance (i.e. company stock may not always be the best currency) thus focusing on alignment with performance development over time rather than on retention … [and] … Introduce forward looking long-term incentive plans for executives and key strategic roles, based on performance achievements beyond total shareholder return metrics.[68]

---

67 IIF, *Principles of Conduct* 49.
68 IIF, *Compensation in Financial Services* Figure 2.

In tandem, the BCBS Range recognises (in common with the EC Recommendation) that poorly calibrated remuneration systems may not reflect the potential for tail-risks or for equity markets to exhibit significant departures from long-term value, and deferral periods are thus crucial.[69] The BCBS Range notes that '[i]ncentive-based remuneration schemes should be adapted to fit the time horizons associated with risks in each business line so as to allow the performance which generates the bonus payment to be validated'.[70] As noted in the original FSB Principles:

> Profits and losses of different activities of a financial firm are realized over different periods of time. Variable compensation payments should be deferred accordingly. Payments should not be finalized over short periods where risks are realized over long periods. Management should question payouts for income that cannot be realized or whose likelihood of realization remains uncertain at the time of payout.[71]

The period of deferral ought to be lengthy enough to allow market- or firm-specific risks to emerge and be quantified. On this basis, the BCBS Range and the IIF compensation principles each recommended that some recognition be made of the power of the leverage and business cycles in

---

[69] BCBS, *Range of Methodologies* 39: 'When designing a remuneration package, the question of the relative proportion in cash and equity instruments (like shares or options) is an important parameter. A key question is the extent to which shares and similar instruments contribute to create appropriate incentives. For purposes of affecting incentives, shares should be subject to a transfer restriction since they differ from cash only during the period when they are subject to transfer restrictions (given that unrestricted shares can be sold and converted to cash). Also, the transfer restriction period should be sufficiently long, to ensure that appropriate incentives are built and to truly differentiate it from a cash payment. However, transfer restriction should not be seen as a substitute for deferral, as deferral permits malus to be applied.'

[70] Ibid. 81. The BCBS argues that risks may be best mitigated through a mixture of *ex post* and *ex ante* adjustments to the wards: 'For many activities, bad-tail risk (low frequency, high impact risk) is difficult to measure ex ante. Deferral could help reduce incentives to take such risks; In the case of risks which are difficult to measure, to model or are simply not known at the time of the award, deferral can be particularly useful because ex ante risk adjustment is less likely to work effectively; Deferral may not be fully effective in constraining the incentives of employees who have the ability to expose the firm to extremely long-term risks, as these risks are unlikely to be realised during a reasonable deferral period. In such cases, ex ante risk adjustments become more important.' See Ibid. C.37.

[71] FSB, *Sound Compensation Practices.*

accelerating executive compensation. For example, the IIF compensation principles voiced the view that compensation ought to 'be based on risk-adjusted and cost of capital-adjusted profit and phased, where possible, to coincide with the risk time horizon of such profit'[72] and the BCBS Range suggests that remuneration structures ought to include specific reference to risk adjustment, taking into account both the nature of the risk involved and the time horizons over which those risks could emerge:[73]

> Deferral practices can be used to address incentives associated with two kinds of risks. In the case of 'ordinary' risks, meaning those that are reasonably well understood and for which severity and time horizon can be assessed, the deferral period and vesting schedule should match the time profile of risk outcomes of the business or have a longer profile, and ideally the ex post adjustments should be tightly linked to the risk outcomes.[74]

There is thus a clear consensus amongst international bodies that remuneration systems ought to recognise that risk which is inbuilt into an institution's profile may not be realised for some time.[75] In this vein, academics have suggested that executive incentive compensation plans should consist only of restricted stock and restricted stock options, with inbuilt deferral periods; this approach, it is argued, will provide incentives for firm executives to act in investors' longer-term interests and 'diminish their incentives to make public statements, manage earnings, or accept undue levels of risk, for the sake of short-term price appreciation'.[76] Furthermore, general measures of financial performance are

---

[72] IIF, *Principles of Conduct* 49.

[73] BCBS, *Range of Methodologies* 36.

[74] Ibid. 113.

[75] On this theme, the UK FCA notes: 'The requirement for assessment of performance to be in a multi-year framework reflects the fact that profits from a *firm's* activities can be volatile and subject to cycles. The financial performance of *firms* and individual *employees* can be exaggerated as a result. Performance assessment on a moving average of results can be a good way of meeting this requirement. However, other techniques such as good quality risk adjustment and deferral of a sufficiently large proportion of *remuneration* may also be useful.' See FCA, *Rem-Code* 19A.3.39.

[76] Romano & Bhagat, 'Reforming Executive Compensation' (contending that a deferral period of 2–4 years would be appropriate to prevent managerial short-termism from unduly affecting risk appetites). See also Bengt Holmstrom, 'Managerial Incentive Problems – A Dynamic Perspective' (1999) 66 REV. ECON. STUD. 169; Bengt Holmstrom, 'Moral Hazard and Observability' (1979) 10 BELL J. ECON. 4.

often unable to capture long-term risks and the BCBS Range, in a similar vein to the EC Recommendation, endorses the use of qualitative metrics to measure performance and determine remuneration rewards:[77]

> The use of indicators like share prices (or similar external measures) may be influenced particularly in the short term by various factors like market sentiment or general economic conditions, not specifically related to firms' or employees' actions … Relative performance measures may increase incentives to take more risk or may, under certain circumstances, reward failure by decoupling remuneration from absolute value generation …[78]

CONCLUSION

This chapter has described the most apposite recommendations for compensation reform released since the GFC by several national and supranational regulatory agencies. The reforms are in varying stages of implementation, yet they are driven by one overarching consideration: to reduce risk within the financial system by providing appropriate incentives in executive compensation contracts.

There are two principal observations to be garnered from these discussions. The first is that all of the corporate governance proposals demonstrate a firm grounding in agency theory. In this way, they are redolent of previous regulatory solutions to incentive problems in employment contracts. Orthodox methods of incentivising executives to act in the interests of firm owners and entrusting the board to monitor management are standard fare in the corporate governance literature. The spectrum of recommendations does not depart from trust in these governance mechanisms.[79]

---

[77] BCBS, *Range of Methodologies* 32.

[78] Ibid. 34.

[79] For example, the terms of reference for the Walker Review left no doubt as to the primary reforms necessary in reducing the likelihood of future financial failures: 'To examine corporate governance in the UK banking industry and make recommendations, including in the following areas: the effectiveness of risk management at board level, including the incentives in remuneration policy to manage risk effectively; the balance of skills, experience and independence required on the boards of UK banking institutions; the effectiveness of board practices and the performance of audit, risk, remuneration and nomination committees; the role of institutional shareholders in engaging effectively with companies and monitoring of boards; and whether the UK approach is consistent with international practice and how national and international best practice can be promulgated.' See 'the Walker Review'.

The second observation of trends within the recommendations is that supervisory authorities appear cognisant of the requirement for mechanisms to be implemented to allow for greater appreciation of long-term risks in the design of executive compensation contracts. Adjustment to remuneration is cited by the majority of regulatory bodies as the appropriate principle under which to align pay with performance more efficiently. The two suggested mechanisms for remuneration adjustment are: (i) deferral of vesting of variable compensation awards; and/or (ii) clawback of pre-awarded compensation. Each mechanism is hindered by considerable practical considerations yet, in principle, they would lead to greater efficiency in the pay-for-performance paradigm. Moreover, regulators in the EU have determined that a cap on variable pay at banks is warranted. There are also several suggestions for wider incorporation of qualitative data into performance appraisals in financial institutions which would, in theory, reduce the reliance on financial metrics of performance which are more manipulable.

The following chapter will make proposals for further reform to executive compensation systems at financial institutions. It will note that the reforms discussed in this chapter exhibit limitations, especially in light of the FIH. In particular, the scope of some of the measures has not been expanded to reflect the unstable character of asset markets and the linkages between those markets and corporate market capitalisations (and by implication how this instability may affect – or be affected by – equity-based remuneration).

7. Reconstituting executive compensation at financial institutions: proposals for reform

INTRODUCTORY REMARKS

The previous chapter outlined the reforms to bank compensation made in each of the major Western financial centres. Characterising the tenor of this reform, Coffee notes that there were two major drivers of the legislative programme following the GFC, namely:

> (1) that the 2008 financial crisis was in substantial part the consequence of flawed executive compensation formulas that gave senior financial managers at major financial institutions perverse incentives to pursue short-term profits by accepting risk and high leverage; and (2) that the market's perception that some financial institutions were 'too big to fail' enabled these firms to obtain capital at a discounted price commensurate with the market's judgment that they would be bailed out. This discount in turn encouraged these firms to take on excessive leverage.[1]

This simple statement encapsulates the motivations underpinning the agenda for reform in the US, UK and EU following the GFC charted in the previous chapter, which will inform the proposals advanced in this chapter. These reforms of course include the introduction of several safeguards to improve the structure of executive compensation in order to focus executives' minds on planning for medium-to-long-term shareholder value. As one would expect from such lengthy processes of planning and implementation, these measures do to some extent address the various issues which fracture the utility of current performance-based compensation calculations, and some of the reforms therefore represent strong progress in this area. The UK, in particular, has implemented some

[1] John C. Coffee, 'Systemic Risk after Dodd-Frank: Contingent Capital and the Need for Strategies Beyond Oversight' (2011) 111 COL. LAW REV. 796, 798–99 (notes omitted).

far-reaching reforms to compensation systems, corporate governance and bank structure.[2]

However, financial crashes will still occur, and compensation systems do not fully reflect this, because they do not take into account the capacity for instability to arise endogenously (as predicted by the FIH) and reveal acute overvaluation of assets.[3] Accordingly, reforms both mooted and implemented since the GFC remain to some extent reflective of the tenets of modern finance theory. On this basis, even those reform proposals which recognise that bubbles may develop in asset markets largely retain the view that optimal contracting, rather than regulatory intervention, is the most appropriate method of preventing future financial instability.[4] The GFC provided regulators with the opportunity to effect meaningful reform to corporate governance in recognition of the failure of market-led solutions to restrain excessive risk.[5] Instead, a good deal of regulatory attention has been caught by measures such as shareholder votes on executive remuneration, which, for reasons to be outlined later in this chapter, will be of limited effectiveness, or the cap placed on variable compensation by the EU Parliament, which may harm the competitiveness of the UK and European banking industries.[6]

---

[2] For example, see the Financial Services (Banking Reform) Act 2013 c.33, which implemented many of the key recommendations of the Independent Commission on Banking (usually referred to as the Vickers Report). See the *Independent Commission on Banking Final Report: Recommendations* (2011).

[3] Alan Greenspan himself noted in 2009 that the GFC was inevitable: 'They [financial crises] are all different, but they have one fundamental source. That is the unquenchable capability of human beings when confronted with long periods of prosperity to presume that it will continue and they begin to take speculative excesses, with the consequences that have dotted the history of the globe basically since the beginning of the eighteenth and nineteenth centur[ies] ... It is human nature ...' See Alan Greenspan, 'Market Crisis "Will Happen Again"' (BBC Interview, 8 September 2009), http://news.bbc.co.uk/1/hi/8244600.stm.

[4] Accordingly, 'bubbles, crashes and rent capture are caused by principal/agent problems [and thus] the solution lies in having the principals change the way they contract and deal with agents.' See John Kay, 'Should We Have "Narrow Banking"?' in Turner et al, *The Future of Finance* 230.

[5] Stefano Pagliari, 'Who Governs Finance? The Shifting Public–Private Divide in the Regulation of Derivatives, Rating Agencies and Hedge Funds' (2012) 18 EUR. LAW J. 44.

[6] For a discussion of this issue, see Kevin J. Murphy, 'Regulating Banking Bonuses in the European Union: A Case Study in Unintended Consequences' (2013) 19 EURO. FIN. MAN. 631. For a thoughtful rejoinder, see Andrew Johnston, 'Preventing the Next Financial Crisis? Regulating Bankers' Pay in

Accordingly, much of the reform to executive remuneration appears to be driven by outrage at perceived 'excess' rather than any discernible objections to the pay-for-performance paradigm.[7] Based on the issues raised in this book, there are far more significant reforms to compensation systems required, which would provide more sustainable solutions to the incentive issues which arise from the current use of equity and stock-related pay.

This chapter will therefore further discuss how, following the GFC, alternative theories of financial markets – particularly the FIH – ought to inform the design of executive compensation systems at large banks which, in concert with proposed and existing macro-financial reform, have the potential to make the economy more stable. On this basis, the chapter will recommend in its proposals that greater emphasis be placed on the capacity of market prices to depart significantly from value for protracted periods, due in particular to the effects of leverage on asset prices and behavioural factors operative in financial markets. The first proposal is to defer variable compensation at banks for a greater time period than is currently mandated, which would reduce the incentives for firm executives to undertake leverage-based expansion which, as charted in previous chapters, is a common precursor to financial crisis. The second proposal is to rely on the prescriptive reforms to bank capital structures instituted since the GFC by global and national bank regulators, in order to implicitly limit the capacity of banks to expand their balance sheets, especially during periods in which the economy exhibits signs of euphoria. This will act as a natural brake or stabiliser of equity-based compensation and/or bonuses linked to returns generated by

---

Europe' (2014) 41 J. LAW & SOCIETY 1. It has become clear that large banks are attempting to sidestep the limits placed on pay by the bonus cap through topping up the salaries of those caught by the cap on variable pay with 'role-based allowances'; these allowances will be counted as fixed pay, yet may be adjusted upwards or downwards in-year. See Daniel Schäfer & Martin Arnold, 'City Bankers to Evade EU Bonus Cap with "Role-based" Allowances', *Financial Times* (London, 13 April 2014) http://www.ft.com/cms/s/0/02213446-c19d-11e3-b95f-00144feabdc0.html#axzz312YDQ4Du.

[7] See, for example, James Moore, 'Fury as Goldman Sachs Unveils Bankers' Pay', *Independent* (London, 15 January 2012); Alistair Gray & Kate Burgess, 'Investor Fury at Executive Pay Policies', *Financial Times* (London, 12 May 2012) http://ft.com. As noted by the IIF: 'The structure and governance of compensation have received far less attention [than bonus levels] and it is the Institute of International Finance's view that these are more important in driving the desired level of prudence in the behaviour of front-line employees, managers and executives.' See IIF, *Compensation in Financial Services* 1.

leverage. The third proposal – to augment the corporate governance of banks through a greater focus on sanctions in promoting more desirable behavioural norms and the incorporation of qualitative indices of performance – will reduce the role of potentially flawed financial market pricing in setting compensation awards. Stiffer penalties for deliberate or reckless decision making that causes significant financial losses will focus the minds of executives at banks on delivering long-term financial returns, whilst an increased use of qualitative indices of performance in determining compensation awards would also reduce the reliance on quantitative metrics, which are often distorted by the forces discussed in previous chapters.

The proposals are designed mainly to guard against the dangers of equity-based governance highlighted in previous chapters and are derived from complementary perspectives relating in some way to the analysis of flawed corporate governance and market pricing systems charted in this book. In considering the following discussions and subsequent proposals three issues must be noted. Firstly, reforms to executive compensation are not a panacea: they must be part of a wide-ranging package of reforms which target key weaknesses in the overarching legal framework under which large banks operate.[8] Secondly, whilst simplification of compensation systems might be desirable, complex pay packages may be unavoidable, because the risk control associated with one form of reward may create additional risk in another area.[9] Thirdly, any reform to compensation structures must be implemented on a global scale, in the form of a supranationally agreed accord. Anything less may find regions of regulatory laxity rewarded with an influx of financial institutions in a

---

[8] In relation to the financial system, for example, for an excellent discussion of existing reforms and insightful proposals for new reform, see Avgouleas, *Governance of Global Financial Markets*.

[9] Stephen Bryan, Lee Seok Hwang & Steven Lilien, 'CEO Stock-Based Compensation: An Empirical Analysis of Incentive-Intensity, Relative Mix, and Economic Determinants' (2000) 73 J. BUS. 661) (hereinafter Bryan et al, 'CEO Stock-Based Compensation') (observing that determining the precise mix of executive pay is difficult, as certain compensation, for example restricted stock, will encourage a CEO to be risk averse, whereas stock options will induce risk taking due to the concavity of potential gains from their use); see also Wilbur Lewellen, Claudio Loderer & Kenneth Martin, 'Executive Compensation and Executive Incentive Problems: An Empirical Analysis' (1987) 9 J. ACCOUNT. ECON. 287, 288 (arguing that diversity witnessed in executive compensation contracts in terms of both composition and time horizons is evidence of the difficulties in determining a standardised form of optimal incentive-based pay).

'race to the bottom' which, in today's vast and interconnected global markets, cannot be tolerated.

PROPOSALS FOR REFORM

Proposal I – Five/Ten-year Deferral of Bonuses, Subject to Clawback

Deferral recommendations are ubiquitous in the reform literature and reflect general industry practice.[10] Deferral provides greater links between pay and performance for two reasons: firstly, it disincentivises the manipulation of earnings or excessive risk adoption by senior managers to capture short-term rewards;[11] and secondly, it allows for the effects of the business cycle to be smoothed out, reducing the possibility that excessive compensation awards are captured on the basis of inflated asset prices. There is convincing evidence to support the use of restricted or deferred compensation awards; for example, managers with greater restricted equity are less likely to engage in earnings management or financial misreporting[12] or embark upon value-destroying corporate acquisitions financed by stock.[13] Clawback policies are also recommended in the major Western financial centres (and mandated in the US). As noted in the previous chapter, the rationale for clawback is simple: excess compensation which has been awarded on the basis of inaccurate financial reports ought to be recouped from senior executives culpable for those inaccuracies. This mechanism therefore ought to assist market informational transparency and increase efficiency.

I concur with the principles that underpin both the deferral and clawback mechanisms, which are patently designed to both disincentivise short-termism and punish the manipulation of data in order to engage in

---

[10] Although deferral of compensation in banks in the US is not mandatory, the adoption of the FSB Principles by large US banks means that, in practice, deferral of variable remuneration is standard practice. Further, banks in both the EC and UK are required to have deferral periods inbuilt into executive compensation systems. However, as will be outlined in the remainder of this chapter, these deferral periods are arguably not long enough.

[11] Romano & Bhagat, 'Reforming Executive Compensation' 363.

[12] Natasha Bums & Simi Kedia, 'The Impact of Performance-Based Compensation on Misreporting' (2006) 79 J. FIN. ECON. 35.

[13] Gregor Andrade, Mark Mitchell & Erik Stafford, 'New Evidence and Perspectives on Mergers' (2001) 15 J. ECON. PERSPECTIVES 103.

rent capture.[14] However, the available evidence suggests that the length of deferral recommended by regulatory agencies, and the somewhat limited circumstances under which clawback may operate, mean that these requirements may not provide sufficient protection against the re-emergence of inappropriate incentive structures, or the adoption of excessive risk. For example, many jurisdictions recommend that elements of compensation ought to be deferred for at least three years;[15] however, 'this restriction appears somewhat arbitrary; three years is not a particularly long horizon in terms of long-term performance'.[16] Naturally, deferral periods will assist in mitigating the effects of increased risk within a sector or institution, but it is clear that these risks may not manifest for protracted periods – many years, in some cases.[17] It is further unclear whether a deferred equity plan which does not cover a significant period of time would increase a focus on the long term, because there would remain a large period of time under which the incentives of senior executives would be the same as with a non-deferred

---

[14] It is clear that the reform agenda has gathered pace over recent years in both the US and EU. See Guido A. Ferrarini & Maria-Cristina Ungureanu, 'Bankers' Pay After the 2008 Crisis: Regulatory Reforms in the US and EU' (2012) J. BANK. LAW & BANKING, http://papers.ssrn.com/sol3/papers.cfm?abstract_id=2001492.

[15] For example, UK banks are advised to have deferral plans of 'two-to-five years'; Dodd-Frank mandates clawback of compensation for 'up to five years'; the EU mandates a deferral period of 'three-to-five years'. However, in practice, in the case of the UK, most large banks defer bonus payments for just three years. Commenting on this in the UK context, Andrew Tyrie, chair of the UK Parliamentary Banking Standards Commission, noted: 'Without much closer alignment of rewards to the maturity of the risk, the structure of remuneration will remain seriously flawed … Fundamental reform is going to be needed to ensure the structure of remuneration can stand the test of a financial and business cycle, incentivising resilience – not excessive risk or poor standards … It will be up to the regulator to get on with the job.' See Sam Fleming, 'Bank of England Is Urged to Clamp Down on Bank Bonuses', *Financial Times* (London, 4 March 2014), http://ft.com. Further, in the US, regulators require only the 'top' executives at large financial firms to defer half of all of their incentive-based compensation and there is no mandatory requirement for them to be paid in the form of equity compensation. See Incentive-Based Compensation Arrangements, 76 Fed. Reg. at 21,170.

[16] Guido Ferrarini, Niamh Moloney & Maria-Cristina Ungureanu, 'Executive Remuneration In Crisis: A Critical Assessment of Reforms in Europe' (2010) 10 J. CORP. LAW STUD. 73, 117.

[17] Ibid.

plan.[18] On this basis, there have been calls in some quarters for deferral periods to last much longer, and for deferral payments to be comprised of instruments which incentivise longer-term investment horizons.[19]

In relation to clawback, there are significant practical constraints imposed on retrieving remuneration that has already been awarded (often years previously) as an *ex-post* adjustment.[20] Moreover, in the main, its implementation has not provided regulators with powers that may have made clawback a more effective tool with which to regulate executive pay packages. No national or supranational agency has recommended the use of clawback in situations other than those involving manipulation or restatements. On this basis, clawback will remain ineffectual as long as regulators allow banks and other financial institutions to apply it only in narrowly prescribed contexts.[21] Where stock prices are inaccurate due to inflation from errors in performance metrics or, for example, the adoption of 'excessive' leverage, no clawback is permitted. Further, where qualitative (non-financial) measures of performance are used as the basis for a

---

[18] James C. Spindler, 'Mandatory Long-Term Compensation in the Banking System – and Beyond?' (2011) Cato Institute Regulation Paper, 42, 44 (hereinafter Spindler, 'Mandatory Long-Term Compensation in the Banking System').

[19] So, for example, the UK Parliamentary Commission on Banking Standards reported in July 2013, and recommended the following: 'much more remuneration [ought] to be deferred and, in many cases, for much longer periods of up to 10 years [and] more of that deferred remuneration to be in forms which favour the long-term performance and soundness of the firm, such as bail-in bonds.' See Report of the Parliamentary Commission on Banking Standards, *Changing Banking For Good (Vol. I)*, HL 27-I; HC 175-I (2013) 9 (hereinafter UK Parliament, *Changing Banking for Good*). However, due to the concurrent implementation of the EU cap on variable compensation the legislature has decided not to implement this recommendation.

[20] Financial Services Authority, *Revising The Remuneration Code, CP10/19* (2010), note 32.

[21] A further criticism of the clawback power under Dodd-Frank § 954 is that all 'executive officers' are subject to its provisions, which casts the net very wide and might lead to the power being used against blameless executives. This might incentivise executives to prefer higher base salaries rather than performance bonuses in lieu of the potential for clawback, thus removing the incentive element of pay. See Stephen M. Bainbridge, 'Dodd-Frank: Quack Federal Corporate Governance Round II' (2011) 95 MINN. L. REV. 1779; Daniel A. Cohen, Aiyesha Dey & Thomas Z. Lys, 'The Sarbanes-Oxley Act of 2002: Implications for Compensation Structure and Managerial Risk-Taking' (2007), http://ssrn.com/sol3/papers.cfm?abstract_id=568483. Moreover, perhaps, the Act's focus on executive officers fails to provide any financial deterrent to senior proprietary traders, who may have greater power and incentives to pursue risk-laden strategies which house the potential to damage their firms.

compensation award which later are revealed to have been inaccurately assessed, clawback could not operate, as no restatement would be required.[22]

Accordingly, it is the contention of this book that all equity-based compensation at financial institutions ought to be deferred from vesting for a more significant period, in order to mitigate fully the effects of the lending cycle. The use of clawback also must be expanded. To give effect to this, variable stock-based compensation awards would be contingent on the fulfilment of a mandatory holding period, with 50 per cent of the rewards being paid out after five years and the remainder being allowed to vest after ten years.[23] The rationale for this is that the market must be permitted sufficient time to adjust and correct any distortions which, as noted in previous chapters, may be pervasive and endure for protracted periods. This would of course also reduce incentives for executives to pursue short-term price-appreciating corporate strategies.[24] The imperfections in the market-pricing mechanism are serious enough that price inefficiency may persist for considerable periods. Moreover, on the basis of the FIH, the financial system, more than any other sector, is prone to exacerbate economic instability, a phenomenon which, as noted in Chapter 5, is arguably made more acute by the perverse incentives in compensation systems. Further, the behavioural and psychological influences highlighted by the FIH discourage prudence and instead encourage a focus on optimism as 'apparent success breeds an inability to imagine the possibility of failure',[25] which makes it extremely difficult to price

---

[22] Jesse M. Fried & Nitzan Shilon, 'Excess-Pay Clawbacks' (2011) 36 J. CORP'TION. LAW 722, 749 (hereinafter Fried & Shilon, *Excess-Pay Clawbacks*). Further, in jurisdictions where clawback is not mandatory, such as the UK, only a minority of companies use them. As of 2012, only 30 per cent of UK FTSE-350 firms had clawback policies. See Deloitte, *Your Guide: Executive Directors' Remuneration in FTSE 250 Companies* (2012) 3.

[23] This was also the recommended deferral period for variable compensation cited by the UK Parliament. See UK Parliament, *Changing Banking for Good.*

[24] Mark Carney, Governor of the Bank of England since 2013, has argued that banks must look to defer at least some part of senior managers' bonuses for a period of greater than five years, commenting that: 'We [the Bank of England] would rather see more deferral, more equity and this ability to take it back when those risks come to light.' Remarks of Mark Carney cited in Shannon Stapleton, 'UK To Look at Longer Deferral for Banker Bonuses – Carney', *Reuters*, 15 January 2014, http://uk.reuters.com.

[25] Joseph V. Rizzi, 'Behavioral Basis of the Financial Crisis' (2008) 18 J. APPL. FIN. 84, 93 (hereinafter Rizzi, 'Behavioral Basis of the Financial Crisis'). This has been confirmed by the FCA (formerly the FSA) in the UK in their

rationally when risk appears remote.[26] Further, research demonstrates that executive compensation contracts encourage risk taking 'to profit from a speculative stock price surge even if at a later date share prices collapse … [and] … stock-based compensation rises in speculative markets'.[27] On this basis, managers of financial institutions have incentives to increase the speculative component of stock prices and increase short-term returns.[28] By reason of these factors, long-term horizons ought to be inbuilt into the vesting of equity-based executive compensation in order to reduce the potential for risk-laden strategies to contribute to the inflation of equity prices and compensation linked to financial returns. These deferral periods must therefore become mandatory across the financial industry, save for particular circumstances.[29]

Ten years has been selected because this strikes the appropriate balance between reining in risk and allowing the financial cycle to 'smooth out' equity and asset prices and financial performance measurements. Some scholars have called for all compensation deferral periods to last for well over a decade with no element of early vesting.[30] This seems excessive. Although there are undoubtedly merits in postponing certain compensation awards, corporations must be allowed to attract and retain talent. Fixed deferral periods would also mean that it would make sense

---

report into the failings of HBOS. The FCA noted that: 'There was a collective denial [within HBOS] of the impact of the financial crisis … The culture of optimism which pervaded the business impeded the identification and effective management of transactions as they became stressed …' See Financial Services Authority, *Final Notice: Bank Of Scotland Plc, Ref.* 169628, 9 March 2012, at 4.116.

26 'The growth of credit derivatives and other forms of risk transfer seem to have made the system more stable. But these gains may have come at the price of increasing uncertainty and potential losses if we end up in the "tail" … It is hard to motivate people to buy more insurance against adverse outcomes when the risks seem remote and hard to measure and when present conditions seem favourable.' Remarks of former President of New York Federal Reserve, Tim Geithner, quoted in Gillian Tett & James Drummond, 'NY Fed President Warns of Risk to Structured Credit' *Financial Times* (London, 12 May 2005) http://ft.com.

27 Patrick Bolton, Jose Scheinkman & Wei Xiong, 'Pay for Short-Term Performance: Executive Compensation in Speculative Markets' (2005) ECGI Finance Working Paper No. 79/2005, 6.

28 Patrick Bolton, Jose Scheinkman & Wei Xiong, 'Executive Compensation and Short-Termist Behaviour in Speculative Markets' (2006) 73 REV. ECON. STUD. 577.

29 For example, retirement on compassionate grounds.

30 Roubini & Mihm, *Crisis Economics* 187.

for a risk-averse manager to refrain from engaging in costly efforts given an uncertain outcome, which may induce widespread risk aversion in the banking sector. Further, managers may alter the timing of their effort dependent upon the stage of the scale of deferment they are at, in order to minimise their risks and maximise their expected gains from their future equity awards.[31] An aggregate deferral period of ten years would arguably make it much more difficult for managers to maintain inefficient levels of risk in their management of their financial institution, as sub-optimal returns to shareholders during that period brought on by excessive risk aversion ought to mean they would be replaced with less risk-averse managers in the meantime (whose rewards will also be deferred and therefore, despite their greater risk tolerance, incentives for 'excessive' risks will remain capped).

Whilst investment risks may take years to emerge, arguably most would become apparent within a time frame of ten years. This lengthened time horizon therefore ought to capture tail-risk and prevent managers from profiting from the effects of a major credit boom. Moreover, the inbuilding into this proposal of a window where 50 per cent of the rewards could be paid at the halfway point ought to reduce risk aversion, and ameliorate the tendency of managers to postpone or reduce innovation in order to maintain future payouts. The ten-year deferral period (for at least half of variable compensation) avoids the costly and difficult

---

[31] As noted in an example of this: 'Suppose a manager of a pharmaceutical firm has two-year restricted stock and has a new potential drug with an expected value of $10 per share. Should the manager begin the testing, approval, and marketing process now or wait until later? Upon announcement, the firm's stock will rise by the expected value – $10 per share – which will then fluctuate as the product introduction process goes either well or badly. Clearly, the risk-neutral shareholders would prefer that she undertake the process now, since idiosyncratic risk does not affect her, and waiting carries some possibility that the firm's product will be pre-empted by the competition. The manager, on the other hand, has nothing to gain in the near term from an announcement and, in fact, [she] will find it costly to bear the risk of the approval process and consequent price fluctuations. Instead, [she] may find it preferable to announce the project and begin the approval process just before [her] stock options vest, such that [she] enjoys the $10-per-share rise with certainty – even if there is some risk of being pre-empted in the meantime.' See Spindler, *Mandatory Long-Term Compensation in the Banking System* 45.

process of risk adjustment within the compensation system in calculating regular grants of deferred compensation.[32]

The deferral proposal would, axiomatically, require the use of clawback. Clawback would only be permitted in the period between the initial vesting of 50 per cent of the bonus (the end of the fifth year) and the end of the assessment period (the end of the tenth year). Its ambit would be extended under this proposal from the current regulatory position in the US, UK and EU (where misconduct or misstatement is required for clawback to be invoked[33]) to recoupment of financial rewards that later transpired to have been captured through short-term price movements, proposals which have been discussed in Anglo-American markets.[34] In particular, it should remain open for financial firms to recoup compensation awarded in periods of economic euphoria where the actions of executives have led to the unsustainable build-up of risk within the institution concerned.[35] No restatement would be needed if a business collapsed due to imprudent risk yet, at present, clawback would not operate in this situation. If it emerged that performance had breached a downward threshold in this period, the clawback system could be invoked

---

32 'Given the uncertainty surrounding accurate risk assessment, the industry may be inclined to shift towards more conservative compensation practices and increased use of deferral.' See IIF, *Compensation in Financial Services* 3.2.1.1.

33 Many global banks have expanded the situations and scope in which clawback clauses may be invoked against errant employees; however, virtually all of these measures still require an element of fraudulent, illegal or reckless conduct. See Liz Moyer, 'Banks Bow to New York on Clawbacks' *Wall Street Journal* (New York, 13 March 2013) http://online.wsj.com/news/articles/SB10001424127887324077704578358791840450814.

34 In the UK, for example, there have been proposals to permit the power to be exercised in the following instances: underperformance in terms of total shareholder return; a fall in the absolute share price beyond a certain level; or, a rise in the credit spread of the company's debt beyond a certain level. See James Barty & Ben Jones, *Executive Compensation: Rewards For Success Not Failure: Policy Exchange Report* (2012). To build up a clawback fund, half of all bonuses would be put in an escrow account and paid out evenly over five years. The company could withdraw the funds if directors underperformed.

35 See Raghuram Rajan, 'Bankers' Pay Is Deeply Flawed' *Financial Times* (London, 9 January 2008) http://ft.com. In fact, even in Europe, efforts to recoup previously paid bonuses in the event of non-compliance with corporate policy or misstatements have been undertaken; Deutsche Bank's employment contracts now permit the bank to claw back bonuses from employees even where those bonuses were earned whilst working at a company other than Deutsche Bank. See Lina Saigol, 'Banks Impose Bonus Forfeits for Bad Deals' *Financial Times* (London, 6 November 2012), http://.ft.com.

to reduce executives' windfalls.[36] Provided that the downward threshold remained breached for the rest of the intervening period, all further bonuses linked to that executive's performance would be forfeited. However, once the ten-year period matured, clawback would cease to operate (in the absence of accounting restatements due to fraud or manipulation in the relevant period).

Further, executives should be prohibited from hedging their exposures to deferred compensation.[37] Whilst there are some countervailing arguments which suggest that limiting executives' ability to hedge will make them too risk-averse,[38] it is clear that the capacity of executives to hedge their exposure to the stock of their own firms may provide serious incentives to take advantage of their insider information to reduce any potential wealth losses (thus transferring losses to shareholders),[39] and insure them against poor decision making at their specific firms.

In addition to mandating deferral periods and encouraging the use of clawback, there have also been calls by some high-profile regulators to switch the focus of calculation of executive compensation at financial institutions from the current standard of return on equity (RoE – discussed in earlier chapters) to a metric arguably more representative of long-term performance, such as return on assets (RoA).[40] This, it is

---

[36] Fried & Shilon, *Excess-Pay Clawbacks*.

[37] Lucian A. Bebchuk, 'How to Fix Bankers' Pay' (2010) 139 DAEDALUS 52, observing at 54 that '[a]n executive who buys a "put" option to sell his or her shares at the current price, as executives are generally free to do under standard pay arrangements, is "insured" against declines in the stock price below current levels … executives should be precluded from engaging in any hedging or derivative transactions that would reduce or limit the extent to which declines in the company's stock price would lower executive payoffs.'

[38] For example, see Viral V. Acharya & Alberto Bisin, 'Managerial Hedging and Equity Ownership', 29 January 2003, http://www.nyu.edu/econ/user/bisina/Stock-review4.pdf.

[39] Carr Bettis, John Bizjak & Swaminathan Kalpathy, 'Why Do Insiders Hedge Their Ownership? An Empirical Examination' (2013) http://ssrn.com/abstract=1364810.

[40] RoA records what level of earnings are generated from invested capital (assets). RoA varies substantially according to the industry concerned. Most corporations are funded by debt and equity. The RoA figure reveals to what extent and how effectively the corporation is earning net income from the money it has to invest. The higher the RoA number, the better, as this indicates the corporation is earning more money on less investment. For example, Company X has £10 million in income and total assets of £50 million, giving it an RoA of 20%; Company Y has £10 million in income and total assets of £100 million, it has an RoA of 10%. In this example, Company X is earning more income per

posited, would reduce the incentives for senior executives to concentrate not on returns to shareholders, but on the returns generated by assets under management.[41] This would arguably expose managers to greater market discipline, because RoA provides a snapshot of the efficiency of the use of firm capital to generate returns, and on this basis, whether leverage is being used optimally.[42] On this basis, a focus on RoA in the financial sector, rather than on RoE, would have resulted in much lower compensation for senior executives at financial institutions prior to 2008, and arguably less risk.[43] It is clear, for example, that focusing on RoA reduces incentives to leverage. This assumption has been tested empirically, and found to be robust.[44]

Mandating a focus on RoA rather than RoE in executive compensation systems at financial institutions is certainly worth exploring, and would arguably make deferral of compensation even more potent. However, it is not a silver bullet. Suppose (as has occurred in the banking sector since the GFC) that all equity-based compensation is deferred for a significant

---

unit of assets, and is therefore using its capital more efficiently. In relation to banks, it is difficult (but not impossible) to magnify RoA through leverage, as although asset levels can be magnified massively by increased borrowing, RoA will not change unless the assets bought through borrowing are relatively more profitable.

41 Andrew G. Haldane, 'Control Rights (and Wrongs)' (2012) 32 ECON. AFFAIRS 47 (hereinafter Haldane, 'Control Rights') observing at 57 that 'it would be a relatively small step for banks to switch from ROE [return on equity] to ROA [return on assets] targets in their capital planning and compensation. Yet the effects on risk-taking and remuneration could be large.'

42 '[M]any managements remain transfixed by the notion of RoE as the primary measure of profitability. They have promised it to their boards and to their shareholders. The targets were written into their remuneration plans. Results fed their bonuses. And there is no doubt about it, all else being equal, higher equity reduces the measure of short term RoE. Never mind that it is the wrong measure and therefore the wrong target.' See Robert Jenkins, 'A Debate Framed by Fallacies', Speech given at the International Centre for Financial Regulation's 3rd Annual Regulatory Summit, London, 4, 25 September 2012 (hereinafter Jenkins, 'A Debate Framed by Fallacies').

43 Haldane calculates that a focus on RoA rather than on RoE in the financial sector would have seen annual CEO pay at the top US banks rise from an average $2.8 million in 1989 to $3.4 million in 2007, rather than to $26 million. See Haldane, 'Control Rights'.

44 Bebchuk & Spamann, 'Regulating Bankers' Pay'; Lin Guo, Abu Jalal & Shahriar Khaksari, 'Bank Executive Compensation Structure, Risk Taking and the Financial Crisis' (2010) http://ssrn.com/abstract=1664191; Christophe Moussu & Arthur Petit-Romec, 'ROE in Banks: Myth and Reality' (2014) http://ssrn.com/abstract=2374068.

period (for example, five years), making it less attractive to undertake short-term leveraged-based expansion to capture higher short-term RoE. Further, assume that the bank's capacity to leverage is also curtailed by new banking regulations, thereby restricting leverage. It becomes much less attractive for bankers in this situation to target RoE, because the much higher risk of default in the intervening period may wipe out any equity-based gains in the intervening five years before payout. In this situation, it is therefore to be expected that banks will behave more conservatively, thus reducing overall risk.[45] However, whilst the risks inherent in targeting RoE in this way are reduced, it is at least arguable whether replacing this with a focus on RoA is either necessary, given the safeguards outlined in the proposals of this chapter or, more significantly, would necessarily reduce long-term risk taking.

In relation to the latter point, where compensation is deferred and linked to a firm's long-run stock price or financial returns, payouts vary with the riskiness of firm assets. In a situation where the incentives to target RoE become much less pronounced, the optimal way for bankers to maintain high levels of pay becomes targeting increased levels of asset risk, rather than manipulation of the capital structure of the firm. On this basis, if banks begin to switch to compensation plans which explicitly target RoA, the portfolio of assets held by financial institutions may become riskier, or they may engage in greater levels of asset substitution, making them harder to monitor.[46] Of course, the risk weighting of assets in capital adequacy rules would go some way to reducing the risks attendant on linking pay to RoA but it is clear that risks relating to assets may be underestimated, especially in euphoric financial conditions. Further, focusing on RoA may also still incentivise the expansion of bank balance sheets on the upward curve of the lending cycle to capture bonuses, particularly due to the effects of mark-to-market accounting in conditions conducive to asset price expansion:

---

[45] Eric D. Chason, 'The Uneasy Case for Deferring Banker Pay' (2013) 73 LOUISIANA LAW REV. 923.

[46] Accordingly, '[r]eturn on assets is positively related to risk in the previous year and even origin risk … Examining asset turnover shows that much of the productivity gain of higher risk firms is that they earn more revenue per dollar of assets … very risky firms have very high asset turnover.' See Ing-Haw Cheng, Harrison Hong & Jose A. Scheinkman, 'Yesterday's Heroes: Compensation and Risk at Financial Firms' (2013) 22–23, http://econ.columbia.edu/files/econ/compensaton__risk_at_financial_firms.pdf (hereinafter Cheng et al, 'Yesterday's Heroes').

> [If] irrational exuberance pushes the price of assets to irrationally high levels, mark to market accounting will swell declared profit in an unsustainable way. A significant element of trading book profits recorded in the years running up to the crisis proved in retrospect illusory. These illusory profits were however used as the basis for bonus decisions, and created incentives for traders and management to take further risk.[47]

As was noted in Chapter 5, not only are asset prices pushed higher by behavioural factors implicit in the FIH analysis of financial markets, but banks actively manage the risk weightings of their assets. Prior to the GFC, for example, it is clear that the risks associated with many forms of asset – especially in the ABS market – were massively underestimated, and RWO may continue in new forms as time progresses.[48] To support this, research has noted that Risk-Weighted Assets (RWA) levels prior to the GFC were not significantly indicative of bank distress. In contrast, unweighted leverage ratios (to be discussed below) were highly indicative of the possibility of default.[49] Focusing on RoA therefore implies a guarantee into the structure of compensation systems at banks concerning the relative riskiness of the bank's assets, a guarantee which may be

---

[47] FSA, *Turner Review* 49.

[48] Securitization of assets increases a bank's RoA by shrinking its balance sheet: 'Accounting sales treatment was seen by some as providing originators/sponsors with additional incentives to securitise. For instance, if an originator was able to achieve off-balance sheet accounting treatment, the removal of balance sheet assets improved certain financial ratios, such as the leverage capital ratio or return on assets.' See BCBS, The Joint Forum Report on asset securitisation incentives (July 2011) 11. Banks' use of asset securitization, of course, was cited as a major cause of the GFC. See Markus K. Brunnermeier, 'Deciphering the Liquidity and Credit Crunch 2007–08' (2009) 23 J. ECON. PERSPECTIVES 77; Douglas W. Diamond & Raghuram G. Rajan, 'The Credit Crisis: Conjectures about Causes and Remedies' (2009) 99 AM. ECON. REV. 606.

[49] Adrian Blundell-Wignall & Caroline Roulet, 'Business Models of Banks, Leverage and the Distance-to-Default' (2013) 2 OECD J. FIN. MARKET TRENDS 1 (hereinafter Blundell-Wignall & Roulet, 'Business Models of Banks'). For this study, the OECD examined a sample of 94 US and EU internationally active commercial banks and broker dealers with market capitalisations of over $5 billion, over the period 2004–11; Andy Haldane & Vasileios Madouros, 'The Dog and the Frisbee', Paper presented at the Federal Reserve Bank of Kansas City's 36th economic policy symposium, 'The Changing Policy Landscape', Jackson Hole, Wyoming, 31 August 2012, 19 (hereinafter Haldane & Madouros, 'The Dog and the Frisbee'); Sonali Das & Amadou N.R. Sy, 'How Risky Are Banks' Risk Weighted Assets? Evidence from the Financial Crisis' (2012) IMF Working Paper WP/12/36.

misleading. Finally, if compensation drops significantly from a switch to compensation based on RoA (as would be expected), there is the danger that banks begin to set lower RoA targets for bankers to meet to set relative compensation levels, thereby simply shifting the incentive problem from one metric to another. In particular, it may be difficult for the market to maintain pay levels based on current RoA correlation with overall bank profits, if it appears that bankers are not being rewarded commensurately with the returns generated for shareholders. This may lead to unwelcome forms of shirking and risk aversion, especially as it is highly likely that base salaries at banks would increase in response to greater deferral of variable pay, making the performance-based element of compensation less important to the bankers concerned.

There are thus some problems with linking compensation to asset returns and incentivising the targeting of RoA may not therefore be efficient in isolation. Focusing on RoA rather than RoE may of course limit the incentives for senior executives to leverage their balance sheets, but in the presence of leverage controls and significant deferral of variable compensation, these risks are reduced. By reason of this, rather than proscribing the focus of bank compensation system formulae, instead, an increase in the length of the deferral period for bonuses based on either RoE or RoA would concentrate the minds of executives on the long term and reduce incentives for profit-seeking, short-term earnings management. Further, it is also clear that calibrating systems to assess risk is incredibly difficult; the proposed deferral period (with attendant clawback) may reduce the need for this calibration.[50]

Of course, practical criticisms regarding deferral and clawback would have to be addressed. As with a ban on hedging, deferring the vesting of restricted stock increases managements' risk exposure to the stock price of the company, leading to potential risk aversion and a reduction in shareholder wealth.[51] Managers may also still use their power to time their stock sales to extract maximum rents from the company, either through trading on inside information or through manipulating the stock

---

[50] 'The challenge facing the industry is how, in practice, to incorporate an accurate measure of risk into the compensation setting process. In relatively simple business areas, there are imperfect yet accepted risk metrics that capture economic capital usage. In more complex business areas, the problem of capturing risk is amplified by product intricacies and deal time horizons.' See IIF, *Compensation in Financial Services* 3.2.1.1.

[51] See Bryan et al, 'CEO Stock-Based Compensation'.

price.[52] Tax considerations also must be countenanced if deferred stock awards are to retain an incentive effect.[53] Moreover, of course, significant compensation deferral may deter talented executives from entry into particular industries, increasing the possibility that banks may leave particular jurisdictions.[54] The costs and requisite time for implementing these reforms are also not inconsiderable. Few financial institutions currently assess performance for bonus purposes over a multi-year framework (just 8 per cent).[55] Over half of IIF members do not incorporate any form of risk adjustment into their bonus pools.[56] It is also clear that while financial institutions generally use deferral mechanisms (76 per cent), on average, only 20 per cent of bonus compensation is deferred,[57] although these figures are expected to change dramatically as financial institutions sign up to industry-wide codes of best practice such

---

52 See generally, Myron S. Scholes, 'Stock and Compensation' (1991) 46 J. FIN. 803.

53 The vesting of restricted stock generally gives rise to a tax liability. See US Internal Revenue Code § 83(a) (2006) (triggering tax liability when 'the rights of the person having the beneficial interest in such property are transferable or are not subject to a substantial risk of forfeiture'). For further discussion see Lucian A. Bebchuk & Jesse M. Fried, 'Paying for Long-term Performance' (2010) 158 UNIV. PENN. LAW REV. 1915.

54 This threat appears more apparent than real: for example, '[It has been posited that] governments must choose between domestic financial stability and the competitiveness of their domestic financial centers. Clearly, if you believe that higher capital requirements damage bank profitability and shareholder returns then you must also fear for the competitiveness of your domestic banking champions, the attractiveness of your country as a global *finanz platz* and the tax take for your treasury. But as we have seen, one need not choose between safer banks and profitable banking … Less leverage will not only be rewarded with a lower cost of capital but also in lower costs for most sources of funding – from bank debt to wholesale deposits. And in terms of market share, the strongest banks are growing their clientele (e.g. revenue) at the expense of weaker competitors. In a world of increased risk awareness, letting your banks off the capital hook will likely damage not enhance their ability to compete. Extend the analogy to your country as financial center: where would clients and counterparties like best to do business? In a stable, well regulated regime? Or in one burying problems and ducking issues because regulators fear their banking system too fragile to fix? Needless to say, the tried and booed alternative – light touch/highly leveraged regimes proved devastating to gross domestic product, the taxman's take and to public confidence in banking and its regulation.' See Jenkins, 'A Debate Framed by Fallacies'.

55 IIF, *Compensation in Financial Services* 3.2.2.

56 Ibid. 3.2.1.1.

57 Ibid.

as the FSB Principles, or are forced to comply with new regulations on bankers' pay such as the EU cap on variable compensation. However, the effects of any potential 'brain drain' or costs of implementation must of course be weighed against the implicit costs of financial bailouts caused by reckless lending, through implicit guarantees, capital infusions during periods of crisis, and the knock-on externalities imposed by failed banks on wider society. These factors in themselves satisfy any burden associated with justifying greater regulation of compensation systems at financial institutions.

Proposal II – Restricting Leverage-based Executive Compensation

This book has postulated that a significant portion of accelerated executive compensation, particularly since the 1980s, is the result mainly of asset value inflation, exaggerated by a massive increase in the use of leverage,[58] which has allowed executives to capture excess rents in an environment of subsidised funding and guaranteed bailouts. As discussed in previous chapters, executive compensation plans may encourage an increase in risk taking, including an increase in leverage.[59] Managers benefit generally from changes in the volatility of their options.[60] This is the case to the extent that the value of the stock price of a levered financial firm may be equated with the value of a call option which increases in accordance with the riskiness of the assets held by the firm.[61] There are therefore risk-taking incentives for executive officers to

---

[58] Margaret M. Blair, 'Financial Innovation, Leverage, Bubbles and the Distribution of Income' (2010–11) 30 REV. BANKING & FIN. LAW 275; Thomas Philippon, 'The Evolution of the US Financial Industry from 1860 to 2007: Theory and Evidence' (2008) http://economics.stanford.edu/files/Philippon5_20.pdf.

[59] Some recent publications on this issue include, Alon Raviv & Elif Sisli-Ciamarra, 'Executive Compensation, Risk-taking and the State of the Economy' (2013) 9 J. FIN. STABILITY 55 (hereinafter Raviv & Sisli-Ciamarra, 'Executive Compensation & Risk-Taking'); Sjoerd Van Bekkum, 'Inside Debt and Enterprise-Wide Bank Risk' (2012) http://ssrn.com/sol3/papers.cfm?abstract_id=1682139; Robert DeYoung, Emma Y. Peng, & Meng Yan, 'Executive Compensation and Business Policy Choices at US Commercial Banks' (2010) FRB Kansas City Working Paper 10-02; Jeffrey L. Coles, Naveen D. Daniel & Lalitha Naveen, 'Managerial Incentives and Risk-taking' (2006) 79 J. FIN. ECON. 431.

[60] Philip G. Berger, Eli Ofek & David Yermack, 'Managerial Entrenchment and Capital Structure Decisions' (1997) 52 J. FIN. 1411.

[61] A point made forcefully in Bebchuk & Spamann, 'Regulating Bankers' Pay'.

increase stock return volatility in order to profit from fluctuations in the value of stock prices, and executives cannot be incentivised to adopt moderate levels of leveraging because of the concave relationship between asset volatility and the value of total compensation. Whilst the first proposal concerning deferral and clawback discussed previously is not without merit, it might not in isolation produce compensation systems which fully reflect the risks of financial crisis generated by expansions in leverage. These risks become much more acute when one incorporates the findings of the FIH in the analysis. As memories of previous crises fade, market actors (including regulators) will be willing to countenance returns to previous compensation structures,[62] particularly if their financial fortunes are linked to the volume of credit in the economy or asset prices. There must therefore be some mechanism, in addition to those proposed by regulators, to restrict compensation linked to asset and equity price levels in periods of economic euphoria. Current BCBS policy is rightly focused on reducing the propensity for credit-based expansion to destroy solidity in the financial system. If it is assumed a priori that the GFC was driven, in part, by flawed incentives, reforming capital requirements might therefore add significant protections to guard against tail-risks generated by poor incentives.[63]

There have been at least three options recommended to cement this form of stabilisation, each of which differs in terms of the mechanisms employed:

(i) To allow the strike price of stock options to be allowed to vary with the price of the debt incurred by the company. Applying this to the proposal concerned, the risk-taking appetite of the executive would be a function of the firm's leverage ratio. As the leverage ratio increased, so would the default probability and the executive would be motivated to assume a lower threshold of risk to compensate.[64]

(ii) To require that managers be paid with debt, rather than equity, which would effectively restrain executives' risk taking by making their compensation contingent on the firm remaining solvent. This

---

62 For example, the EU bonus cap is to be reviewed in 2016.

63 Felix Salmon, 'The Biggest Weakness of Basel III', *Reuters*, 24 September 2010, http://blogs.reuters.com/felix-salmon/2010/09/15.

64 Alon Raviv & Yoram Landskroner, 'The 2007–2009 Financial Crisis and Executive Compensation: Analysis and a Proposal for a Novel Structure' (2009) NYU Working Paper No. FIN-09-003.

would theoretically reduce the incentives to leverage because higher leverage levels carry a relatively increased threat of bankruptcy.[65]

(iii) To require that the compensation of CEOs (and, presumably, other top-ranking corporate executives) be linked to the firm's CDS spread.[66] Deferred bonuses of CEOs would be placed in a stand-alone fund by the company and then paid out under a pre-specified formula dependent on whether the companies' CDS spread deviated from the average companies' spread. In other words, the higher the default spread (and, by proxy, the riskier the firm), the lower the executive's variable compensation. Empirical analysis confirms that market participants believe that linking executive compensation to the risk of default will reduce firm riskiness.[67] Higher leverage would, in most cases, present to analysts an increased risk of default and therefore credit spreads on its bonds would widen.

Whilst these proposals are certainly not without advantages over current compensation systems, what remains abundantly clear is that market-based compensation systems have largely failed to rein in excessive risk taking, and the limits to the systems of risk limitation discussed above are commensurate with the limits to market pricing and behavioural factors traced earlier in this book. Each of the proposals relies on the market-pricing mechanism to some degree to inform their design. Based on the observations charted in this book, particularly the tenets of the FIH, this would appear to be a flawed approach to regulating compensation, in particular because market inefficiency might prevent the appropriate stabilisation of executive compensation based on the metrics discussed. In the context of the use of CDS spreads, for example, it is clear that in the run-up to the GFC, bank CDS spreads were not immediately indicative of distress amongst the portfolios of financial institutions. Whilst financial instability began to increase rapidly (calculated based on equity-to-market value of assets) in the final quarter of 2006, it was not until the third quarter of 2007 that CDS spreads began to

---

65 Alex Edmans & Qi Liu, 'Inside Debt' (2011) 15 REV. FIN. 75. See also Frederick Tung, 'Pay for Banker Performance: Structuring Executive Compensation for Risk Regulation' (2010) Emory Public Law Research Paper No. 10-93 (2010); Bebchuk & Spamann, 'Regulating Bankers' Pay'.

66 Patrick Bolton, Hamid Mehran & Joel Shapiro, 'Executive Compensation and Risk-Taking' (2011) FRB New York Working Paper No. 456.

67 Ibid. 2.

react.[68] For this reason, it would appear that trusting market-based mechanisms to regulate elements of compensation systems which relate to or are dependent on leverage may not result in sufficient incentives to reduce risk. Accordingly, meaningful reforms must be imposed through regulation, rather than market-based mechanisms. The most appropriate route to regulation is, in my view, to build upon existing reform of regulatory capital levels at banks (in combination with the previously discussed deferral and clawback provisions) in order to reduce incentives for leverage-based expansion, and thereby exert 'natural' downward pressure on bankers' compensation.[69]

Firstly, the Basel III Accord increases the proportion of Tier One capital which must be held by banks from 4 per cent to 6 per cent of their RWAs. Further, at least 4.5 per cent of Tier One capital for the purposes of capital regulation must now be comprised of common equity or retained earnings, up from 2 per cent under Basel II.[70] In relation to executive compensation, this has major implications. Firstly, the requirement for higher capital levels will axiomatically limit the capacity of banks to expand their balance sheets to the same degree that was possible pre-Basel III because the new rules mean that banks must hold a higher proportion of top-quality capital to withstand losses from asset write-downs. Whilst there have been some studies which suggest that economic growth will be impacted negatively by these higher capital requirements, the fact that capital regulations remove incentives to expand balance sheets to capture higher RoE – and thereby higher executive compensation packages – will go some way to counteracting these trends and,

---

68 Mark J. Flannery, 'What to do about TBTF?', Paper presented at the Federal Reserve Bank of Atlanta 2010 Financial Markets Conference, 'Up from the Ashes: The Financial System after the Crisis', Atlanta, Georgia, 12 May 2010, Figure 4. As noted by the manager of hedge fund Scion Capital LLC, which made over $800 million shorting US sub-prime mortgages, it was inconceivable that CDS spreads failed to reflect the default probabilities on the CDOs written by Wall Street's banks until June 2007: 'I was in a state of perpetual disbelief. I would have thought that someone would have recognized what was coming before June 2007. If it really took that [long] to cause a … realization, well, it makes me wonder what a "Wall Street analyst" really does all day.' See Michael Lewis, *The Big Short: Inside The Doomsday Machine* (Allen Lane, 2010) 198.

69 For a more detailed statement of this proposal, see Avgouleas & Cullen, 'Excessive Leverage and Bankers' Pay'.

70 BCBS, *Basel III: A Global Regulatory Framework For More Resilient Banks and Banking Systems* (2011) (hereinafter BCBS, *Basel III*).

moreover, ought to make the financial system more stable.[71] Further, the requirement that common equity and retained earnings make up such a large portion of Tier One capital (at least relative to Basel II), means that the incentives to engage in RWO are much reduced which, as discussed in Chapter 5, resulted in large banks holding levels of capital which did not actually conform to the principles of prevailing capital regulations.

Basel III also introduces a 'capital conservation buffer' (CCB), 'designed to ensure that banks build up capital buffers outside periods of stress which can be drawn down as losses are incurred'.[72] The move was driven largely by the behaviour of banks prior to the GFC, as they continued to make distributions in the form of share buybacks, dividends and discretionary bonus payments, despite the fact that both their individual capital positions and systemic capital levels had become severely weakened.[73] The CCB is designed to ensure that banks build up capital reserves in benign economic conditions, and to enforce the rebuilding of those reserves following an economic downturn. The CCB prevents banks which have depleted their capital buffers from using predictions of future economic recovery to justify awarding either dividend payments to shareholders or bonus payments to staff. The CCB requires that banks set down an additional 2.5 per cent of Tier One common equity capital (thereby raising the Tier One common equity capital ratio to 7 per cent). The lower the proportion of Tier One common equity capital held above the 4.5 per cent floor to comprise the CCB, the

---

[71] Leonardo Gambacorta, Jing Yang & Kostas Tsatsaronis, 'Financial structure and growth' (2014) BIS Q. REV. 21 (finding that up to a point, banks and markets both foster economic growth, but beyond that limit, expanded bank lending or market-based financing no longer adds to real growth); Siong Hook Law & Nirvikar Singh, 'Does Too Much Finance Harm Economic Growth?' (2014) 41 &J. BANK. & FIN. 36 (finding a threshold effect in the finance–growth relationship, which means that the level of financial development is beneficial to growth only up to a certain threshold; beyond the threshold level further development of finance tends to adversely affect growth); Jean-Louis Arcand, Enrico Berkes & Ugo Panizza, 'Too Much Finance?' (2012) IMF Working Paper WP/12/161 (finding that finance starts having a negative effect on output growth when credit to the private sector reaches 100% of GDP); and Stephen G Cecchetti & Enisse Kharroubi, 'Reassessing the Impact of Finance on Growth' (2012) BIS Working Paper No. 381 (finding that the level of financial development is good only up to a point, after which it becomes a drag on growth, and in advanced economies a fast-growing financial sector is detrimental to aggregate productivity growth).

[72] BCBS, *Basel III* 54.

[73] Monica Mars, 'Procyclicality' in Richard Barfield (ed), *A Practitioner's Guide To Basel III And Beyond* (Sweet & Maxwell, 2011) 245–46.

more restricted the ability of banks to make discretionary payments, including bonuses. Table 7.1 shows the minimum capital conservation ratios that apply in determining the proportion of permitted distributions which may be made.

Table 7.1 Calculation of distributable earnings

Core Tier 1 assets above minimum 4.5%	% earnings distributable
0 – 0.625	0
0.626 – 1.24	20
1.25 – 1.824	40
1.825 – 2.49	60
2.5+	100

Accordingly, the buffer constrains the ability of bank boards to issue discretionary payments following stress periods, and incentivises the build-up of high quality capital as banks make profits in benign economic conditions (a corollary to the 'euphoric' stages identified by the FIH). Whilst holding this additional Tier One capital is discretionary, in practice, financial institutions will be required to make bonus and dividend payments by the market and, on this basis, the CCB provides a highly effective tool to prevent the whittling away of high quality capital.

Linked to the CCB is a 'countercyclical buffer' (CB), which may require banks to build up at least 2.5 per cent of additional Tier One capital in times of 'excessive' credit growth.[74] The rationale underpinning the CB is that bank failure and the business cycle are often closely correlated, and a linkage between bank capital requirements and the macroeconomic cycle may prevent the accumulation of credit in the upswing of the cycle, and by implication, protect the financial system from deleveraging during crisis:[75]

> Losses incurred in the banking sector can be extremely large when a downturn is preceded by a period of excess credit growth. These losses can destabilise the banking sector and spark a vicious circle, whereby problems in the financial system can contribute to a downturn in the real economy that

---

[74] National regulators are charged with assessing credit levels and taking appropriate action.

[75] Simon Gleeson, *International Regulation of Banking: Capital and Risk Requirements* (2nd edn, OUP, 2012) 6.49.

> then feeds back on to the banking sector. These interactions highlight the particular importance of the banking sector building up additional capital defences in periods where the risks of system-wide stress are growing markedly.[76]

The CB will be triggered based upon a credit-to-GDP ratio: where the volume of credit within a country breaches a certain level in relation to its GDP, the buffer will be activated and financial institutions will be forced to conserve capital. The amount of capital to be conserved under the CB will depend upon the extent of the build-up of systemic risk. The CB is thus designed to promote macroeconomic stability; accordingly, it is 'the most potent regulatory weapon so far to counter bubbles and the debilitating effects these have on the financial sector once they diminish …'.[77] Whilst the CB is not the only tool available to national supervisors to use in the identification and treatment of excessive credit,[78] it arguably provides a formidable frontstop tool to prevent banks from excessive lending and the inflation of (certain) asset classes, particularly the property market.[79] Moreover, as with the CCB, the CB increases the minimum buffer required of banks to meet capital requirements at precisely the time that asset markets show signs of overheating. This, in the context of executive compensation, will arguably reduce focus on RoE, as the requirement to hold additional equity capital, together with the effect that restrictions on credit growth may have on asset prices, will reduce the capacity of bankers to profit by extending loans in these 'euphoric' expansionary economic periods.

Basel III has furthermore introduced a non-risk-based leverage ratio of 3 per cent of Tier One assets.[80] Any bank with a leverage ratio of assets to capital of less than 3 per cent will be deemed to be undercapitalised. The leverage ratio adds a further layer of capital control, because the

---

[76] BCBS, *Basel III* 136.

[77] Avgouleas, *Governance of Global Financial Markets* 325–26.

[78] The Basel Committee recommends that supervisors also monitor various asset prices, funding and CDS spreads, credit-condition surveys, real GDP growth, and data on the ability of non-financial firms to meet payments under their credit agreements. See ibid. 328.

[79] Charles A.E. Goodhart, 'The Macro-Prudential Authority: Powers, Scope and Accountability' (2011) 2 OECD J. FIN. MARKET TRENDS 1.

[80] BCBS, *Basel III* 61. For discussion, see Martin Hellwig, 'Capital Regulation after the Crisis: Business as Usual?' (2010) Max Planck Institute For Research on Collective Goods, Bonn 2010/31. The leverage ratio is defined as the quarterly average total assets less deductions that include goodwill, investments deducted from Tier One capital, and deferred taxes.

effects of risk-weighting of assets are stripped out of the ratio calculation. The use of the ratio therefore has two interlinked consequences: firstly, it prevents the expansion of bank balance sheets without a commensurate increase in the amount of capital held by the relevant banks and secondly, it provides significant safeguards against modelling errors related to asset risk-weighting.[81]

The implementation of the ratio is at various stages in different jurisdictions, although the Basel III Accord does not require full compliance until 2018. Despite this extended timescale, some jurisdictions have opted to go further than the recommended 3 per cent ratio under Basel III. For example, in the US, the leverage ratio has been set at 4 per cent of total assets. Moreover, under a recent final rule, bank holding companies (BHCs) with more than $700 billion in consolidated total assets or $10 trillion in assets under custody (covered BHCs), are required to maintain a Tier One capital buffer of at least 2 per cent above the minimum supplementary leverage ratio requirement of 3 per cent, resulting in a total leverage ratio of 5 per cent.[82] Swiss financial regulators also insist upon more strict leverage ratios than those required under Basel III, although it has become apparent that Canadian financial regulators are prepared to adopt it.[83] In the EU, leverage ratios are under

---

[81] 'The more advanced and complex the models become, the greater the need for such a baseline. The leverage ratio ensures that a capital backstop remains even if model errors or other miscalculations impair the reliability of risk-based capital. This is a crucial consideration – particularly as we work through the implementation of Basel II standard. By restraining balance sheet growth, the leverage ratio promotes stability and resilience during difficult economic periods.' Remarks by Sheila Bair, Chairman, Federal Deposit Insurance Corporation before the Basel Committee on Banking Supervision, Merida, Mexico, 4 October 2006.

[82] Regulatory Capital Rules: Regulatory Capital, Enhanced Supplementary Leverage Ratio Standards for Certain Bank Holding Companies and Their Subsidiary Insured Depository Institutions, 79 Fed. Reg. 24,528 (Final Rule: May 1, 2014) (12 C.F.R pts. 6, 208, 217, 324). Failure to exceed the 5% ratio would subject covered BHCs to restrictions on discretionary bonus payments and capital distributions. In addition to the leverage buffer for covered BHCs, the proposed rule would require insured depository institutions of covered BHCs to meet a 6% supplementary leverage ratio to be considered 'well capitalised' for prompt corrective action purposes. This proposed rule would currently apply to the eight largest, most systemically significant US banking organisations.

[83] In Canada there has been a strict leverage ratio of assets (including off-balance sheet items) to capital of 20:1, although Canada's main bank regulator has indicated that the jurisdiction will adopt the leverage ratio recommended under Basel III. See Katia Dmitrieva, 'OSFI to Replace Canada

implementation via the Fourth Capital Requirements Directive ('CRD IV')[84] and as in the US, EU regulators use the Basel III Accord as a template for action. However, although CRD IV requires that institutions calculate and report on their leverage ratios, CRD IV has not yet mandated a minimum leverage ratio. The European Banking Authority is to monitor developments and the implementation of Basel III to evaluate whether the 3 per cent minimum leverage ratio is appropriate for European financial institutions. On this basis, the UK has followed the lead of the EU Commission, and no recommendations for higher leverage ratios have been announced.[85]

Increased leverage is symptomatic of an increasingly fragile financial structure, which, as predicted by the FIH, escalates the potential for financial crisis. This is all the more important because evidence indicates that leverage is strongly pro-cyclical and thus contributes to both bubbles and crashes.[86] On this basis, each of the measures discussed have the capacity to limit excessive credit growth and, in this way, to indirectly reduce the incentive to link compensation to metrics such as RoE, a practice which contributes to higher risk taking. When viewed in conjunction with the proposals concerning deferral of compensation, it is these aspects of suggested reforms to executive remuneration which go farthest in reducing the propensity for economies to become over-leveraged during euphoric periods, and thereby unstable. Accordingly, this proposal resonates with the principles of the FIH, which regards the

---

Leverage Rules With Basel III', Bloomberg, 14 January 2014, http://www.bloomberg.com/news/2014-01-14/osfi-to-replace-canada-leverage-rules-with-basel-iii.html. For discussion, see Allan Crawford, Chris Graham & Étienne Bordeleau, 'Regulatory Constraints on Leverage: The Canadian Experience' (2009) BANK OF CANADA FIN. SYS. REV. 45. In Switzerland a leverage ratio of 4% at the consolidated bank level is required by the national regulator, although regulators have discussed raising the ratio to 6–10%. See Kersten Kellermann & Carsten-Henning Schlag, 'Occupy Risk Weighting: How the Minimum Leverage Ratio dominates Capital Requirements – A Swiss Example' (2013) 21 J. FIN. REG. & COMPLIANCE 353.

[84] Directive 2013/36/EU of the European Parliament and of the Council of 26 June 2013 on access to the activity of credit institutions and the prudential supervision of credit institutions and investment firms, amending Directive 2002/87/EC and repealing Directives 2006/48/EC and 2006/49/EC, OJ L176/338 (27 June 2013).

[85] Bank Of England Prudential Regulatory Authority, *Capital and Leverage Ratios for Major UK Banks and Building Societies, Supervisory Statement SS3/13* (2013).

[86] Tobias Adrian & Hyun Song Shin, 'Liquidity and Leverage' (2010) 19 J. FIN. INTERMEDIATION 418.

adoption of increasingly unstable financial structures by economic units as the precursor to crisis. Progressively higher leverage levels, of course, are a manifestation of this pattern.

There are some arguments against both mandating an increase in capital levels at banks and enforcing more strict leverage ratios. The most significant objection is perhaps that increasing bank capital and restricting leverage will reduce the amount of credit available for loans and project finance, and thereby reduce investment.[87] There are also significant tax and liquidity advantages to operating with high leverage as opposed to high capital ratios.[88] There are further objections raised on the basis that increasing capital requirements and introducing strict leverage ratios will incentivise bankers to engage in higher-risk lending, on the basis that this will capture for them higher RoE.[89] Indeed, recent reports suggests that large US banks have reduced the proportion of 'safe' assets they hold as a proportion of their total asset levels, indicating that their balance sheets are becoming progressively riskier.[90] Thus, introducing a leverage ratio might result in the generation, rather than elimination, of perverse incentives. However, these costs must be weighed against the counterfactual scenario, which is that the costs of the externalities resulting from bank failure are often many multiples of the supposed benefits.[91] For example, whilst restricting credit through these methods

---

[87] International Institute of Finance, *The Cumulative Impact on the Global Economy of Changes in the Financial Regulatory Framework* (2011), predicting a cumulative loss in GDP of 2.9% through capital regulation reforms by 2020.

[88] Gary Gorton & George G. Pennacchi, 'Financial Intermediaries and Liquidity Creation' (1990) 45 J. FIN. 49. For a recent discussion of this, see Harry DeAngelo & René M. Stulz, 'Liquid-Claim Production, Risk Management, and Bank Capital Structure: Why High Leverage is Optimal for Banks' (2013) Charles A. Dice Center for Research in Financial Economics Working Paper No. 2013-03-08.

[89] Haldane & Madouros, 'The Dog and the Frisbee' 19.

[90] Tracy Alloway, 'US Banks Take On More Risk As New Rules Bite' *Financial Times* (London, 16 January 2014) http://ft.com.

[91] Anat R. Admati, Peter M. DeMarzo, Martin F. Hellwig & Paul Pfleiderer, 'Fallacies, Irrelevant Facts, and Myths in the Discussion of Capital Regulation: Why Bank Equity is Not Expensive' (2013) Rock Center for Corporate Governance at Stanford University Working Paper No. 161 (hereinafter Admati et al, 'Fallacies, Irrelevant Facts and Myths'). Estimates by Nicholas Nassim Taleb suggest that banks have never made a profit in the history of banking; he notes that 'the incentive scheme commonly in place does the exact opposite of what an "incentive" system should be about: it encourages a certain class of risk-hiding and deferred blow-up. It is the reason banks have never made money in the

may reduce economic activity, it is not clear that this will necessarily reduce allocative efficiency in the economy. Put simply, there can be too much credit, and there is an optimal upper bound of aggregate credit beyond which output decreases, rather than appreciates (see above for discussion). Recent studies also suggest that increased capital regulation will not have any adverse impact on economic growth.[92] It is also unclear that regulating capital and leverage more closely might incentivise bankers to pursue riskier projects, as the incentives to leverage themselves add to the agency costs of banking, leading to an environment where senior executives directly favour low-quality, high-yield loans over high-quality but low-yield loans.[93]

Moreover, there are several other convincing factors which would support the introduction of leverage ratios. Firstly, leverage-based incentives in compensation contracts not only encourage managers to amplify equity risk, but also contribute to the build-up of asset risk[94] within investment portfolios, and thereby systemic risk.[95] Empirical evidence

history of banking, losing the equivalent of all their past profits periodically – while bankers strike it rich. Furthermore, it is that incentive scheme that got us in the current mess.' See Nicholas Nassim Taleb, 'How Bank Bonuses Let Us All Down' *Financial Times* (London, 24 February 2009) http://ft.com.

[92] David Miles, Jing Yang & Gilberto Marcheggiano, 'Optimal Bank Capital' (2013) 123 ECON. J. 1; Georg Junge & Peter Kugler, 'Quantifying the Impact of Higher Capital Requirements on the Swiss economy' (2012) MIMEO, http://wwz.unibas.ch/fileadmin/wwz/redaktion/makro/Papers/G_Junge_P_Kugler_July_02_2012_V3_fina.pdf; Anil Kashyap, Jeremy C. Stein & Samuel G. Hanson, 'An Analysis of the Impact of "Substantially Heightened" Capital Requirements on Large Financial Institutions' (2010), MIMEO, http://www.people.hbs.edu/shanson/Clearinghouse-paper-final_20100521.pdf; Douglas J. Elliot, 'Quantifying the Effects on Lending of Increased Capital Requirements' (2009) Pew Financial Reform Project Working Paper, The Brookings Institution; Jochen Schanz, David Aikman, Paul Collazos, Marc Farag, David Gregory & Sujit Kapadi, 'The Long-term Economic Impact of Higher Capital Levels' (2009) BIS Working Paper No. 60.

[93] Admati et al, 'Fallacies, Irrelevant Facts and Myths'.

[94] Marc Chesney, Jacob Stromberg & Alexander F. Wagner, 'Managerial Incentives to Take Asset Risk' (2012) Swiss Financial Institute Research Paper No. 10-18, 28. See also Clifford W. Smith & Rene M. Stulz, 'The Determinants of Firms' Hedging Policies' (1985) 20 J. FIN. QUANT. AN. 391; Robert A. Haugen & Lemma W. Senbet, 'Resolving the Agency Problems of External Capital through Options' (1981) 36 J. FIN. 629.

[95] Christopher S. Armstrong & Rahul Vashishtha, 'Executive Stock Options, Differential Risk-taking Incentives, and Firm Value' (2012) 104 J. FIN. ECON. 70.

confirms that, in periods of tranquillity (as explained by the FIH), bankers target the maximum level of asset risk to benefit from higher RoE, which is most easily achieved through increased leverage.[96] Borio and Lowe document that 'sustained rapid credit growth combined with large increases in asset prices appears to increase the probability of an episode of financial instability'.[97] Secondly, leverage ratios are simple to apply and by stripping out RWAs, they reduce the capacity of bankers to manipulate capital levels.[98] Moreover, RWA levels were not as predictive of bank distress as leverage ratios prior to the GFC, which would suggest that, despite being the more crude measure of financial strength, leverage ratios are more adept indicators of the potential for bank collapse.[99]

Relying on current protections enshrined in Basel III would reduce reliance on incentive-moulding regulation of all executive compensation contracts and simultaneously institute extra defences against future periods of systemic instability by forcing management of banks to maintain appropriate capital and leverage ratios. As noted in relation to removing structures which inhibit reactions to high-impact events: 'Chief among the obstacles are short-term compensation systems which reinforce behavioural biases [which] leads to a fatal neglect of the longer-term build-up of risk.'[100] If leverage-based expansion can be contained by reducing the ability of investors and executives to herd (which often amplifies leverage) or engage in other strategies which inflate asset and stock prices, greater stability and lower price distortion will result. Limiting discretionary awards of stock- or asset-based compensation awards to executives at financial institutions in periods of euphoria will promote a more risk-based approach to corporate investment strategies.

Proposal III – Incentivising Sustainable Behaviours

Whilst a discussion of the ethics of banking are beyond the scope of this book, additional measures may be introduced alongside reform to compensation structures to complement the proposed reforms, such as more prescriptive ethical signposting to guide bankers' behaviour in their

---

96 Raviv & Sisli-Ciamarra, 'Executive Compensation & Risk-Taking'.

97 Claudio Borio & Philip Lowe, 'Asset Prices, Financial and Monetary Stability: Exploring the Nexus' (2002) BIS Working Paper No. 114.

98 Andrea Beltratti & Giovanna Paladino, 'Why Do Banks Optimize Risk Weights? The Relevance of the Cost of Equity Capital' (2013) MPRA Working Paper No. 46410.

99 Blundell-Wignall & Roulet, 'Business Models of Banks'.

100 Rizzi, 'Behavioral Basis of the Financial Crisis' 95.

decision making and investments. Western financial systems are run on the basis of the perceived ability of executives to run profitable businesses. This view of corporate organisation has held sway for decades yet short-term performance indicators have supplanted long-term sustainability as the chief driver of economic existence. It is unsurprising, therefore, that the pursuit of financial gain has, in some instances, clouded the judgment of some boards and executives, and denuded their appreciation of risk.

Moving forward, reforms to corporate governance should not happen in a vacuum, and it may be necessary to contextualise reforms to pay at financial institutions by emphasising the importance of value-enhancing behaviours, through measures such as compulsory training of bank executives on the societal costs of their operations, and through recognition of measures of value creation and sustainability beyond analysis of profit and loss. There is convincing evidence, for example, that signalling via sanctions can be used as a powerful mechanism to drive behavioural and cultural changes.[101] On this basis, there are, in my view, two simple tools which may be implemented in addition to reform to bankers' compensation: (i) emphasising ethical principles through corporate governance guidelines backed by (criminal) sanctions for non-compliance; and (ii) rewarding sustainable behaviours through a higher degree of qualitative assessment in determining performance-related pay.

(i) Governance reform (including criminalisation of certain conduct)

With regard to the first tool, it is clear that reforms to corporate governance following the GFC have so far been largely cast in the traditional and deliberately amorphous and non-descript language characteristic of codes and guidelines, which rely to a large extent on executives

[101] Joel van der Weele, 'The Signaling Power of Sanctions in Social Dilemmas' (2012) 28 J. LAW ECON. ORGAN. 103; Dirk Sliwka, 'Trust as a Signal of a Social Norm and the Hidden Costs of Incentive Schemes' (2007) 97 AM. ECON. REV. 999; Michael Wenzel, 'The Social Side of Sanctions: Personal and Social Norms as Moderators of Deterrence' (2004) 28 LAW & HUMAN BEHAV. 547; James Andreoni, William T. Harbaugh & Lise Vesterlund, 'The Carrot or the Stick: Rewards, Punishments and Cooperation' (2003) 93 AM. ECON. REV. 893; Roland Bénabou & Jean Tirole, 'Intrinsic and Extrinsic Motivation' (2003) 70 REV. ECON. STUD. 489; Uri Gneezy & Aldo Rustichini, 'A Fine is a Price' (2000) 29 J. LEGAL STUD. 1; In-Koo Cho & David. M. Kreps, 'Signaling Games and Stable Equilibria' (1987) 102 Q. J. ECON. 179.

and boards of directors working towards the overarching goal of shareholder value. In the UK context, for example, the Walker Review[102] devoted an entire chapter to discussing reform of compensation arrangements in the financial sector, and made 12 recommendations in respect of remuneration.[103] However, none of the recommendations involved the common sense language of what *ought* to be done – what guiding principles banks ought to use when directing performance. Indeed, ultimately, in the overall analysis, Walker concluded that the (old) Combined Code on Corporate Governance 'remains fit for purpose' – overlooking, in an instant, the fact that the code was wholly ineffective last time the financial world crashed. Whilst these new rules seek transparency, avoiding paying more than necessary, and linking pay to individual and corporate performance, what principles do these guidelines espouse? What do they reveal to investors about the corporate strategy of a firm in relation to the recruitment and compensation of its executives? There is no mention of key values to guide behaviour or purpose in leadership, or sanctions for failure. No values to underpin firm remuneration policies are outlined; instead, the guidance retreats to the trusted corporate language of 'structures', 'performance objectives' and 'disclosure', language familiar to analysts of corporate governance in public corporations.[104] Proposals to empower shareholders to vote on

---

[102] David Walker, *A Review of Corporate Governance In UK Banks and Other Financial Industry Entities: Final Recommendations* (2009).

[103] Ibid. chapter 7, recommendations 28–39. On the issue of the remuneration committee at banks, for example, the Review states: 'The remuneration committee should provide the packages needed to attract, retain and motivate executive directors of the quality required but should avoid paying more than is necessary for this purpose … Remuneration committees should judge where to position their company relative to other companies. They should be aware what comparable companies are paying and should take account of relative performance. But they should use such comparisons with caution, in view of the risk that they can result in an upward ratchet of remuneration levels with no corresponding improvement in performance … Remuneration committees should be sensitive to the wider scene, including pay and employment conditions elsewhere in the group, especially when determining annual salary increases.'

[104] Moreover, the ethos underpinning pay practices subsisting in the financial sector has continued to influence compensation cultures across industries, and therefore reform to the root may also inculcate reform of the branch. Roger Bootle has found this reflected in senior corporate executives outside the BOFI sector, stating: 'The pay culture of the City has affected expectations elsewhere. The whole climate is relevant here, because bad practices drive out the good … If, wherever you look, you see people lining their pockets rapaciously, without any thought for what is right, then if you do the right thing, you are made to feel

executive pay packages, for example, common to all of the recommendations reviewed in the previous chapter, follow in the traditional footsteps of corporate governance theory, surveyed earlier in this book. According to this view of governance, shareholders should be granted increased powers to ratify or reject the compensation of key executives and board members; as the owners of firms, they are regarded as the ultimate disciplining force with which to balance the power of management.[105] Indeed, shareholder power and influence in disciplining management is positively correlated with superior firm performance: firms with stronger shareholder rights have higher firm values, higher profits, higher sales growth, lower capital expenditures and make fewer corporate acquisitions.[106]

However, the framing of this issue proceeds from the position that only shareholders have the necessary incentives and detachment from the board to regulate executive pay effectively, despite there being a good deal of evidence suggesting that shareholder power, as a risk-reducing mechanism, is limited in practical terms.[107] I have written elsewhere in the context of the corporate governance of European banks about the

---

stupid. Your wife thinks you are stupid, your friends at the golf club think you are stupid … executive pay reflects a deeper underlying failure revealed by the banking crisis. The whole system of boards and non-executives has been a major failure. And scrutiny by shareholders hasn't worked.' See Ruth Sutherland, 'Invasion of the Booty Snatchers: How Greed Is Spreading Out from the City' *The Observer* (London, 18 April 2012) http://www.theguardian.com.

[105] Lucian A. Bebchuk, 'Letting Shareholders Set the Rules' (2006) 119 HARV. LAW REV. 1784; Lucian A. Bebchuk, 'The Case for Increasing Shareholder Power' (2005) 118 HARV. LAW REV. 833; Kym Sheehan, 'Say on Pay and the Outrage Constraint' in Jennifer Hill & Randall Thomas (eds), *Research Handbook on Executive Compensation* (Edward Elgar, 2012) (hereinafter Hill & Thomas (eds), *Research Handbook on Executive Compensation*).

[106] Paul A. Gompers, Joy L. Ishii and Andrew Metrick, 'Corporate Governance and Equity Prices' (2003) 118 Q. J. ECON. 107.

[107] Lucian A. Bebchuk, 'The Myth of the Shareholder Franchise' (2007) 93 VIRGINIA LAW REV. 675; Marcel Kahan and Edward B. Rock, 'How I Learned to Stop Worrying and Love the Pill: Adaptive Responses to Takeover Law' (2002) 69 UNIV. CHICAGO LAW REV. 871; Stephen M. Bainbridge, 'Director Primacy: The Means and Ends of Corporate Governance' (2003) 97 NORTH-WESTERN UNIV. LAW REV. 547. For rejoinders to these see Leo E. Strine Jnr., 'Towards a True Corporate Republic: A Traditionalist Response to Lucian's Solution for Improving Corporate America' (2006) 119 HARV. LAW REV. 1759; Theodore N. Mirvis, Paul K. Rowe & William Savitt, 'Bebchuk's "Case for Increasing Shareholder Power": An Opposition' (2007) Harvard Law School Discussion Paper No. 586.

pitfalls in relying on shareholder engagement to act as disciplining force in relation to managerial conduct.[108] For starters, shareholders (particularly institutional shareholders) lack the information, time and incentives to perform comprehensive due diligence on their investments.[109] Moreover, the structure of institutional investors also prevents effective dialogue between owners and agents. Mutual funds, for example, are a form of collective investment scheme that pools money from many different investors and entrusts the investors' wealth to an asset management company, which itself constructs the contracts between the fund and the investors. Investors hold shares in the fund in proportion to the value of their investment. These investors have no direct relationship with any of the companies that the collective investment scheme to which they belong invests in. This insulates directors and executives from the force of shareholder activism. At an individual level, fund managers are in competition with other fund managers and the performance of their funds is normally benchmarked to their peers. They will therefore have very few incentives to attempt to discipline management.[110] Further, the investment horizons of fund managers are usually not long term; their performance is often evaluated annually and they do not therefore have incentives to engage in destabilising battles to oust management.[111]

Perhaps the biggest problem with entrusting shareholders to monitor management is that they have (particularly institutional investors) few incentives to rein in excessive risk taking by executives. As noted by Coffee:

---

108 Emilios Avgouleas & Jay Cullen, 'Market Discipline and EU Corporate Governance Reform in the Banking Sector: Merits, Fallacies, and Cognitive Boundaries' (2014) 41 J. LAW & SOCIETY 28 (hereinafter Avgouleas & Cullen, 'Market Discipline').

109 See Avgouleas, *Mechanics and Regulation* 30–32; for discussion of this behavioural bias in the context of institutional investors, see Brad M. Barber & Terrance Odean, 'All That Glitters: The Effect of Attention and News on the Buying Behavior of Individual and Institutional Investors' (2008) 21 REV. FIN. STUD. 785.

110 Avgouleas, *Mechanics and Regulation* 32.

111 John C. Coffee, 'Liquidity versus Control: The Institutional Investor as Corporate Monitor' (1991) 91 COLUMBIA LAW REV. 1277 (hereinafter Coffee, 'Liquidity versus Control'); Ronald J. Gilson & Reinier Kraakman, 'Reinventing the Outside Director: An Agenda for Institutional Investors' (1991) 43 STANFORD LAW REV. 863; Bernard S. Black, 'Shareholder Passivity Reexamined' (1990) 89 MICHIGAN LAW REV. 520.

> There is a dominant, prevailing scenario shared by Congress, the public, and academics: reckless managers driven by compensation assumed excessive leverage. Shareholders are assumed to be cautious, prudent, and long-term oriented, while managers have shifted to risk-taking through incentives. The first is true, the second is a fairy tale. But [it shapes] a good deal of … legislation.[112]

On this basis, studies find that 'compensation and risk-taking are not related to governance variables but co-vary with ownership by institutional investors who tend to have short-termist preferences and the power to influence firm management policies'.[113] Therefore, powerful shareholders will normally favour managers who take risks, as opposed to more conservative managers, a preference which is reflected in the structure of compensation.[114] This problem is exacerbated by the short-term holding of firm securities in Anglo-American markets, particularly in relation to bank stocks. In both the UK and the US large investors typically hold shares in banks for an average of three months.[115] Accordingly, institutional investment reduces the effectiveness of shareholder engagement with company management.[116] The absence of long-term forward investment horizons not only undermines any attempts to align the interests of managers and the investor class, but may lead to serious issues of complexity and manipulation.[117] As I (together with a co-author) have noted in the context of shareholder engagement with bank performance and executive pay prior to the GFC:

> There is strong evidence that those within financial institutions, who understood the potential of the financial revolution, pushed it to its limits in a rent-seeking exercise, inflating institutions' profits and traders' and managers'

---

[112] Remarks of John C. Coffee, 'Governance, Executive Compensation, and Excessive Risk in the Financial Services Industry: A Research Symposium' Columbia Business School (27–28 March 2010) http://www4.gsb.columbia.edu/rt (hereinafter Columbia Symposium, 'Governance, Executive Compensation and Excessive Risk') 10.

[113] Cheng et al, 'Yesterday's Heroes'.

[114] Remarks of Lucian Bebchuk, Columbia Symposium, *Governance, Executive Compensation and Excessive Risk* 11.

[115] Haldane, 'Control Rights'.

[116] Kenneth Froot, Andre Perold & Jeremy C. Stein, 'Shareholder Trading Practices and Corporate Investment Horizons' (1991) NBER Working Paper No. 3638.

[117] Eitan Goldmana & Günter Strobl, 'Large Shareholder Trading and the Complexity of Corporate Investments' (2013) 22 J. FIN. INTERMEDIATION 106.

> salaries. Yet outsiders, mostly institutional investors, did not delve deeper to ascertain the source of financial institutions' strong profitability that generated the hefty dividends and market price appreciation that boosted their returns from financial stocks. They also invariably approved in general meeting-after-general meeting executive compensations plans.[118]

Whilst, in theory, the market for corporate control may assuage some of these difficulties, in practice, of course, it suffers severe limitations to its effectiveness, the most serious of which is institutional shareholder passivity: there are limited incentives for institutional investors to launch takeover bids for firms or to remove poorly performing management.[119] Naturally, it is cheaper to sell stock than engage in costly attempts to rein in or restructure management,[120] due to the so-called 'free-rider' problem.[121] The dispersed ownership structure of Anglo-American companies renders concerted shareholder activism largely redundant. It is difficult to envisage shareholders acting in concert to change board composition at banks, or to resist compensation demands from executives and traders. In the absence of prescriptive rules to govern conduct – which admittedly would be hugely difficult to formulate – regulators must adopt a system of credible sanctions to punish reckless behaviour. Incentives matter, of course – but on the same basis, so do sanctions, if the threat of their use is deemed credible.[122]

There are signs that recognition of this dilemma is beginning to occur, at least in the UK. Paradoxically, despite the destruction wrought by the GFC, it took two relatively smaller financial scandals to energise UK regulators and provide the impetus for wholesale reform. The LIBOR and

---

118 Avgouleas & Cullen, 'Market Discipline' 42.

119 Gregory Jackson, 'A New Financial Capitalism? Explaining the Persistence of Voice over Exit in Contemporary Corporate Governance' (2008) 5 EUR. MAN. REV. 23.

120 Albert O. Hirschmann, *Exit, Voice and Loyalty: Responses to Decline in Firms, Organisations and States* (Harvard University Press, 1970). As Hirshmann explains at 4: 'Voice is costly and conditioned on the influence and bargaining power customers and members can bring to bear within the firm from which they buy or the organisations to which they belong.'

121 Anat R. Admati, Paul C. Pfleiderer & Josef Zechner, 'Large Shareholder Activism, Risk Sharing, and Financial Market Equilibrium' (1994) 102 J. POLIT. ECONOMY 1097.

122 For any sanction to be effective it must meet four conditions: the person infringing the standard has to be detected; the enforcer has to decide that it is worth spending valuable time and other resources in bringing an action; the action has to be successful; and the sanction has to be meaningful.

PPI mis-selling scandals prompted the establishment of the UK Parliamentary Commission on Banking Standards, to attempt to address some of the issues undermining confidence in the banking sector.[123] Its report, published in June 2013, contained some far-reaching recommendations, which included severe sanctions for senior individuals in bank management who act in ways which endanger bank solvency. Most of these recommendations were adopted by the UK Parliament and have found their way into the Financial Services (Banking Reform) Act 2013, which includes:

(i) the establishment of a 'Senior Managers Regime' at banks (extending the 'Approved Persons regime under FSMA 2000[124]), members of which must assume all key responsibilities, liability for which cannot be delegated;[125]
(ii) subjecting Senior Managers to the full range of civil remedies available to regulators, including fines, restrictions on responsibilities and industry bans;
(iii) the introduction of a new criminal offence making Senior Managers liable for taking a decision which leads to the failure of a bank, or failing to prevent such a decision being taken, if that Senior Manager was aware of a risk that the implementation of the decision may have caused failure. Senior Managers found guilty of this offence may be jailed for up to seven years;[126] and
(iv) in cases of financial institution failure, the burden of proof now lies with the Senior Manager, rather than the regulator, in demonstrating that the Senior Manager was not guilty of reckless misconduct.

---

[123] The LIBOR scandal concerned the deliberate manipulation by global commercial banks of the so-called LIBOR ('London Interbank Offered Rate') benchmark, which is used across global financial markets to determine contractual payments due under a host of financial contracts, including swaps, futures, options, loans, mortgages and credit cards, and many products traded over-the-counter. Indicatively, the aggregate size of financial contracts which utilise LIBOR as the base rate for determining interest payments is in the order of $350 trillion. The PPI (Payment Protection Insurance) scandal has concerned only British banks, which engaged in the deliberate mis-selling of financial products to retail customers and small-to-medium-sized businesses, most commonly to insure against loan default, or to hedge against interest rate and foreign exchange rate changes.

[124] Financial Services and Markets Act 2000 c.8, s.31.

[125] Financial Services (Banking Reform) Act 2013 c.33, s.33.

[126] Ibid. s.36.

General civil sanctions, such as fines for institutions have not generally provided effective deterrence to misconduct in other areas of corporate regulation, weakening the stigma attached to poor behaviour. Without sanctions for recklessness, it would seem unrealistic to expect a substantial change in individual or collective conduct, and attempts to change the culture of banking on other grounds would almost certainly be doomed to fail.[127] The criminal standard attached to the UK offence, and the lack of strict liability, ought to ensure that the threat of prosecution does not deter talented people from taking up senior positions at financial institutions. Even if prosecutions on the basis of these legal provisions are rare (which is likely[128]), it will arguably focus the minds of senior bank managers on inculcating an environment of compliance with both the letter and spirit of banking regulation (the latter apparently having been jettisoned some years ago), as regulators will retain the residual power to launch actions for prosecution in instances of very serious failings. Moreover, the capacity to ban individuals from the industry, which seems

---

[127] On this, see Dan Awrey, William Blair & David Kershaw, 'Between Law and Markets: Is There a Role for Culture and Ethics in Financial Regulation?' (2013) 38 DEL. J. CORP. LAW 191. The authors assert that banks ought to try to internally drive changes in their organisations to constrain socially undesirable behaviour and produce a more 'ethical culture' within finance. This line of argument also regards sanctions as important in fostering changes in banking practices, but relies on reforms to the traditional corporate governance apparatus (for example, the mandatory introduction of ethics committees) and 'soft' sanctions, such as reputational threats and counterparty monitoring, to achieve this. The authors' view is that legal measures to enforce greater trust and information efficiency in markets (including in relation to disclosure, product regulation and bank capital regulations) have so far failed to rein in excessive risk taking and reforms since the GFC are therefore limited in their likely effectiveness. However, it is submitted that whilst ethical signposting can be effective in providing a guide to professional conduct, the ingrained nature of banking culture (in particular, its ultra-competitiveness and intense focus on financial returns) means it is likely to be highly resistant to the forms of 'ethical' change the authors recommend. Instead, alterations to incentive structures and (credible) sanctions for failure (as well as the structural reforms that I have mentioned) stand more chance of avoiding the excessive risk taking that characterised the pre-GFC financial environment.

[128] Prosecution for this offence is expected to be used 'in cases involving only the most serious of failings, such as where a bank failed with substantial costs to the taxpayer, lasting consequences for the financial system, or serious harm to customers. The credibility of such an offence would also depend on it being used only in the most serious cases, and not predominantly against smaller operators where proving responsibility is easier, but the harm is much lower.' See UK Parliament, *Changing Banking for Good* 244.

a likelier punishment for anyone found to have transgressed this law, will be as great a sanction as imprisonment.

There are also possibilities for this power to be applied beyond the UK. Whilst the EU has displayed reticence in the past to criminalise individuals for misconduct, preferring instead to fine corporations,[129] it is clear that the public mood appears generally supportive of the introduction of some form of individual sanctions beyond the civil remedies currently available to prosecutors against bankers guilty of recklessness. In the US, similar calls for introducing more punitive measures have been made, although the powers afforded to prosecutors prior to the GFC were already much wider than those in the UK.[130] Despite this, and a promise from the US Federal Agencies to adopt a much more proactive approach to prosecuting bank executives for alleged criminal conduct, few prosecutions have been undertaken.[131] The EU and US lawmakers might

---

[129] For example, in the EU, the cartel offence under Article 101 TFEU carries only civil sanctions against corporations, whereas the same offence in the US and UK carries criminal sanctions for individuals. There have been recommendations, however, to extend criminal penalties in the EU to members of 'hard-core' cartels. See Eleanor J. Morgan, 'Controlling Cartels – Implications of the EU Policy Reforms' (2009) 27 EURO. MAN. J. 1.

[130] As noted: 'Beyond traditional bank fraud [18 U.S.C. § 1344] and embezzlement [18 U.S.C. § 656] statutes, prosecutors [in the US] can also base charges on a wide range of banking and general fraud violations including making false statements [18 U.S.C. § 1001(a)(2)], or concealing material facts [18 U.S.C. § 1001(a)(1)], making false entries in bank books and records [18 U.S.C. § 1005], receipt of commissions or gifts for procuring loans [18 U.S.C. § 215], mail or wire fraud [18 U.S.C. §§ 1341, 1343], and … newly created offenses related to fraud connected with TARP funds [15 U.S.C. §§ 77q(a), 77x].' See Chip F. MacDonald, Henry W. Asbill, Martha Boersch, Jean-Paul Boulee, Garrett L. Bradford, Charles M. Carberry, R. Christopher Cook, Richard H. Deane Jr., Randy S. Grossman, Jonathan B. Leiken, George T. Manning, Theodore T. Chung, Daniel E. Reidy & Brian A. Sun, 'Criminal Actions Against Failed Bank Executives' (Mondaq, 19 April 2011), http://www.mondaq.com/unitedstates/x/129978/Corporate+Crime/Criminal+Actions+Against+Failed+Bank+Executives.

[131] See Nate Raymond, 'Judge Criticizes Lack of Prosecution against Wall Street Executives for Fraud', *Reuters*, 12 November 2013, http://www.reuters.com/, quoting Federal Judge Rakoff: 'The failure of the government to bring to justice those responsible for such a massive fraud speaks greatly to weaknesses in our prosecutorial system that need to be addressed.' In continuance of this vein, see the July 2014 settlement between the French bank BNP Paribas and courts in the US. In summary, BNP pleaded guilty to state and federal charges of violating US law in relation to sanctions imposed on transactions with the Sudanese government. According to the superintendent of

therefore be advised to follow the UK path, in legislating explicitly on the issue of individual recklessness within financial institutions.

(ii) Qualitative behavioural assessments

With regard to the second tool, it is clear that reliance on quantitative measures of performance led executives to a dangerous obsession with short-term performance measurements. As discussed in previous chapters, equity-based governance was arguably a cardinal cause of the GFC. On this basis, together with the more prescriptive proposals outlined above, the adoption of qualitative indices of performance may assist in alleviating the over-reliance on stock options and other stock-based compensation: 'It is … clear that [these sorts of] recommendations from supervisors would help solve the collective action problems relative to the adoption of pay mechanisms that are not directly tied to wealth maximization purposes …'[132] To this end, post-GFC several supra-national bodies have recommended the use of qualitative indicators of executive performance rather than wholesale reliance on financial data in designing compensation. The use of qualitative data is already standard practice across financial institutions; the BCBS Range noted that 'Both qualitative and quantitative performance measures should be considered [in compensation structures]. While performance measures are normally focused on financial metrics, it is also important that financial institutions

New York's Department of Financial Services, which investigated the case, 'BNP employees – with the knowledge of senior executives – engaged in a longstanding scheme that illegally funnelled money to countries involved in terrorism and genocide.' Despite these charges, and despite the bank admitting its guilt and agreeing to pay an $8.9 billion fine, no individual was prosecuted in relation to the sanctions violations. As noted by one commentator at the time: 'This was a missed opportunity. If no one goes to jail and the fine does no permanent damage, the settlement becomes more a transaction tax than a deterrent. It is unlikely to be seen as justice in the eyes of the public – people who tend to go to prison when they break the law. Will it change behaviour? Time will tell. Will it deter BNP employees and others with respect to the area of sanctions violations? Probably. Will it deter wrongdoing in finance more generally? I fear not.' See Robert Jenkins, 'An opportunity missed rather than a case settled', *Financial Times* (London, 1 July 2014) http//:ft.com.

[132] Guido Ferrarini, 'Bankers' Compensation and Prudential Supervision: The International Principles' in Hill & Thomas (eds), *Research Handbook on Executive Compensation* 130.

include non-financial metrics in developing the risk-based remuneration hurdles.'[133] Similarly, the EC recommended that:

> In order for remuneration policy to be in line with the objectives, the business strategy, the values and the long-term interests of the financial institution, other factors, apart from financial performance, should be considered, such as compliance with systems and controls of the financial institution, as well as compliance with the standards governing the relationship with clients and investors.[134]

Existing foundations must be built upon, with targets that focus not only on financial performance, but on all areas that are critical for future corporate success.[135] Research from cognitive sciences questions seriously the capacity of quantitative performance-based pay – in isolation – to ever work.[136] The bounded rationality and bounded ethicality[137] of market participants may lower the incentive effects of bonuses based upon monetary targets. It has been demonstrated that targets based on financial performance indicators may lead to narrow focus, motivate risk taking, encourage unethical behaviour and shorten time horizons.[138] In addition, the incentive effects of compensation based on a 'bonus culture'

---

133 BCBS, *Range of Methodologies* 58.

134 EC Commission, Recommendation on Remuneration Policies in the Financial Sector (C(2009) 3159) 17.

135 'Rewards for success should be better focussed on generating long-term benefits for banks and their customers. Where the standards of individuals, especially those in senior roles, have fallen short, clear lines of accountability and enforceable sanctions are needed.' Remarks of Andrew Tyrie, Chair of the Parliamentary Commission on Banking Standards cited in Parliamentary Business, 'Banking Commission Publishes Report on Changing Banking For Good', 19 June 2013, http://www.parliament.uk/business/committees/committees-a-z/joint-select/professional-standards-in-the-banking-industry/news/changing-banking-for-good-report/.

136 Jaap Winter, 'Corporate Governance Going Astray: Executive Remuneration Built to Fail' in Hill & Thomas (eds), *Research Handbook on Executive Compensation*.

137 Max H. Bazerman & Don Moore, *Judgment in Managerial Decision-Making* (8th edn, John Wiley & Sons, 2009).

138 Lisa D. Ordonez, Maurice E. Schweitzer, Adam D. Galinsky & Max H. Bazerman, 'Goals Gone Wild: The Systematic Side Effects of Overprescribing Goal Setting' (2009) 23 ACAD. MAN. PERSP. 6; Maurice E. Schweitzer, Lisa Ordonez & Bambi Douma, 'Goal Setting as a Motivator of Unethical Behavior' (2004) 47 ACAD. MAN. J. 422.

may wane over the long term, and actually demotivate employees.[139] Non-monetary-based targets provide an additional benefit: by incentivising executives to deliver customer-focused results, rather than concentrating their minds completely on increasing profits for shareholders, the potential to inculcate an improvement in business culture would arise. More responsible compensation policies and a greater customer focus might improve trust in corporations; this has been a problem for many businesses in recent years, particularly financial institutions.[140] Compensation policies ought to focus on targets which encourage integrity[141] and trust,[142] each of which enhances productivity and creates value.

Non-financial indicators of performance currently form approximately 23 per cent of determined bonus awards in banks for 'front office employees' (which include sales, marketing and customer services staff).[143] However, it is clear that the most senior staff and those that engage in significant risk taking at banks receive bonuses almost exclusively on the basis of the financial returns they generate.[144] Future

---

139 Bruno S. Frey & Reto Jegen, 'Motivation Crowding Theory: A Survey of Empirical Evidence' (1999) Univ. of Zurich Institute for Empirical Research in Economics Working Paper No. 26 (1999); Charles A. O'Reilly III, Brian G. Main & Graef S. Crystal, 'CEO Compensation as Tournament and Social Comparison: A Tale of Two Theories' (1988) 33 ADMIN. SCI. Q. 257. The obsession with bonuses may eventually lead to serious health problems for the employee concerned. See Alexandra Michel, 'Transcending Socialization: A Nine-Year Ethnography of the Body's Role in Organizational Control and Knowledge Workers' Transformation' (2011) 56 ADMIN. SCI. Q. 325.

140 Merryn Somerset Webb, 'Trust Index Sinks to an All-time Low' *Financial Times* (London, 29 June 2012) http://ft.com.

141 Werner Erhard, Michael C. Jensen & Steve Zaffron, 'Integrity: A Positive Model that Incorporates the Normative Phenomena of Morality, Ethics and Legality' (2009) Harvard Business Sch. NOM Working Paper No. 06-11.

142 George Baker, Robert Gibbons & Kevin J. Murphy, 'Subjective Performance Measures in Optimal Incentive Contracts' (1993) NBER Working Paper No. 4480.

143 In assessing the performance of front office employees, the measures used ordinarily include: 'The franchise nature of the employee's business (client oriented businesses are favoured over proprietary trading); Quality of revenues (businesses with large illiquid risks appear to be discounted qualitatively in addition to the quantitative liquidity charges); Performance appraisals from managers and colleagues; Resources and behaviours used to achieve the results; Teamwork; Individual employee compliance with controls or adherence to the rules; and Track record/multiple years of performance.' See BCBS, *Range of Methodologies* 91.

144 IIF, *Compensation in Financial Services* 12.

compensation systems therefore ought to '[i]ncrease [the] weighting of non-financial input and output criteria'[145] in calibrating awards. On this basis, in the UK, the FCA has recommended that:

> Non-financial performance metrics should form a significant part of the performance assessment process and should include adherence to effective risk management and compliance with the *regulatory system* and with relevant overseas regulatory requirements. Poor performance as assessed by non-financial metrics such as poor risk management or other behaviours contrary to *firm* values can pose significant risks for a *firm* and should, as appropriate, override metrics of financial performance.[146]

Of course, criticisms of qualitative performance appraisal remain: the absence of quantitative data might make the process too subjective and difficult to benchmark. Further, there are certainly latent dangers that 'soft' targets are more malleable than hard, financial data. Nevertheless, increasing the consideration of qualitative performance metrics in relation to the more senior staff at banks might go some way to alleviating the problems associated with over-reliance on financial indices and give recognition to other measures of value addition.

In practical terms, many businesses already utilise non-financial performance indictors in setting pay levels.[147] Currently, many businesses utilise the 'balanced scorecard approach',[148] which emphasises four key measures of performance: (i) financial measures (including shareholder returns); (ii) innovation (this could include, for example, the number of patents granted or the cost savings made in restructurings); (iii) employee measures (including satisfaction and retention); and (iv) customer satisfaction (satisfaction, retention and profitability). It is apparent that the use of this approach to setting pay has become more prevalent at some financial institutions, although how widespread the practice is remains

---

145 Ibid. Figure 2.

146 FCA, *Rem-Code* Sysc 19A. 3.37.

147 See Thomas L. Albright, Christopher M. Burgess, Aleecia R. Hibbets & Michael L. Roberts, 'Four Steps to Simplify Multimeasure Performance Evaluations Using the Balanced Scorecard' (2010) 21 J. CORP. ACC. FIN. 63; Adrian Payne, Sue Holt & Pennie Frow, 'Integrating Employee, Customer and Shareholder Value through an Enterprise Performance Model: An Opportunity for Financial Services' (2000) 18 INT. J. BANK MARKETING 258.

148 Robert S. Kaplan & David P. Norton, 'The Balanced Scorecard – Measures that Drive Performance' (1992) 70 HARV. BUS. REV. 71.

open to debate.[149] Further qualitative measures used to gauge performance might include the contribution of an employee to a firm's corporate social responsibility (CSR).[150] Following high-profile corporate collapses and notable instances of corporate abuse, CSR has become a common indicator of good governance and corporate awareness. The resultant reputational advantages enjoyed by corporations through the positive impact generated by employees reaching CSR benchmarks and ensuring active compliance with ethical and legal standards therefore ought to be rewarded.[151]

Allying greater consideration of qualitative performance indicators with the previous proposal of this book for an increase in the deferral period relating to variable compensation would lower the incentives for short-termist executive behaviour. Instead of large-scale reliance on quantitative metrics to determine short-to-medium-term incentives, future compensation design arguably ought to focus to a higher degree than is currently the case on 'softer' measures of value creation. This would reduce incentives for executives to concentrate on financial variables, which is often a source of short-termism, theoretically reducing risk to financial institutions. Moreover, when performance is based upon several forms of metric, rather than focused primarily on financial indicators, 'gaming the system' is more difficult.

---

149 HSBC, for example, proposed reform to the pay of senior staff as far back as 2011, to include assessment of non-financial performance targets, with the *Financial Times* commenting that 'HSBC's leading investors are broadly supportive of the changes, particularly the widening of targets beyond current shareholder return and profit measures to an unspecified basket of "balanced scorecard" measures. "Moving away from purely financial metrics is a good thing," said one.' See Masa Serdarevic & Patrick Jenkins, 'HSBC Proposes Pay Shake-up', *Financial Times* (London, 22 March 2011) http://www.ft.com/cms/s/0/c97c607c-54bf-11e0-b1ed-00144feab49a.html?siteedition=uk#axzz312YDQ4Du. In 2014 the Barclays CEO also pledged to include the balanced scorecard approach to setting pay levels of certain staff. See Martin Arnold, 'Antony Jenkins' Steel and Passion Tested in Barclays Results', *Financial Times* (London, 11 February 2014) http://www.ft.com/cms/s/0/c937bf64-928b-11e3-8018-00144feab7de.html#axzz312YDQ4Du.

150 R. Edward Freeman, *Strategic Management: A Stakeholder Approach* (CUP, 2010).

151 Donna J. Wood, 'Corporate Social Performance Revisited' (1991) 16 ACAD. MAN. REV. 691.

CONCLUSION

The foregoing analysis, on the basis of the regulatory response to the GFC in the context of executive compensation discussed in the previous chapter, has made proposals for further reform in order to insulate the financial system from the damaging effects of perverse incentives. The chapter has noted that impressive steps have been made in tackling the issue of flawed incentives and that reform to executive remuneration packages has rightly focused on the issues caused by market short-termism. In this way, therefore, policies recommending deferral of bonus payments and the clawback of certain variable compensation are to be welcomed, although the length of the applicable periods of deferral, and the circumstances under which clawback may be utilised, need to be expanded. 'Piggy-backing' on recent reforms to bank capital regulations will also act as a risk-reducing mechanism in relation to executive compensation, and will not require extensive actions by regulators, other than to ensure that those regulations – which in any case have as their cardinal aim to ensure greater financial stability – are complied with, both in letter and spirit. Finally, the introduction of greater sanctions for reckless behaviour, as well as more consideration of non-quantitative indices of performance in determining pay, would arguably both incentivise a more prudent approach to the business of banking, and provide a more holistic view of employee contributions to firm success. If these issues are not addressed, flawed incentives will continue to weaken corporate governance and may increase economic instability over the long term. However, these proposals would go some way to mitigating those risks.

8. Conclusion

I began this book by querying some of the fundamental assumptions of financial market theory, and thereby questioning the application of those theories to the regulation of securities markets. On this basis, my aim has been to demonstrate that the market pricing mechanism is an inefficient tool upon which to base executive compensation at financial institutions. Specifically, to achieve this task I have attempted to provide answers to three key questions, namely: firstly, how the dominant view of the operation of the market determines the use of equity-based compensation schemes in financial institutions; secondly, why this view is flawed in light of alternative theories of asset and securities markets behaviour, which explains how market prices may become distorted (particularly the FIH); and thirdly, whether those alternative financial market theories ought to be considered by regulators in the design of future compensation systems following the GFC, which exposed the limitations of market discipline and the futility of relying on market pricing to deliver optimal compensation awards.

Until recently, absolute faith was placed in modern finance theory (which contends that the market is comprised of an agglomeration of supremely rational, calculating and self-interested beings) and free market principles underpinned the regulation of corporate governance.[1] Market discipline was trusted to deliver optimal governance arrangements through the actions of shareholders, board engagement, the influence of the market for corporate control, and the role of creditors and other outside corporate monitors. Whilst this view of the firm regards

[1] This view was not without its logical flaws. Alan Greenspan, former Chairman of the US Federal Reserve System, claimed in the months following the GFC that 'the modern risk-management paradigm held sway for decades … The whole intellectual edifice, however, collapsed in the summer of last year [2008].' This statement encapsulates the collective ideological myopia characteristic of certain modern finance adherents. Prior to 2008 there were numerous failures of risk management at public and private corporations. Certain of these crises – whilst not as serious as the GFC – also threatened to collapse the entire financial system. See Edmund L. Andrews, 'Greenspan Concedes Error on Regulation' *New York Times* (New York, 23 October 2008) http://nytimes.com.

investors and market participants through the lens of modern finance theory, governance theorists recognised that costs are inherent whenever companies are managed by agents who do not own them. Structural problems also exist which dent the capacity of the market to regulate agents' conduct. Agency theory was thus conceptualised with regard to the firm to explain the problems derived from the separation of ownership and control; shareholder value theory was proffered as the solution to these problems. In order to prevent corporate managers from exploiting the benefits of control, it was suggested that they ought to share in the financial success of the firm. The most efficient method in aligning principal and agent interests was to grant agents rewards of equivalence with principals; in the case of corporations, this meant company stock, or bonuses linked to stock performance. However, stock-based remuneration – a central plank of shareholder value theory – created incentives for executives to engage in short-termist strategies and dubious investments in order to capture rents from corporations. Instead of aligning the interests of managers and owners, stock-based compensation schemes provided serious incentives to adopt risk-laden corporate strategies.

I therefore consider the dominant views concerning incentives-based compensation, especially in relation to large and complex financial institutions, to be misguided. Cardinally, these views neglect the fact that financial markets, far from being stable and equilibrium seeking (as posited by modern finance theory), are afflicted by multiple problems which undermine the pricing mechanism. The EMH, used as the basis for the regulation of financial markets, and deriving its predictive authority from rational choice theory, provides a flawed approximation of systemic behaviour. Instead, financial markets are prone to pronounced volatility and exhibit extreme swings in price and capital allocation. Some of these issues are caused by investor behavioural traits and the pro-cyclicality of investment strategies. These strategies often drive asset bubbles and price distortions. Moreover, Minsky and his FIH predict that, by their very nature, financial markets are prone to instability, and explain how financialised economies progress from debt-fuelled periods of expansion to inevitable collapse, through increased leverage adopted by risk-averse speculators. Moreover, the FIH may be used to explain how equity-based compensation systems may exacerbate financial crises by making executive rewards contingent on the inflation of asset prices.

On this basis, the GFC demonstrated the acute failure of modern finance theory to account for financial instability and for its role in devising inappropriate regulatory structures. Many of the failed incentives which contributed to the banking collapses of 2008 were driven by compensation awards. These awards were often contingent on inappropriate assumptions of risk or short-term myopia within financial markets. The issue was further exacerbated by investor cognitive limitations and extreme financial product complexity. Equity-based compensation awards played a significant role in the incentives misalignment which led to over-leveraging and eventual financial collapse. Therefore, not only may excess rents be captured by executives in upward markets, executive reward systems themselves may play a decisive role in driving asset bubbles. The paradox here remains all the more powerful when it becomes apparent that it does not actually matter whether executives believe that asset prices are inflated, or conspire actively to inflate them. Cognitive boundaries may blur the capacity of market participants – shareholders, institutional investors and other corporate monitors – to recognise that instability within an economy has increased, particularly in a highly financialised environment. This book therefore recognises that the power of market discipline cannot be relied upon to establish appropriate compensation structures.

In examining the regulatory response to the GFC in the context of executive compensation and the attempts to insulate the financial system from the damaging effects of perverse incentives, I have found that progress on these issues remains mixed. Some impressive steps have been made in tackling the issue of flawed incentives and reform to executive remuneration packages has rightly focused on the issues caused by market short-termism. In this way, therefore, policies recommending deferral of bonus payments and the clawback of certain variable compensation chime particularly well with the thrust of the book. In the absence of these reforms, flaws in corporate governance may have continued to threaten financial stability. On the other hand, governance reform casting shareholders in the traditional role of monitors of management, and the ill-conceived bonus cap in the EU are bound to create more problems than they solve. Accordingly, I made three proposals to guard against the dangers of equity-price-based governance, and it is hoped, provide some concrete and sensible suggestions to tackle this issue – which appears still to captivate the public at large.

On this basis, I have attempted to provide a theoretical explanation and practical solutions to the flaws in equity-based compensation at banks; however, this book cannot answer all questions regarding the failure of incentives to guard against systemic instability. Further research into the role of flawed incentives would assist in compiling a more accurate picture of the causes of financial distress in large banks. It would be useful to ask, for example, in light of the multitude of corporate governance failures that have plagued securities markets over the past decade, whether wholesale reform to corporate governance and executive compensation packages is even worthwhile. There remains a marked reliance on market discipline to constrain corporate behaviour. Despite the failures evident in the run-up to the GFC, regulators contend that any reforms to financial regulation must be 'grounded in a commitment to free market principles'.[2] It appears these regulators still devolve much of their responsibility for maintaining market stability to the markets themselves, and are instead concentrating their efforts on providing liquidity backstops and insolvency guarantees for large financial institutions which have, paradoxically and unfortunately, become larger and thereby more unmanageable since the GFC. Certain measures emanating from the BCBS appear to be steps in the right direction, although it is clear that the banking lobby remains powerful and highly resistant to further moves to increase capital or impose leverage constraints.[3]

It of course also be recognised that executive compensation was but one of a plethora of interconnected factors which can be implicated in causing the GFC. The issues that were generated through the aforementioned failures and collective regulatory inertia permitted executives to ride credit bubbles until they burst. However, many of the factors responsible for the GFC – including fiscal laxity and financial institutions drunk on leverage – were facilitated by the appetite and greed of humans for ever higher financial rewards, which eventually span out of control and in this way were common to many other recent crises of Anglo-American capitalism. Failed incentives were the reason that structural weaknesses in the financial system were not tackled: greed, recklessness and market myopia were translated into a credit binge, which eventually collapsed a large portion of the global economy. Reform to incentive structures at financial institutions, particularly equity-based compensation, therefore ought to be prioritised. This will aid the long-term viability and sustainability of the economy, improve market welfare and in the process ensure that profitable enterprise is preserved for the long term.

---

[2] G-20, 'The Declaration of the Washington Summit on Financial Markets and the World Economy', November 15, 2008, Washington DC, http://www.un.org/ga/president/63/commission/declarationG20.pdf.

[3] Sam Fleming & Gina Chon, 'Banks Win Basel Concessions on Debt Rules', *Financial Times* (London, 13 January 2014) http://ft.com.

Index